MW00973317

MY ANCHOR HOLDS

Irene,
Hope you enjoy my
story.
God is faithful!!
Michelle Ironside Hy

MICHELLE IRONSIDE HENRY

WESTBOW®
PRESS
A DIVISION OF THOMAS NELSON
& ZONDERVAN

Scripture quotations taken from the New American Standard Bible®, Copyright © 1960, 1962, 1963, 1968, 1971, 1972, 1973, 1975, 1977, 1995 by The Lockman Foundation. Used by permission. (www.Lockman.org)

WestBow Press books may be ordered through booksellers or by contacting:

WestBow Press
A Division of Thomas Nelson & Zondervan
1663 Liberty Drive
Bloomington, IN 47403
www.westbowpress.com
1 (866) 928-1240

ISBN: 978-1-4908-5360-4 (sc)
ISBN: 978-1-4908-5359-8 (hc)
ISBN: 978-1-4908-5361-1 (e)

Library of Congress Control Number: 2014917337

Printed in the United States of America.

WestBow Press rev. date: 10/07/2014

I dedicate this book to the two Davids in my life:

- In memory of my father, David Stewart Ironside, a man who walked closely with God and modeled for me what it means to live life abundantly through the power of Christ.
- In honor of my husband, Guy David Henry III, with deep appreciation for his faithful care throughout my illness and his undying love.

"But as for me, the nearness of God is my good; I have made the Lord God my refuge, that I may tell of all Thy works." Psalm 73:28

Introduction

In December 2009, at the age of 45, I heard the words no one wants to hear, "You've got cancer."

Physically active and a happily married mother of two, I ate right and exercised religiously. I worked three part-time jobs, took care of my family, volunteered for worthy causes and taught Sunday school. And I almost *never* got sick. Before cancer, my pharmacist joked that the only prescriptions he filled for me were birth control pills or prenatal vitamins.

Then colorectal cancer came knocking at my door.

The diagnosis was surprising because I didn't fit the profile. Colorectal cancer is most common in people over age 50. Risk factors include things like a family history of colorectal cancer, diabetes, and eating a diet high in fat and cholesterol and low in fiber. People are at increased risk if they drink alcohol, smoke, don't get enough exercise, or are overweight.

None of those categories described me, my history or my lifestyle. Nevertheless, I had Stage IV cancer – the most advanced and deadly form of the disease. According to the American Cancer Society, only about 6 percent of people diagnosed with Stage IV colorectal cancer survive five years or more.

The cancer started in my colon, spread to my liver and later moved to my lungs. To date, I've undergone rigorous chemotherapy twice, a six-week session of chemo and radiation together, and endured four major surgeries. I still have cancer in my right lung.

As I write this, almost five years after my initial diagnosis, doctors say it's a miracle I'm still here. And it is. The bigger miracle, though, and the one that makes me want to shout my story from the mountaintops is how near God has been to me throughout my journey.

Section One

"You've got cancer."

January 1, 2010 – January 12, 2012

"Yea, though I walk through the valley of the
shadow of death …" Psalm 23:4

Before diving into my story, I'll start by explaining that this book is a chronicle of my journey with cancer, covering more than four years, from diagnosis to restoration of health. Each step along the path begins with a journal entry and ends with my present-day reflections on that entry.

As you follow my story, there are times when my quirky sense of humor and typically positive attitude make it fun and easy to read; there also are times when it is hard to believe that everything I endured could happen to one person. As I have left everything unvarnished, this book is sometimes happy, sometimes sad. *My Anchor Holds* captures a true picture of my heart at the time the words were written, and you will see how I learned and grew in the process.

The journal entries were originally published on CaringBridge, a website that serves as a platform for information sharing and support for those facing major health issues such as cancer, premature birth or serious injury. It works by allowing individuals to host a private site through which they share updates and information about their health status. Others then can read the posts and share their own words of encouragement, love and support. Each site is unique to the user, and there are many options available to personalize the look of the site. For mine, I chose the theme of "Hope." This word, and all it embodies, defines my journey so well that I continue to use it as a life theme today.

A dear friend suggested I use CaringBridge just after my diagnosis. She said it would be a great way to keep people updated without having to spend a lot of time on the phone repeating the same story. I had no idea at the time that her simple suggestion would so dramatically impact my entire journey with cancer.

Through my journal on CaringBridge, I've detailed my battle with this ugly disease. I have shared my heart, pulled back the curtain on my fight with cancer, and made it possible for others to walk with me on a path that has at times been rocky and arduous and at others a mountaintop experience. This book is my invitation for you to journey with me, while I share the battle, the blessings and the lessons I've learned.

⚓ **Friday, January 1, 2010, 6:31 p.m.**

New Year's Day seems a fitting time to start the process of keeping a journal of my battle against cancer.

As I launch into a new year and this journal, it is still a bit surreal to think that I have a disease that could kill me. Or that, even if I do survive (which I believe I will), 2010 will likely be the hardest year of my life. I've always been the healthy person who rarely even catches a cold – the one who prays for others that are sick. It will be tough to be on this side of the fence. This is where I find myself, however, so I will try to make the best of it.

Starting this journal is also daunting, because I really don't like talking about myself, and I hate talking about health problems. However, I hope that doing so will not only be therapeutic for me but also helpful for others. Knowing that it will keep friends and family informed of my progress and help them better pray for me is reason enough to take on the task.

As I write this, I'm not feeling too bad. I had a pain pill about an hour ago, so I'm good to go for a little while. Here's a brief update:

I was diagnosed with colorectal cancer in mid-December, when a colonoscopy revealed a tumor that my gastroenterologist, Dr. Meade Edmunds, described as "huge." I could tell that it must be serious when he had me wait in his office while he called to make an appointment with an oncologist. Clearly, there was no time to waste.

My oncologist, Dr. Richard Antonucci, also did an amazing job of getting the treatment process underway as quickly as possible. I had a PET scan on Monday and a chemo port implanted on Wednesday. The port is really cool. They'll hook it up to a chemo pump that attaches to my belt, and I'm on my way. No sitting for hours, which is a good thing for me. I'd much rather be on the go.

Originally, my treatment plan was as follows:

1. Radiation;
2. Chemotherapy;
3. Surgery; and
4. More chemotherapy.

I heard yesterday that the PET scan showed "something" in my liver. Now, I go for a CT scan on Wednesday, January 6. After that, I'll see my doctor and we'll start chemotherapy. I really don't mind the change of plans; I'm just ready to start treatment.

Stay tuned...

Before landing my job at Moxley Carmichael, one of the leading public relations firms in East Tennessee, I had to take a Caliper Profile personality test to see if I was a good match for the company and the PR profession. In addition to helping get me hired, the test revealed that I have a very high sense of urgency and a very low sense of caution. The test was dead-on.

After learning I had cancer, I just wanted to get on with whatever I needed to do to get better. Caution didn't enter the equation. I didn't read medical literature for possible side effects or risks. I didn't visit online colorectal cancer forums to see what others had to say about treatment. In short, I was just ready to go full steam ahead with whatever my doctors suggested. Fortunately, I had some of the best doctors in the business and their recommended strategy was right.

But blindly trusting a doctor is what got me to the point of needing some of the top docs in Knoxville to help keep me alive. For years I struggled with alternating constipation and diarrhea and a generally unhappy stomach. About two years prior to my diagnosis, the symptoms worsened and included some bleeding. That made me concerned enough to visit a gastroenterologist. My work at Moxley Carmichael had me researching various gastrointestinal disorders, and I realized that rectal bleeding could be an indicator of cancer. When the doctor diagnosed irritable bowel syndrome (IBS), I felt a bit foolish for having worried and was glad that it was nothing more serious. "That's great news," I said. "I just wanted to be sure I didn't have something that would kill me." He assured me I was healthy and dismissed me with a pat on the back and a prescription for some little blue pills that were supposed to settle my stomach.

The pills didn't really help, but my stomach did seem to do much better if I avoided eating fats. So for nearly two years I watched what I ate and complained that IBS was a pain. Then, pain in the figurative sense became literal. My stomach started hurting. A lot. My bowels were constantly changing and, for lack of a better description, just looked weird. When I sat for any length of time, my legs throbbed. Yes, I know. Throbbing legs don't seem related to a stomach malady, but looking back, I can tell you that the as yet undiagnosed tumor was so large that it somehow affected my legs when I was in a sitting position.

I knew I needed to do something to control the symptoms of what I still believed to be IBS, but didn't see the point in wasting time with another visit with the gastroenterologist. Years before, I had seen an acupuncturist for neck pain and liked the holistic approach of Eastern medicine. "Western medicine sure hasn't helped with IBS," I thought. "I'll see what an acupuncturist can do."

The acupuncturist said that the symptoms would probably get worse before getting better but that acupuncture would help over time. I went for treatments during my lunch break several times a week. I remember going back to work feeling just awful. By about week four with symptoms continuing to escalate and getting to the point where I could barely eat anything, the acupuncturist said, "I don't think you have irritable bowel syndrome. I suggest you get a colonoscopy and that you do it soon."

Foolishly, I called the gastroenterologist who had diagnosed me with IBS. I shared my symptoms with the nurse and asked for an appointment as soon as possible. She didn't share my sense of urgency and set an appointment for more than a month away. Ugh.

My mother suggested that I call a different doctor at another facility called Gastrointestinal Associates of Knoxville, where my father went. My father had a long history of colon polyps, which, as part of my family history should have been a red flag to the original gastroenterologist. At any rate, Gastrointestinal Associates scheduled an appointment within a few days. When I saw Dr. Edmunds, he was furious. "You diagnose irritable bowel syndrome after ruling out everything else. I can't believe he didn't suggest a colonoscopy," he said of my original doctor.

My colonoscopy was scheduled and I was given instructions for cleansing my bowels. When people talk about a colonoscopy, they're quick to say that the test itself isn't bad but the prep is dreadful. I dutifully took the laxative pills, drank Gatorade laced with MiraLAX and spent the night on the toilet.

People were right. The prep wasn't fun, but the colonoscopy was a piece of cake. The propofol rendered me quickly and completely unconscious, and I enjoyed a nice little nap. When I awoke from the anesthesia, Dr. Edmunds was at my bedside to talk with my husband, David, and me. The doctor explained that he found a large tumor but couldn't complete the colonoscopy because my colon wasn't cleaned out enough. He wanted to do a follow-up colonoscopy the next day to be certain of the extent of my condition. That was a true low point. I felt terrible, I was afraid, and I dreaded going through the prep all over again. I remember finally breaking down and crying as David and I were getting in the car. David helped talk me through it, and I managed to rally enough to soldier on.

That afternoon, our Basset Hound, Henry, gave us a good laugh and reminded me of an important truth. When we got home from the colonoscopy, David gave Henry a really big dog bone. Henry was hilarious. He roamed all over the house looking for the perfect spot to hide his bone, all the while eyeing us suspiciously. He ended up hiding it under the cushion of an upstairs sofa. His stubby legs couldn't manage to get the cushion back in place, so his secret hiding place was not so secret. "We gave him the bone," I laughed. "Why in the world does he think he needs to hide it so we won't take it away from him?" Then it dawned on me. James 1:17 says, "Every good thing bestowed and every perfect gift is from above ...." My health, my family, my job, all those things were gifts from God, and I could trust Him to take care of me.

Remarkably, the next day I felt better physically than I had in a long time. The huge tumor in my rectum had severely hindered waste from leaving my body, which was a big part of why I was so sick the past few months.

Although the laxatives provided temporary relief, there were serious issues to be addressed. Dr. Edmunds immediately identified the oncologist and surgeon he wanted me to see and even made an appointment with the oncologist. He couldn't have chosen better doctors, and I sit here today thankful for the team – including Dr. Edmunds – that has helped make it possible for me to be here writing my story.

⚓ Sunday, January 3, 2010, 12:29 p.m.

Before I got sick, my days were filled with constant activity. Most days, I finally stopped and sat down around 10:00 p.m. – earlier in the winter, but I still stayed fairly active until around 8:00. I now log a lot of hours on the couch, and I got really excited when I discovered a new method of layering my blankets that keeps me warm and cozy. How times change!

The thing that hits me now is, what was I doing, and why was I spending so much time doing it? The house is fine. Surprisingly so. The boys are fed. Sure, they're eating out some and making good use of the fryer, but no one is in danger of going hungry. I haven't worked out in what seems to be ages, and poor Henry hasn't had his beloved walks. The dog is putting on some weight, but with my newfound lack of appetite the lack of exercise isn't affecting my waistline.

For years now, my mother and I have vowed to make more time for fun. My friends and I have promised each other that "this year" we would get together more often. I've planned to spend more time studying and reading the Bible, not just when preparing to teach Sunday school. But all of my cooking, cleaning, working, and constant activity kept getting in the way. Now that I can't stay constantly on the go, I recognize that the world hasn't stopped spinning, and my time could have been better spent. I'm sure this won't be the last revelation to come my way.

Some might say my cancer diagnosis was a lousy Christmas present. The good thing about it, though, was that I got to see a lot of close friends and family members not long after getting the news. They were very encouraging. One of my good friends – whom I love dearly but don't see nearly often enough – said, "Maybe now we will finally make the effort to get together!" Yes, maybe now I will slow down even when I'm not forced to and spend time focusing on things that really matter. If I can just get off the couch.

My temperament is such that I feel best about myself when I'm extremely busy and my day ends with a bunch of checkmarks on my mental to-do list. The more, the better. Nothing wrong with that, right? Wrong. I think for many Christians and for myself in particular, Satan's best strategy is to keep us so busy with the good that we miss the best.

At heart, I'm a writer. It's a God-given talent that was evident when I was a mere fourth-grader banging out stories on the typewriter that was my favorite Christmas gift. I believe that God's best for me often includes writing, but so often I'm tempted to do "bigger" and "better" things. Even after quitting a job to write this book, I find myself wanting to volunteer for efforts that aren't meant for me, at least not right now.

About 15 years ago I had a job that included a lot of down time, leaving me mostly alone with nothing to do. I felt called to use that down time to write notes of comfort to people who were hurting. I'm so glad I answered that call. Although it was years ago, I still hear from people who say they were deeply touched by those notes. So I know that not only am I a writer, but that God has and will use my writing to make a difference.

When my younger son, Evan, went to a private Christian school, there were two divergent mom groups. One was the Parent-Teacher organization, the group of doers who worked hard and volunteered for everything. The other was Moms in Touch, a group that met for prayer once a week. The groups' different interests had them battling at times. Those who prayed didn't volunteer for work. Those who worked didn't go to prayer group. Each group complained about the other. Despite the fact that I had a part-time job, I somehow ended up in both groups.

Among many other tasks, through the working group I helped establish a large annual auction and fundraising event that raised a lot of money to pave the way for low-income children to attend the school. It was important work and no doubt good. It also honed my event planning and organizational skills and bolstered my resume.

While the working group was good and necessary, I believe the time invested in the prayer group was better. The prayer group took place on Wednesday mornings, my day off. I used Wednesdays to run through my to-do list and at first didn't want to give up any of that time. But I felt led to join the group and a little reluctantly attended the first session. You could feel the Spirit in that room as we moms joined together in prayer not only for our own children but also for all those in the school. I noticed, too, that if I invested that time in prayer, the rest of my day went well. I accomplished much more on the days I attended the prayer group than on those when I didn't. I don't think it was coincidence. I believe it was God showing me that the prayer time mattered.

I may not be able to list note writing and praying on my resume, and I certainly won't get any public recognition for those endeavors, but I know it was the highest and best use of my time. I also know that while cancer has been a beast, it has been a blessing in that it has forced me to slow down and really think about how God wants me to use my time.

"If the devil can't make us bad, he will make us busy." –Corrie ten Boom

⚓ **Monday, January 4, 2010, 5:43 p.m.**

When I got married (26 years ago!), everyone said I was the most laidback bride-to-be they had ever seen. And I was. Right up to the moment I walked down the aisle and stood in front of 500-plus people. I was shaking so badly, I couldn't hold the wedding bouquet steady. Thankfully, David reached over and helped me hold it still.

It was the same way when our first son, Drew, was born. I was the Queen of Calm throughout the pregnancy, but when I went into labor, I felt a little panic-stricken. David, however, was calm, cool and collected. His strength and calmness helped me overcome my fears. So much so, I spent the entire afternoon at the pool before giving birth that evening!

Now, David's strength is helping to carry me through this cancer diagnosis. He's been right there with me as we've heard not so good news from doctors; as I've prepped for yet another test; as I've lounged on the couch in my grungy sweats and nappy hair; and as I've tossed and turned unable to sleep because of the pain. (That problem has been solved, by the way. Thank you, hydrocodone!)

David has also taken over the tasks of going to Sam's Wholesale and the grocery store, which have to be my two most hated activities. He helps keep the house clean and happily eats soup from a can with no complaint.

It is very difficult for me to talk about my health and tell others how I'm doing. David has been great to help spread the word so that I don't have to. And, with this new outlet of CaringBridge, I'm able to speak through the written word, which is far more comfortable for me.

As I write this, I am thankful. Thankful for a husband who loves me for better or worse, in sickness and in health, and thankful for all the people who are praying for me and supporting me through this difficult time.

My family has gained much insight – and gotten quite a few laughs – from studying the four temperaments through *Personality Plus* by Florence Littauer and *The Spirit-Controlled Temperament* by Tim LaHaye. The theory of four distinct temperaments, or humours, dates back to Hippocrates, the ancient Greek physician considered by many to be the father of medicine. Hippocrates believed a person's health and personality were determined by the balance of black bile, phlegm, yellow bile and blood in their body.

While the four temperaments paint with a very broad brush, they do a good job of explaining who we are at our core and why we think and act the way we do. I've heard it explained that the temperaments are the skeleton of who we are. Just as we can't change our height or bone structure, we can't change our temperaments. We can, however, vastly change our appearance by gaining or losing weight, changing our hair, or even by the clothes we wear. Similarly, our life experiences, such as education, family history, birth order and faith, can cause us to act very differently from someone else with the same temperament.

In a nutshell, the four basic types are described as follows:

Sanguine – Extrovert. Sanguines are talkative, creative, emotional, energetic, optimistic, fun-loving people. In the world of Winnie the Pooh, Tigger is a sanguine.

Melancholy – Introvert. Melancholies are logical, deep, quiet and thoughtful. They are perfectionists and pessimistic by nature, foreseeing problems before they happen and counting costs before going forward. Eeyore is melancholy.

Choleric – Extrovert. Cholerics are powerful, take-charge and self-confident individuals who speak their mind. They are decisive and quick to action. Rabbit is choleric.

Phlegmatic – Introvert. Phlegmatics are easygoing, well balanced, quiet, calm and peaceful. They are the easiest of all temperaments to get along with. Winnie the Pooh is most definitely phlegmatic.

David and I are complete opposites. I am almost entirely choleric, with a little sanguine thrown in. I know I can be bossy, and I've already confessed that I am high on sense of urgency and low on caution. I want things to happen – fast. David is a fairly equal blend of phlegmatic and melancholy. Where I am fast, he is slow. I am energized by spending time with people; he needs time alone to recharge. I fearlessly push forward to achieve an end result; he carefully researches and plans before making a decision. He is definitely my heavenly sandpaper, helping to smooth away those things like my innate impatience that aren't like Christ. He also balances me out.

While David and I are opposites in so many ways, we share a common and deep commitment to God and to the vows we made before God and those 500-plus people who made me shudder with fear all those years ago. I won't say it has always been easy, and as is the case in almost all marriages, there have been times when either of us could have made a very plausible excuse to give up on the marriage and walk away. I'm so glad we didn't. David has been a rock and faithful companion, and I can't imagine going through this battle without him by my side.

⚓ Sunday, January 10, 2010, 7:24 p.m.

How do you tell your children you have cancer? When I told them a few weeks ago, I decided to handle it like I do everything else – with as little drama as possible. No family meeting, no big speech, just tell them straight up when they got home.

Drew, 20, was the first to arrive. In short, I told him that I had colorectal cancer, but that it was very treatable and that the chances for a full recovery were excellent. The pain showed in his eyes. "I'm so sorry," he said, and I felt his deep sympathy. Then he went upstairs.

Evan, 17, arrived about 30 minutes later. After I told him, he said, "Next time you tell me something like that, start with 'It's very treatable, but ... ' You about gave me a heart attack!" Then he sat down and asked questions for about 20 minutes, one of which involved whether or not I would lose my hair. When I told him that I probably would, he looked at me like he didn't even want to think about it. (I agree. It won't be pretty.)

They've both handled everything wonderfully, just as I would have expected. They are fine young men, and I am very proud of them.

Evan has taken up cooking and is becoming quite adept in the kitchen. The other day, my lunch was chicken fried rice that he had made, and my supper was half a cheeseburger I found leftover when I got home from work. I learned later that Evan was saving the cheeseburger for himself. When I apologized for eating it, he said, "How many meals have you fixed for me over the years? How could I possibly get mad?"

Drew, noticing that I was a bit stir-crazy last weekend, came upstairs with a funny movie and sat down to watch it with me. He also has decided that he wants to try to find a full-time job so that he can start paying more of his own expenses. I believe it is the way he wants to contribute to the family, so this is one of those times when I'm going to have to step aside and let him do it.

Just a little while ago, I watched the amazing happen when the University of Tennessee men's basketball team beat Kansas even though UT was without four of its best players. It is amazing what can happen when a team functions as a team, with all the players contributing. Now that I'm not able to run around doing everything for everybody, our family is functioning like a team more than ever before. And, in the end, I am confident we'll be victorious.

Before I got sick, I truly did just about everything for my family. I realized how spoiled they were when, after 26 years of marriage, David asked, "So, you just put the dish in the dishwasher?" I said that someday Drew's and Evan's wives would thank their lucky stars I got sick because it forced them to learn some domestic duties. Drew's wife still laughs at some of the things he's never had to do.

As a "doer," it has been hard for me to stop doing for my family. Ridiculous as it may seem, when I'm not feeling so great I feel guilty to be lying on the couch while someone else is cleaning the kitchen, vacuuming or doing laundry. It's been tough admitting I can't do everything and accepting help.

The toughest thing by far, however, was telling my sons I had cancer. I felt like I was letting them down somehow. Their mom, who was supposed to be invincible and rarely even got sick, had something that could kill her. How do you soften the blow of that news? Even now, it's much harder for me to share bad news with them than it is to get bad news from the doctor.

By the way, the "something" in my liver that I referred to in my January 1 post was later confirmed to be cancer. Reading through my old posts, I find it curious that I never even mentioned that fact. I wasn't trying to hide bad news. I believe I was just so focused on my family and how my cancer would affect them that the news about my liver barely registered.

⚓ Monday, January 11, 2010, 7:05 p.m.

About 10 years ago, I wrote a humor book, *The Fashion Police Handbook*. In it, I poked fun at everything from "Improperly Contained Fat" to "Contributing to the Tackiness of a Minor." I also made fun of the infamously ugly fanny pack. I am now sporting a fanny pack; and, yes, it probably serves me right. More details in a minute.

I went today for my first chemo treatment. Everything went very well. They loaded me up with anti-nausea medicine, and I don't feel sick at all. After they administered some of the drugs on-site, they filled my pump with the medicine I will receive until I go back in tomorrow. Then, they'll deliver some chemo on-site, fill my pump, and send me on my way. I go back in Wednesday for them to remove the pump. Then I have a week off and the whole process starts again the next week.

When they pulled out the fanny pack and prepared to wrap it around my waist, I had to laugh out loud. "I have to wear this thing?" I asked. I had expected something the size of a cell phone that would discretely fit on my belt with no one being the wiser. Wrong! Anyway, at least it's only for a few days. I suppose with the chemo card, people won't make fun of me. The one exception would be my younger brother, Phillip. He would take one look at me and come up with the funniest remark you could imagine. I may send him a photo. I always love a good laugh, even if it's at my expense!

Notes: Those of you who know about cancer have asked what kinds of chemo I'm on. One of the nurses said the combination of chemo I'm receiving is known as Folfox. The main drugs are Avastin and Eloxatin.

My new treatment regimen will be chemotherapy (probably for about 10-12 weeks) and then surgery. Radiation is now out of the picture. If chemo does the trick on the cancer in my liver, surgery on my liver will not be necessary, which would be a good thing.

While I wrote that post intending to be funny, I really was bothered by the fanny pack. Looking back on it now, I realize how foolish I was to be focused on the fashion-worthiness of the device delivering chemotherapy through my body. I also realize how fearlessly I jumped into the entire treatment process. I showed up on a Monday morning – by myself – assuming that they'd fill my chemo pump with whatever toxins the doctor prescribed and send me off to work. I didn't even know what kind of drugs they were giving me, and didn't even have it right after talking to the nurse. I was getting Folfox, a combination of three drugs, plus Avastin.

The nurse warned me that Oxaliplatin, one of the drugs in the combination, could cause sensitivity to cold. She suggested that I always wear gloves when outdoors and avoid drinks with ice. I remember a funny tingling in my hands as I entered the chilly parking garage, a feeling that greatly intensified when I opened the car door. "I will have to start wearing gloves," I thought. Then, without thinking, I took a big gulp of the ice water that had been sitting in my car. Yikes! It felt like I had swallowed glass. Undaunted, I drove on to work and was still more concerned about how I looked in the fanny pack than anything else. I remember complaining about a mild headache, but I managed to work until 5 p.m.

⚓ Tuesday, January 12, 2010, 9:48 a.m.

I'm sending out an SOS. I was up sick all night and my head is killing me. I'm leaving shortly to go back to the doctor. Please pray that they can tweak the dosage so that it doesn't make me feel so bad. I love all of you and thank you so much for your prayers and concern.

I'm so glad I included that post. People often mistakenly assume that I only share good news and try to put a positive spin on my situation. "How do you really feel?" is a question that drives me crazy. I'm always honest about how I feel. On the morning of January 12, I felt lousy.

⚓ Tuesday, January 12, 2010, 3:46 p.m.

All went well at the doctor today. Because David drove me, they were able to give me some "happy juice" to kill the pain and knock me out all afternoon. I'm feeling better, but expectedly weak. We have a new game plan for next week that we hope won't make me so sick. Many thanks for all your prayers and concerns. I appreciate you!

That happy juice was some good stuff. I felt much better by that afternoon.

⚓ Thursday, January 14, 2010, 4:55 p.m.

I've run into and talked to a few people today and yesterday who were concerned about me since my "SOS" post. Sorry I didn't update sooner. I slept most of the day and evening on Tuesday and then went back to work yesterday feeling fine. I probably overdid it a little yesterday, because I basically passed out when I got home from work, but other than being tired, I felt fine. I feel fine today, too.

I had two very pleasant surprises today. I ran into my best childhood friend. She was so encouraging, telling me about her brother who survived a serious scare from colon cancer. There are so many survivors out there, and I love hearing stories about each of them.

I also had another friend stop by my office to catch up and share her concern. I am constantly touched and amazed at the number of people who are praying for me and care about me. I am overwhelmed and grateful.

On a lighter note, I've commented to several people lately that if it's true that pets have an inner sense about their owner's health and wellbeing, there is no need to worry about me. Henry, our aging basset hound, sees my time on the couch only as an opportunity to demand more of my attention. He also hovers closely whenever I'm eating because he knows I won't finish it and he'll likely get a bite. No compassion or concern out of this hound. I'll take that as a good sign!

"There is one who speaks rashly like the thrusts of the sword, but the tongue of the wise brings healing." Proverbs 12:18

Words matter. The words of my friends that day lifted me up and gave me hope. How many times do we think about calling a friend, or sending a note, or just saying something nice to someone we're with but fail to follow through? Knowing how words have lifted me up, I try to be extra diligent in sharing words of healing whenever possible.

As to the first part of the verse, I'll start by confessing that with my choleric temperament there are times when my words are like the thrust of a sword. Many unfortunate words have escaped my lips over the years, and I wish dearly that I could take them back. Age and experience have helped make me a little better at holding my tongue, and my sickness has made me much more likely to think before I speak. I wish I could say the same for many others.

I often say that some of the most inappropriate comments made are those spoken to pregnant women, people with cancer and people who have just experienced the loss of a loved one. I've actually had more than one person say something along the lines of, "Oh, I had a friend with colorectal cancer. Hers got better, but then it came back worse than ever and she died."

⚓ **Sunday, January 17, 2010, 4:43 p.m.**

For the past several years, my family has carried on a Labor Day tradition of staying with my brother, Phillip, and going to Six Flags

Over Georgia. This past Labor Day, my stomach was giving me fits (although I had no idea it was from cancer), and it would have been easy for me to decide I didn't feel up to the trip. Instead, I plied myself with Imodium AD and forged ahead as planned. Evan took a friend, and I took my niece, Tejah, 10. We rode every ride there and had a fabulous time.

In December, my mother, sister and I took my nephew Parker, 6, to see the "Polar Express" at a private showing at the Bijou Theatre sponsored by U.S. Cellular. It was a fun day. Parker was so happy he skipped all the way to the car. I wasn't feeling too great that day, either, but I was so glad that I went ahead as planned.

Today, my mother and I went to a wedding shower. Typically not at all my idea of a fun time, but it was very uplifting and I was glad we went.

I realize that in the days ahead there will be many times when my body won't allow me to do what I want to do, and I'm going to be careful to respect that. However, I do plan to carve out time for family and friends and sometimes go forward with things even when I don't feel like it. I believe the good memories and positive energy will help me in the long run.

Striking a balance between rest and activity has been a challenge and, I believe, an important part of what has helped me do so well throughout my treatment and recovery. There were a lot of days when I could have stayed home in bed because I felt so bad, but instead I chose to carry on – whether it was going to work, enjoying something fun or maintaining my exercise routine. I typically was glad I forged ahead and felt better because of it. I am convinced that, had I declared myself sick and unable to do things, it would have been a self-fulfilling prophecy.

At times, however, David had to insist that I slow down; at others, I recognized it myself. I've had to learn to push myself just enough to get stronger without pushing myself so hard that I deplete everything I have. It's a delicate balance that I continue to fine-tune.

⚓ **Tuesday, January 19, 2010, 4:58 p.m.**

Like all the Ironsides, I'm quite competitive. The fact that my cancer is Stage IV – the most advanced stage – hardly represents a victory to me, however. The good news is that we met with the doctor today, and he is every bit as enthusiastic about my complete recovery as he was before we discovered the cancer spots on my liver.

On Monday, I go back for Round Two of chemo, and we'll continue every other week for at least two more rounds after that. Then, we'll do a scan to see how the cancer is responding to the chemo and begin discussing surgery.

There will be a six-week wait period before we can do surgery because the chemo affects the body's ability to heal. So, it looks like surgery will take place in the spring. Maybe I can spend some recovery time out by the pool.

Satan is clever. He knows when and how to attack us, where we're most vulnerable. I am competitive, and there's a part of me that wants to be better than any other cancer patient. I want to be stronger, smarter, more independent, quicker to recover, more resilient and have a more miraculous recovery. My gut reaction when I hear news about someone with cancer is to compare theirs with mine and count the ways that I come out on top.

"She has to have someone sit with her while she has chemo? I can drive myself and I sure don't need someone there holding my hand."

"They found the cancer at Stage I? That's nothing."

"He's having surgery with no chemo or radiation? It should be a breeze."

It sounds despicable and it's not easy to admit, but it's true. I share it because this book is intended to reveal the real me, warts and all. I will add that I am getting better at quickly identifying and confessing those kinds of thoughts as the sin that they are and replacing them with only love and concern for those who are suffering.

"Be of sober spirit, be on the alert. Your adversary, the devil, prowls about like a roaring lion seeking someone to devour. But resist him, stand firm in your faith, knowing that the same experiences of suffering are being accomplished by your brethren who are in the world.

"And after you have suffered for a little while, the God of all grace, who called you to His eternal glory in Christ, will Himself perfect, confirm, strengthen and establish you." I Peter 5:8-10

⚓ Saturday, January 23, 2010, 9:56 a.m.

Appearances can be deceiving. People are shocked when they find out I have cancer. "You look too healthy!" they all say. I do look healthy. Even my blood work, blood pressure, etc. are excellent. Under a PET scan that lights up when cancer is present, however, it becomes apparent that I'm not.

Our pastor often tells us that we have no idea what the people around us are going through. Job losses, depression, health issues, loss of loved ones – so many people are hurting and we often never even know it.

I'm fortunate that people know what I'm going through because it affords me an unbelievable amount of support. These days, I'm making more of a conscious effort to treat with kindness everyone I encounter. You never know what they may be going through, and even a simple smile might brighten their day.

As an aside, the chemo seems to be working. As I write this I feel good, and I feel a little better each day. I go back in for more chemo on Monday, and I'm actually excited about it because I know that it's helping.

Many thanks for your prayers! They're helping, too!

As I've battled cancer, there have been many times I've looked much better than I felt. I remember one day when I was climbing the hill from the parking garage to work. I didn't realize I was walking slowly, but I must have been. Two or three young people hurried around me as if to say, "Out of my way, old lady."

Before that day, I had never felt particularly old and never really worried about my age. I realized, though, that those young people saw me as just another old person impeding their progress. It's an attitude I've had more times than I like to admit. That occurrence and many like it have made me look very differently at the people I encounter each day.

The store clerk is a little rude? Maybe she has some issues at home that are weighing her down. A coworker snaps when I ask a simple question? Maybe mine was one in a long line of disruptions for someone struggling to meet a deadline. He's being a jerk? Maybe it's because he's a jerk, but that doesn't mean I have to respond with meanness. My family says my sickness has softened me up, which I say was sorely needed.

"Therefore, however you want people to treat you, so treat them."
Matthew 7:12

⚓ Monday, January 25, 2010, 5:03 p.m.

Just a short and sweet update to let you know that I did not have chemo today. I have to wait until next week because my white blood count is too low. White blood cells are the ones that fight disease in your body. The doctor and nurses didn't seem too concerned. They just told me to avoid being around too many people, particularly those who are sick. And, I can't clean our chinchilla's cage. Darn!

While far from earth-shattering, the news that I couldn't go through with chemo as scheduled forced me to slow down and think.

⚓ Tuesday, January 26, 2010, 5:50 p.m.

Yesterday's events made me a little reflective, and today I've come to the following conclusions:

1. Vanity is going to have to go out the window. First, it was the fanny pack. Now, I have to wear a face mask when I'm in large crowds. Next, I'll probably lose my hair (although for now it's holding on pretty well). But I will be thin!

2. I'm going to have to change my ways. Caution is not my strong suit. However, I have to be careful about germs, which probably means I'll give up going to church for the short-term and definitely wear the aforementioned mask when I'm around a lot of people.

3. I have to remember that my treatment and getting better are the most important things right now. When I first heard about the change in my chemo schedule, I was bothered by the fact that it would interfere with a board meeting schedule at work. I now realize that there will be plenty of other board meetings and plenty of work for me to do so long as I take care of myself and get well.

4. I've been too quick to treat my cancer as something I could just fit in with the rest of my schedule and carry on with life as normal. While I'll do everything in my power to keep life as "normal" as possible, I'm going to give the disease and its treatment the respect they both deserve. So, the girl who's been a daredevil since before she could walk will tone it down a bit – just until I'm well. Then, everybody better look out!

It was still so early in the disease when I wrote that post; I had no idea how much cancer would change my life. I often catch myself tracking time based on my cancer diagnosis. I'm much more likely to say, "That was before I got sick," than "That was more than four years ago." It's not that I let cancer run my life or that every waking moment is spent thinking about it; it's just that cancer is always there – the nerve pain that causes a sudden stab in my side, the scars across my abdomen and back, the frequent doctor visits, or the realization that at any time it could strike hard and knock me sideways.

When you peel back all the layers, though, the main thing that cancer has taken away is my sense of control. Like Jacob, I suppose I've wrestled with God a bit over this giving up of control. Yes, it seems ridiculous that I believed I could better manage my life and my days than the One who created the universe, but somehow I did. Even today, I catch myself trying to get back in the driver's seat, to flex my muscles a bit and show how strong I am. When I humble myself, though, I realize that I am not the master of my fate, and without Him I can do nothing.

"But as for me, I shall sing of Thy strength; yes I shall joyfully sing of Thy lovingkindness in the morning, for Thou hast been my stronghold, and a refuge in the day of my distress.

"O my strength, I will sing praises to Thee; for God is my stronghold, the God who shows me lovingkindness." Psalm 59:16-17

⚓ **Thursday, January 28, 2010, 6:19 p.m.**

I have to start by explaining that I have three jobs:

1. Four days a week, I work at the Knoxville Area Urban League, a non-profit agency dedicated to empowering communities and changing lives.
2. One day a week, I work at Moxley Carmichael, a public relations firm.
3. From home, I serve as executive director for Executive Women's Association, a group of about 150 of the top women executives in Knoxville and surrounding areas.

Most people say so many jobs must make me crazy. I say it makes me perfectly content, more so in light of recent events.

At the Urban League, I work for the CEO, Phyllis Nichols. She is an amazing lady whom I admire very much. She is extremely supportive and encouraging, and she actually shoos me out the door if she thinks I look too tired and need to go home.

The staff members at the Urban League have also been great. Just yesterday, our Housing Director – a man who is in a lot of pain from recent back surgery – came to me and said he plans to do a cancer walk in September in honor of me and a couple of his friends who died from the disease. He's going to try to get a lot of the staff involved. I am so touched by that, and my expectation is that I'll be right out there with them for the walk.

The ladies of Executive Women's Association have blown me away with their support. Within an hour of sending an email to the membership about my cancer, I had at least 50 emails – many of them from cancer survivors and all of them full of heartfelt and encouraging words. Emails and cards continue to come in daily. At yesterday's meeting, they showered me with love and concern, and their genuine care showed in their eyes.

Today my colleagues at Moxley Carmichael presented me with a "Sunshine Basket," a huge, gorgeous, handmade basket full of wrapped presents. They instructed me to take a present each time I go to chemotherapy so that I have something to be excited about. I was so overwhelmed with their generosity and kindness I nearly cried.

I could go on and on about all the other people who are doing so much for me – my parents, siblings, friends, the Soul Sisters (my Sunday school class), neighbors, and even complete strangers. Earlier this week I received a hand knit blanket from a cancer survivor who now makes blankets and prays for the person she's making the blanket for as she knits.

I know that being surrounded by so much love is helping me stay strong and feel good. To everyone, I offer my sincerest thanks!

I quit my four-day-a-week job at the Urban League so I would have time to write this book. It was incredibly difficult to do so, and there were times I wondered if I would have the courage to take such a giant leap of faith.

In late December, David and I agreed that, if we could secure health insurance, I would quit my job to allow time to write. The decision was made soon after we returned from a weeklong cruise when we both were relaxed and refreshed. Following our decision, the Urban League was closed for the holidays, giving me additional time to think about my resignation. Doubts began to nag me, and I felt guilty that my departure would be difficult for my employer and coworkers.

I should point out I feel a huge sense of responsibility for just about everything. Something needs to be done? I'll do it. There's a problem? I'll solve it. Someone's unhappy? I'll make them feel better.

My sense of responsibility is particularly keen when it comes to work. I have a hard time resting until every task is complete, and it kills me to think someone else will have to pick up the slack for something I've failed to do. Outrageous as it may sound, there were times when I tweaked the timing of infusions, appointments and even surgery to better accommodate my work schedule.

All of that came into play when I devised an alternate plan to work 16 to 20 hours a week instead of resigning. I can try to spin it any way I want, but deep down I know Plan B was disobedience. God had called me to resign and write a book. I was going to work less and write a book.

When I offered Plans A and B to my boss, she was caught quite off guard. And, I think, hurt a bit. Phyllis Nichols and the Urban League had been with me throughout this journey, too. We had worked very closely for a number of years and worked well together. She was not pleased with either proposition. We spent a stressful few days filled with meetings and back-and-forth negotiations until I was forced to make a decision: Did I trust God's leading, or didn't I? Was I willing to walk away from my job, or not?

God gave me the courage to quit my job. Like the Israelites, though, I remained fickle. Fear started creeping in, and I started to worry my reputation would be damaged or people would make the assumption I had been fired rather than resigning. In short, I started to doubt. But

God was faithful. It felt like the heavens had opened up and God's voice came straight to my ears when my mother and a godly friend told me on the same day, "God will protect you."

God showed His protection in one area only a few days later. When choosing health insurance, David and I were very careful to select a plan that included all my doctors. After confirming with two insurance representatives that my doctors were on the plan in question, we finished the online application and attempted to make payment to finalize the process. Much to my chagrin, problems with the website prevented that from happening.

Shortly thereafter, my mother heard the tail-end of a newscast about a cancer patient having trouble using her new insurance. Alerted to a potential problem, we made more calls and learned we had been given bad information. My doctors were not on the selected plan. Because we had been unable to pay for the insurance, we were able to change the plan before it was too late.

"And Peter got out of the boat, and walked on the water and came toward Jesus. But seeing the wind, he became afraid, and beginning to sink, he cried out saying, 'Lord, save me!'" Matthew 14:29-30

⚓ Saturday, January 30, 2010, 2:32 p.m.

Our pastor had just finished an excellent sermon on love. He asked us, "Do you love God?" "Do you love your neighbor?" "What are you willing to do to reach your neighbors for Christ?"

As we stood to sing our hymn of invitation, I could hear God asking me, "Do you love me?" *Of course, I do, Lord.*

"Do you love your neighbors?" *Yes, Lord.*

"Are you willing to do anything to bring them to me?" *Yes.*

It was a significant moment that really shook me to my core. I knew that I was signing up for something, although I had no idea what I had just agreed to do.

Matthew 5:16 says, "Let your light shine before men in such a way that they may see your good works, and glorify your Father who is in Heaven." That's how I've tried to live my life. I've let people know that I'm a Christian and tried to let them see Jesus in me by the way I live. Sometimes I've succeeded; sometimes I've failed miserably.

After the sermon, I was prepared to change how I reached people, although I didn't know what that would entail.

Meanwhile, my job at Moxley Carmichael had me writing full-page health features for the *Shopper-News*. Each week, I would talk to people whose lives had been changed – often in an instant – by some sort of health tragedy.

In October, my sister's father-in-law died unexpectedly from a heart attack. I kept being reminded that we just don't know how or when our lives will change – or even end.

Shortly after that, it was my turn to teach the quarterly breakfast meeting that included several adult Sunday school classes. I told them about the health stories and my sister's father-in-law, and exhorted them to find God's purpose for their lives every day. I could barely get the words out because they were coming from a place so deep in my soul that it made me cry. I knew I was speaking the words as much to myself as I was to them.

When December came and the doctor told me I had cancer, I somehow wasn't shocked by the diagnosis. Not because I suspected I had cancer, but because I expected that something in my life was going to drastically change, and God had been preparing me for the diagnosis months in advance.

Now I see the cancer as a way for me to reach out to even more people. I also see this outlet of CaringBridge as a way to offer hope – not just to my family and friends, but to other people who have cancer and to those whose family members have it.

Don't get me wrong. I'm not saying I'm glad I have cancer, but I look at my cancer diagnosis like this: I could get angry. I could get angry at the disease for attacking me, the healthy one who eats right and exercises. I could get angry at God for allowing this disease to come my way. But anger will get me nowhere and will actually hinder my progress. Instead, I choose to trust that God has a plan for me, that He will bring me through this difficult time and that He will use me to reach others for Him in the process.

I remember writing this post with tears pouring down my face. I'm not typically an emotional person, but I do get teary when I'm really speaking from the heart. This was definitely one of those times. It is so easy to give lip service to reaching the lost or following the Lord, but it's far easier to let the mundane concerns of daily living silence that still, small voice and crowd out the higher purpose to which we are called. Like hamsters on a wheel, we're all so busy going nowhere.

While I maintain the position that I'm not glad I got cancer, I do see that so much good has come out of it. In addition to strengthening my faith and making me a better person, cancer has given me a platform to share my faith and help others. I often hear from people who say that a particular post has spoken to them or that following my journey has helped them stay positive in the midst of adversity. It is my hope and prayer that this book will take those posts and multiply their blessings, similar to the feeding of the 5,000 with five loaves and two fish.

"In this is love, not that we loved God, but that He loved us and sent his Son to be the propitiation for our sins. Beloved, if God so loved us, we also ought to love one another." 1 John 4:9-10

⚓ Tuesday, February 2, 2010, 5:49 p.m.

The Fanny Pack is Back!

Yes, I'm in day two of my second round of chemo and day two of the dreaded fanny pack. I have to say, though, that I'm already getting a little numb to it and a little less embarrassed. And, since it goes off tomorrow morning, I can't really complain. The good news is that my white count was up enough to start treatment again.

The bad news is that I had another migraine last night following the chemo. As I lay suffering on the couch, David suggested that I take some Tylenol. "I already took a pain pill and it didn't do a thing," I moaned. He then suggested that I might be better off going to the bedroom where it was dark and quiet. "I'm fine," I groaned.

Then I decided to have David call the doctor on call to see what I should do. Guess what the doctor said? "Take some Tylenol and go to a dark, quiet room." Suppose I should have listened to "Dr. Dave." Anyway, it worked. I got up this morning feeling fine. Today, they lowered my dose of steroids to see if that helps with the headache. So far, so good.

Sunshine Basket Updates: I was like a little kid all weekend – looking at my gift basket, fighting the urge to open all my presents at once, and trying to decide which I would open first. I ended up using the blind draw method. My first present was a DVD, "Bride Wars." Definitely a chick flick. Having grown up in a house full of boys and now living in a male-dominated household, chick flicks aren't something I often see. Guess I'll get in touch with my feminine side after all!

Today I opened a box of shortbread cookies – my favorite! Even though I don't technically get chemo tomorrow, I do have to get two shots, one to raise my red blood count and one to raise my white blood count. They say that for some patients the white blood count shot can cause pain and achiness similar to the flu. I'm hoping to be one of the exceptions. Still, I think having to get two shots deserves another present, don't you?

I was the kid who, if allowed, would open all of her presents on Christmas Eve and eat all of her Halloween candy soon after carrying in the haul. I did manage to muster some much needed self-control for the gift basket, which was good because those gifts were a definite pick-me-up throughout the treatment process.

One, a Queen Elizabeth statuette, provided a good laugh just last year. The Queen, a gift from my boss, Cynthia Moxley, is holding a solar-powered handbag. When sunlight hits the handbag, the queen gives a royal wave. She sits on my desk at home. On a snow day last winter, I heard a loud clicking sound coming from my office. After a little investigation, I discovered that the sun was reflecting very brightly off the snow and coming straight to the queen's handbag. She was waving for all she was worth.

⚓ **Wednesday, February 3, 2010, 7:15 p.m.**

This 'n That

We seem to have found the right chemo mixture. I had no problems after yesterday's treatment. I also suffered no side effects from the shot I got today to raise my white blood count. Hooray! It's funny, though, I've been taking enough pain pills to put down a small farm animal and have still been able to work and function as normal. But when I took the allergy pill Claritin – which for some reason helps prevent the muscle aches from the shot – it nearly knocked me out.

More gifts! Today I chose the largest gift in my basket. It is a set of photo books. Maybe now I'll organize all those photos that have found their way into boxes and drawers!

I also had a funny surprise in today's mail. I'll explain.

When my cousin Tracy and I were kids, we had our tonsils out at the same time. Certain that she was going to die, Tracy went to church the Sunday before surgery and put all of her money in the offering plate. After surgery, Tracy acted like she was about to die. I, on the other hand, was unfazed by any of it. In fact, while I was still supposed to be in bed recovering from surgery, I jumped up and ran across the hospital room to get a box of Whoppers malted milk balls my father had brought me. Everyone yelled at me to get back to bed and told me I couldn't eat anyway. Today, my aunt Shirley, Tracy's mother, sent me a box of Whoppers. Thanks, Shirl!

A lot of people tend to treat cancer patients with kid gloves, all kind words and somber looks. I much prefer to approach my sickness with a healthy sense of humor and appreciate it when others do, too. That box of Whoppers was a perfect gift.

One day when I was cleaning out the kitchen at work, I unearthed someone's leftovers that looked more like a science experiment gone awry than something that had once been consumable. "Breathe that in," said a coworker. "It should do a better job of killing cancer than the chemo you're taking." We both got a good laugh.

Last spring my brother, Phillip, also gave me some much needed comic relief. I was in an unbelievable amount of pain and had just texted friends and family to let them know that I had gone back in the hospital to try to get some relief. Phillip texted, "A tough person would just bite down on a stick." I laughed out loud and read it to my friend. "That would make me mad," she said with disgust. Not me. It was perfect.

"A joyful heart is good medicine, but a broken spirit dries up the bones." Proverbs 17:22

⚓ **Sunday, February 7, 2010, 12:30 p.m.**

My mom has been by my side for all the big purchases – my first bra, my first "big girl" outfit that didn't include a football jersey (I was quite the tomboy growing up), my wedding clothes and my maternity clothes. It was perfectly fitting that she was with me yesterday when we purchased a wig. Yes, it's true. Yesterday, my mother bought me a wig.

I'm not bald yet, but I am becoming increasingly follicly challenged. I look like I'm having a perpetually bad hair day, as my normally thin and baby fine hair falls out by the handful every time I blow dry and brush it. After I get ready, the bathroom looks like the floor of a military barber shop!

Surprisingly, the wig doesn't look half bad. I wore it home yesterday, and David really liked it.

And if I grow tired of my normal looking wig, I always have other options. My friend Mary Lee offered to loan me her son's mullet wig and to draw on a tattoo! Other friends have reminded me that I have a plethora of options available thanks to my many years of dressing up for Halloween – Cher, Martha Stewart and Grandma (the one who got run over by a reindeer) are just a few of the wigs available in my Halloween stash.

My friend Sybille is going to knit some caps, and I also plan to buy a few head wraps for the days when I'm not in the wig kind of mood.

I am encouraged by the fact that the women I know who lost their hair from chemo have not only grown back full heads of hair, but actually have prettier hair than they had before. Who knows? Maybe this time I'll inherit my mother's thick, gorgeous head of hair!

Until then, bring on the head cover!

My mother is a beautiful woman, inside and out. She was a fashion model for many years and always looks impeccable. When I was growing up, Mom was always fair and honest about everything, including how I looked. Most of my friends were short and petite, while I was tall and broad shouldered. When I wanted to buy clothes like those my friends wore, Mom would politely point me in the other direction. "That doesn't really flatter you," she'd say with a smile. "Try this."

When I started losing my hair and suggested that I might just wear head wraps or scarves, Mom leaped into action and took me to buy a wig. She was right, of course. My head is disproportionately small for my body, and I never could have pulled off a wigless look.

That fact was brought home to me one day when I was speaking to a group of middle school students about keeping a journal. Using my CaringBridge posts as an example, I pulled up the post that talked about telling my sons I had cancer because I thought it would resonate with the students. Before I could move on to another post, one little boy raised his hand. "I'm picturing you without hair," he said. "And it's not a pretty picture."

I also remember a funny guestbook post from my friend, Tami Hartmann. Tami told about a friend whose grandmother always kept several wigs by the front door to pop on like hats as she left the house. She had a grocery shopping one, a Sunday go-to-meeting look and a Zsa Zsa Gabor style for when she was feeling a bit flirty. One day, the weather turned chilly while the grandkids were outside playing at Grandma's house. When their mother came to pick up her young children, she found them playing on the rope swing wearing Grandma's gloves and "hats!"

A happy footnote, I never lost all my hair. Better yet, what fell out has grown back much thicker and prettier than before, just as I had hoped.

⚓ Thursday, February 11, 2010, 7:09 p.m.

If – and this is a big IF – I could sing, my song tonight would be, "I Feel Good!" It's true. I'm feeling really good, especially considering I'm on chemo. And I can tell that it's working. As of this week, I am officially off pain pills because I no longer need them. Given the fact that only a few weeks ago I had to take something every four hours just to get through the day, I deem this a huge achievement and one worth celebrating.

Other than the fact that I'm feeling good, I have no real medical news to report. I start back on chemo on Monday and am hoping that their new mixture does the trick and I don't have another migraine. I'm also hoping that the shot to raise my white blood count did the trick and my counts are good enough for treatment.

Someone recently said they appreciated the fact that I try to keep my posts upbeat to help everyone feel better about me. I assured her that I'm not *trying* to keep my posts upbeat. My posts are a direct reflection of what's in my heart and on my mind at the moment. So, there may be days, such as the day I sent out the SOS, when my posts are not so cheerful. Rest assured, though, that I'll always be upfront and honest about how I'm feeling and what I'm dealing with medically.

And, yes, brutal honesty is an Ironside thing. Those of you who know us well are probably smiling as you read this.

It's time for you to meet the Ironsides, the family of my birth. I'll start by sharing some interesting history. My father hailed from England, and his lineage traces back to a king. Charles Dickens told about King Ironside in *The Child's History of England*. Here's an excerpt:

> Was Canute to be King when Ethelred the Unready died? Not over the Saxons, they said; they must have Edmund, one of the sons of the Unready, who was surnamed Ironside, because of his strength and stature.
>
> Edmund and Canute thereupon fell to, and fought five battles—O unhappy England, what a fighting-ground it was!—and then Ironside, who was a big man, proposed to Canute, who was a little man, that the two should fight it out in single combat. If Canute had been the big man, he would probably have said yes, but, being the little man, he decidedly said no. However, he declared that he was willing to divide the kingdom— to take all that lay north of Watling Street, as the old Roman military road from Dover to Chester was called, and to give Ironside all that lay south of it. Most men being weary of so much bloodshed, this was done.
>
> But Canute soon became sole King of England; for Ironside died suddenly within two months. Some think that he was killed, and killed by Canute's orders. No one knows.

My siblings, while not yet in any history books, are nonetheless an interesting lot.

Kevin, 14 months older, was a straight-A student and the kind of kid who actually changed into play socks before going outside so he wouldn't stain his good ones. I always looked bad compared to Kevin. Today, the star pupil is an environmental engineer. He has a beautiful wife, Pamela, and seven sons, four biological and three adopted from Uganda where the family served as missionaries for two years. In the temperaments, Kevin is a choleric/melancholy, a very strong leader with a penchant for perfectionism.

Phillip, three years younger, paid me the tremendous favor of coming along in time to keep my parents' attention diverted from me and the comparisons to Kevin kept to a minimum. I was apt for mischief; in addition to finding creative ways to get in trouble, I talked too much in school and frequently came home from play injured and dirty. Compared to Phillip, however, I looked pretty good. Phillip's lack of effort in the classroom was extraordinary. And, when he went outside to play, he didn't just get dirty, he destroyed whatever he happened to be wearing. I remember a pair of "indestructible" boots that lasted only a day.

Today, Phillip is a very successful high school football coach. He is married to Tashia, whom he met while she was training for the Olympics and he was a college football player. They have a son and daughter and live just outside of Atlanta. Phillip is an easygoing phlegmatic who can always make me laugh.

Growing up between Kevin and Phillip had a definite impact on me. It most certainly made me tough, something that has served me well, especially in this fight against cancer.

Kristen, the baby of the family, came along when I was 12. In Kristen, my mom finally got the "real" girl she always wanted. While I was a complete tomboy, Kristen liked to wear dresses and play with dolls. Kristen is married to Tommy, who is about the same age as me and is very good for her. She has a son from a prior marriage and two stepdaughters, Lauren and Lindsey Vandergriff. Kristen is a fun-loving, emotional sanguine. She and I are very different in many ways, but very close.

My mother, Barbara, is an amazing lady who is loved by all. A woman of rock-solid faith, she modeled for us what it means to live for Christ and to love others. She was a devoted homemaker and an excellent cook. Mom's temperament is a little hard to nail down, because she lacks a lot of the weaknesses that make it easy to define the rest of us. If I had to guess, I would assume that she is an easygoing phlegmatic with a hint of perfectionist melancholy.

My father, David, was a devoted father and husband who worked hard to provide for his family and still managed to spend a lot of time with his children. Dad was a strong choleric, and there was no doubt that he was the head of our household. My cousin Tracy and I laugh about how scared we were of my father when we were children, but I expect it was only because we were so mean and knew we couldn't get away with anything on his watch. Dad died from Alzheimer's last year. Watching him leave us little by little was one of the hardest things I have ever endured.

Mine was a very idyllic, Cleaver-like childhood. Only when I was much older did I realize how tremendously blessed I was to be raised in a household like mine.

I realize this introduction was a bit lengthy, but I believe my formative years had a lot to do with making me who I am today. Without knowing my family, it's not possible to fully know me.

⚓ Monday, February 15, 2010, 9:33 p.m.

It's a good day. Today I started round three of chemo, which means:

1. My white blood count was up enough to have chemo. Yay!
2. I got to open another gift. Yay! This time it was a satirical book that has fictitious news releases. It is definitely my brand of humor and actually had me laughing out loud in the chemo room.
3. I don't feel as good as I did the past few days, but I didn't get a migraine this time. So, that's another Yay! in my book.

Thanks to all of you for your prayers, cards, emails and posts. I feel them carrying me through this battle.

I assume the chemo treatment room at my doctor's office is like most others. It's a large room lined with roughly a dozen recliners that are typically full of patients receiving infusions. The times I've been there, the patient population has been quite diverse. Some patients were old and some were young; some looked fairly healthy and upbeat while others seemed despondent and looked near death; and some simply slept soundly and snored loudly.

Most of the time, I felt like the old Sesame Street song, "One of these things is not like the others." I didn't look or act sick, and I enjoyed laughing and talking with the nurses. On the day I opened up my copy of *The Onion*, a gift from Scott Bird, a coworker with a wonderfully dry sense of humor, I laughed out loud at several of its satirical news reports. I then shared with the nurses the headlines and quotes that I found particularly funny. One article, for example, talked about Depends not being so dependable. It included the quote, "I started having major problems with the Depends on Friday, which is taco day at the nursing home."

Speaking of the nurses, I would be remiss if I didn't say that my oncology nurses are amazing. Their medical knowledge is encyclopedic; they never stop moving; and despite having tremendously stressful jobs, they always are smiling and pleasant. I remember someone telling me soon after I was diagnosed that they would be praying for my nurses because a good nurse can make all the difference in your treatment. Amen to that.

⚓ **Friday, February 19, 2010, 11:14 a.m.**

More good news! I was starving at 11:45 and had to eat lunch early. This is the first time in a long time that I've eaten because I'm hungry and not because someone is telling me I need to eat. If not for my mother's delicious pound cake and vegetable beef soup, I can't imagine how much weight I would have lost by now. I was laughing to my brother about how all my pants fit. He nailed it when he compared it to M.C. Hammer, the rap singer famous for his sagging pants.

The shot to raise my white blood count and the chemo knocked me down a peg or two on Wednesday afternoon and yesterday, but today I'm feeling better. I'm proud of myself for having sense enough to take long naps and go to work at 11:00 yesterday instead of 8:30. Yes, you can teach an old dog new tricks!

Other updates:

- My hair continues to hang on, although it is thinning. For a fleeting moment I was actually hoping it would fall out so I would need the expensive wig my mother purchased. Now, I'll be thankful for whatever hair I keep and be glad I have a wig if I need it.
- On a prior post, I mentioned that the Ironsides are known for our "brutal honesty." My mom thought that sounded a little harsh. For the record, her honesty is not as brutal as the rest of ours!

Mom is the nicest member of our family. After I wrote the post that talked about our brutal honesty, she was a bit mortified, similar to how she felt when I wrote *The Fashion Police Handbook*. Any time that book is mentioned, Mom is quick to say, "She's not really that mean."

To be honest, I hope I'm no longer as mean as the person who scribed the book that pokes fun at just about everybody. As Christians, we are meant to spend every day being conformed more and more to the image of Christ. In my case, perhaps it took something as strong as cancer to help make that happen.

"And we know that God causes all things to work together for good to those who love God, to those who are called according to His purpose … to become conformed to the image of His Son." Romans 8:28-29

⚓ Monday, February 22, 2010, 6:54 p.m.

When I was a kid, I ordered a clown cash register. Then, every day for about the next year, I sprinted down our mountainous driveway in anticipation of finding my cash register in the mailbox. I'd yank open the mailbox in hopes of finding my treasure, only to have my hopes dashed. It took some time, but I finally realized the cash register was not coming.

Now my trips to the mailbox are adventurous again – without the disappointment! Every day, I get cards in the mail – some funny, some sweet, but all very meaningful. I'm saving every card, which is another change for me. In my former life, I'd always go on cleaning sprees and throw out things like that.

I also enjoy opening my email and reading my guestbook on this site. It's always a treat to hear from friends and family!

I was supposed to go to the doctor tomorrow, but he had to go out of town. I'll see him on Monday before my next round of chemo and will give an update then. Overall, I'm doing well with few side effects. I am a little tired, but I expect it to pass shortly like it did last time.

Thanks again for your prayers and support!

It happened so many years ago, but we still laugh about the clown cash register. The story makes me appreciate that little girl who, undaunted by repeated disappointment, continued to run to the mailbox every day in hopeful expectation. That same resilient attitude serves me well today.

I still have the cards – hundreds of them – that people have been kind enough to send over the years. One of my favorites came from Amy Rose, a friend I worked with more than 20 years ago. On the front is a picture of a woman in a pair of boots and the inscription, "Wear some cool boots. Cool boots make you feel like you can handle anything." Inside it reads, "Or at least kick it really hard!"

⚓ Friday, February 26, 2010, 11:10 a.m.

Yesterday my boss, Phyllis Nichols, was named Person of the Year, a much deserved honor. In her acceptance speech, she got a little emotional as she said that she owed much of who she is to her parents.

I, too, owe much of who I am to my parents. They are amazing people who model faith, service and love. Just yesterday, I stopped by to pick up my pound cake (Yes, I know. I'm going to have to kick the pound cake addiction when I'm better!) and found them babysitting my nephews, ages 3 and 4. My mother had spent the morning volunteering at the Western Heights Baptist Center, baked a cake for her daughter, and she and my father were keeping two youngsters for the night, all with happiness and no complaint.

When my father had prostate cancer, he and my mom modeled the faith that I have today. They've always modeled a strong faith, and I know that seeing their faith has helped to strengthen mine. When my son Evan first learned of my cancer diagnosis, he commented that he might be more scared if he hadn't seen how well my father had handled his cancer. So, the legacy continues.

I am thankful to have parents that raised me well and now support me unconditionally. I am blessed.

By the way, I'm feeling very good today. I expect a good weekend before starting chemo again on Monday. It's always nice to have a few days of feeling really good – it makes it easier to handle the days when I'm not.

When my parents celebrated their 50th wedding anniversary, I made them a photo book that incorporated lots of pictures and a brief synopsis of their remarkable love story. In talking about their love, I chose the verse from 1 John 3:18: "Little children, let us not love with word or with tongue, but in deed and truth." That verse sums up how my parents loved each other and their children. Not that they didn't say, "I love you," it's just that they did so much more than say the words.

When I recently heard a sermon by Rick Warren (pastor and best-selling author of *The Purpose Driven Life*) in which he said that we demonstrate love by giving our time and attention, I thought about my parents. I also thought that I show love the same way they showed it to me, not so much by words but by actions. If I love you, I may not say it a hundred times a day, but I'll show it every time I set aside my wants for yours or put aside my agenda to meet your needs. That's probably one of the reasons it has been so hard for me to be sick; because I show love by doing, it feels like I'm not giving love when I'm not doing.

⚓ **Monday, March 1, 2010, 6:26 p.m.**

I had a very good visit with Dr. Antonucci today. He said my blood work looked "great," he was very impressed with the fact that I'm completely off pain pills, and overall he was very pleased with the progress I'm making. Me, too!

Because I'm tolerating the chemo so well, the doctor wants to get two more rounds in me before doing a PET scan. Guess that means a little more bonding time for me and my fanny pack!

Assuming all goes as planned, my surgery will take place sometime around mid-May.

Thanks again for your prayers and good wishes. I think we may be beating this thing!

It really was remarkable how much better I felt after four rounds of chemotherapy. Shrinking that humongous tumor made a world of difference. Although I didn't know it at the time, there were to be many tough days ahead, but I can honestly say one of the things that surprised me most about cancer was the treatment wasn't nearly as bad as I had feared.

Going into chemo, my expectation was something similar to what I had seen in movies, with people vomiting the whole time they got treatment. Fortunately, that expectation was way off base. Thanks to advances in science, it is no longer a prerequisite of treatment that you feel lousy.

In my case, the steroids that were supposed to make me feel better were actually giving me migraines. Rather than just assuming the chemotherapy was supposed to make me sick, the doctor and nurses kept tweaking my treatment until I was better able to tolerate it.

Another thing that helped me, I think, is that I didn't read all the possible side effects of the medications. Instead of reading about possible problems and looking for them to happen, I waited for issues to arise and then researched and talked to my doctor to determine if the medicine was the culprit. Most often it was the chemo, but I'm convinced I was better able to ignore minor issues because they weren't already on my radar waiting to be discovered.

⚓ Wednesday, March 3, 2010, 10:48 a.m.

More good news on the medical front! When I went to the doctor on Monday, he said he wanted to do a CBC (Cancer Blood Count) test to see what my levels are. At the time of my diagnosis, the count was 20-something, which is very high. Today, I just received news that the count is normal! Hallelujah!

I had to have another Neulasta shot to raise my white blood count today. (Boo!) The shots help, and I know they're worth it, but they do drag me down a bit. I'll have to treat myself to another present when I get home!

I continue to be amazed at how well everything is going and the level of support that I'm receiving. Thank you, thank you!

This post shows my ignorance at the time. It wasn't a CBC blood test, it was a CEA test. Carcinoembryonic antigen (CEA) is a protein produced by developing babies during pregnancy. Because CEA is not produced in large quantities by healthy adults but is produced by some types of cancer, particularly colorectal cancer, CEA levels can be a good diagnostic tool. Anything below 5 is considered normal. If memory serves, my level before chemotherapy was 28.

When cancer recurred in my lungs, my CEA counts again shot up in the 20s. At the time, Dr. Antonucci assumed there was more cancer present than showed up on the scans because the counts were so high. In surgery, they discovered that the cancer was no worse than the scans indicated. Dr. Antonucci said that mine are the most sensitive CEA counts he has ever seen, making them an excellent tool for staying on top of any future cancerous activity in my body.

⚓ Wednesday, March 10, 2010, 6:38 p.m.

There are days when I feel so good that I almost forget I'm battling a dreadful disease. Then, there are days like today when cancer reminds me that beating it is no easy battle.

Last night, feeling good and a little cocky, I ate a bowl of soup that was a bit spicy and even put in some tortilla chips – things I typically would avoid. Then, I proceeded to eat the Twizzlers which I had been craving and Evan kindly bought for me. Interesting combination, huh? My stomach didn't like it either. Today, my stomach is killing me and I feel like the guy in the old Alka-Seltzer commercials who says, "I can't believe I ate the whole thing."

One good thing about having my stomach hurt like this – it reminds me how far I've come. My stomach hurt for months before I knew what was wrong. Now, I feel good enough to complain when it does me this way for one day.

At any rate, I have learned my lesson. I won't be rolling the dice on what I put in my mouth and on my stomach any time soon!

When David and I went on our most recent cruise, the boarding time was pushed back by a couple of hours because the ship was late returning to port. We ended up standing outside in a very long, very slow line for the embarkation process. I kept saying things like, "It could be worse; it could be pouring rain." Or, "At least we're making progress." David struck up a friendly conversation with the couple in front of us. Meanwhile, the lady behind us just kept griping. Needless to say, our wait in line was much more pleasant than the wait for the couple behind us.

At the risk of sounding like I'm bragging on myself, I do think that attitude matters, and I firmly believe that my positive attitude has helped make my treatment easier to tolerate and more successful. Just as a long line was a reality we had to deal with to enjoy our cruise, treatment is a reality I've had to deal with in order to get better. No matter the situation, we are all much better off if we find something to be thankful for and make the best of it.

I will be quick to add that my faith has made it much easier to have a positive attitude. Because I trust God, it is natural for me to assume there's more to the picture than I'm seeing at the moment and in the end things will work out for the best, perhaps not my idea of best, but the best nonetheless.

"Rejoice always; pray without ceasing; in everything give thanks; for this is God's will for you in Christ Jesus." I Thessalonians 5:16-18

⚓ **Monday, March 15, 2010, 6:47 p.m.**

> *Praise God, from Whom all blessings flow;*
> *Praise Him, all creatures here below;*
> *Praise Him above, ye Heavenly Host;*
> *Praise Father, Son, and Holy Ghost.*
> *Amen.*

If - again a big IF - I could sing, tonight my song would be the doxology above. Ever since I went to the doctor today, it's been going through my head.

The doctor said he's never seen anyone respond to therapy as well as I have. I told him I have about a gazillion people praying for me, and I know it's making a difference. Gazillion is perhaps a slight exaggeration, but not by much! I feel your prayers all day every day. They uplift me and carry me through the good times and bad!

Twizzler Update - Lest I give Twizzlers – and spicy soup – a bad name, the doctor said my poor dining choices of Tuesday night had nothing to do with the resulting stomach problems that lasted through the weekend. They also had nothing to do with a stomach bug, which I was convinced I had. Instead, he said it is toxicity building up in my body from the chemotherapy. We lowered the dose a bit today, and I'm doing great!

Thanks again for all your support! I am constantly amazed and humbled at the level of care and concern that come to me every day!

In talking about how I've responded to treatment, my doctors often use the word miraculous. It is a miracle that I've done so well, and I credit much of that to all the prayers that have gone up on my behalf.

In prayer, we often ask God to intervene in some way, be it miraculous or small. I wonder, though, how often we really expect our prayers to be answered.

In Acts 12, we read that James, the brother of John, became the first of 12 disciples to be martyred when King Herod had him killed. Soon thereafter, Herod had Peter arrested. The people of the church prayed fervently on Peter's behalf.

Verses 6-13 describe Peter's miraculous rescue through the help of an angel who appeared the very night Peter was to have been killed. Interestingly, Peter was asleep when the angel showed up. He wasn't awake worrying; he trusted God.

But did those people praying on his behalf really believe that God would save him? Apparently not.

> And when Peter came to himself, he said, "Now I know for sure that the Lord has sent forth His angel and rescued me from the hand of Herod and from all that the Jewish people were expecting."
>
> And when he realized this, he went to the house of Mary, the mother of John who was also called Mark, where many were gathered together and were praying.
>
> And when he knocked at the door of the gate, a servant-girl named Rhoda came to answer.
>
> And when she recognized Peter's voice, because of her joy she did not open the gate, but ran in and announced that Peter was standing in front of the gate.
>
> And they said to her, "You are out of your mind!" But she kept insisting that it was so. And they kept saying, "It is his angel."
>
> But Peter continued knocking; and when they had opened the door, they saw him and were amazed." Acts 12:11-16

I can't begin to explain how God works. I do know, however, there are many examples in the Bible that teach us prayer changes things, and I believe I have personally experienced the power of prayers sent up on my behalf.

"Worry about nothing. Pray about everything." – Charles R. Swindoll

⚓ Sunday, March 21, 2010, 7:56 p.m.

Since I promised to share the good, the bad and the ugly, I'll let you know that today is a bit ugly. Last night I was up all night with my stomach killing me (no Twizzlers involved this time) and have spent the entire day on the couch feeling pretty lousy.

The stomach problems are a result of the chemo. Fortunately I only have one more round to go. So this too shall pass.

Thanks for your continued prayers and support.

When I speak about my chemotherapy, I usually say that it wasn't that bad. Reading through these posts, however, reminds me that there were times when it was far from a piece of cake.

⚓ Tuesday, March 23, 2010, 11:56 a.m.

It's funny. I'm terribly musically challenged, but it seems that hymns speak to me so much these days. (My thanks to those of you who are musically gifted for sharing your talent!)

When I'm feeling the worst, two hymns go through my mind over and over: "On Christ the Solid Rock I Stand" and "It Is Well with my Soul." Those hymns went through my head a lot the past few days.

I'm happy to report that I'm feeling better – not great, but better – and am back at work today. I'm wondering if my body has had all the chemo it can stand and is telling me "enough already!" I see the doctor on Monday and will learn then if we go forward with one more round. Pray that we make the right decision.

My thanks and love to you all!

More than any others, "On Christ the Solid Rock I Stand" and "It Is Well with My Soul" have strengthened me, encouraged me and helped define my battle with cancer.

While visiting my father at hospice shortly before his death, I ran into a friend of my parents. She and I ended up talking about her daughter, Brooke Griffith, an artist. When I later looked up Brooke's work on the Internet, I was immediately struck by her print, "It Is Well with My Soul." The print depicts a ship in the midst of rolling waves and a fierce storm; the paper on which it appears is the hymn, "It Is Well with My Soul."

Although many people are aware of the story behind the hymn, it is so inspirational it bears retelling.

> Horratio Spafford was a successful Chicago attorney and devout Christian. He and his wife lived in a beautiful home with their son and four daughters. Wealthy and happy, they led what seemed to be a charmed life up until the time that their only son died of scarlet fever in 1870.
>
> Only one year later, the Great Chicago Fire consumed thousands of buildings, took 300 lives, left 100,000 homeless, and destroyed property valued at nearly $200 million. With it, the fire took almost all of the Spaffords' wealth, which was largely invested in real estate. Nonetheless, the family freely gave from what little they had to help the many Chicago residents who faced losses more devastating than their own.
>
> In 1873, the Spaffords planned a much needed European vacation which included a visit with famed evangelist D.L. Moody at a revival he was holding in England. Interestingly, Moody also was a Chicago resident at the time of the Great Fire. In fact, it was the fire that prompted him to hold his first revival in the United Kingdom in 1872.
>
> Shortly before the family was to set sail, Spafford learned of unexpected business that required his attention. He sent his wife and daughters ahead and made plans to join them later.
>
> Before leaving to join his family, Spafford received the devastating news that all four of his daughters were killed when the ship on which they sailed was involved in a collision that sunk it in the Atlantic. Only his wife survived.

As he sailed to meet his grieving wife, Spafford wrote the hymn that has touched so many and speaks to us still today, "It Is Well with My Soul."

I bought the print for my mother, and she has it displayed in a prominent place. Each time I look at it, I am reminded of God's gift of peace that passes all understanding and how He has kept our family secure through so many struggles these past few years.

It is that print that helped inspire the title to my book. If all goes as planned, that same print will adorn this book's cover.

⚓ Monday, March 29, 2010, 7:56 p.m.

Isn't this a wonderful time of year? Saturday was beautiful; the forecast for the rest of the week is grand; the flowers are blooming; the grass is turning green; and Easter is Sunday. Now, the lyrics going through my head are: "Lift High the Cross, the Love of Christ proclaim, Till all the world adore His sacred name."

I went to the doctor today, and he and I agreed that one more round of chemo is the way to go. I felt like I had my answer when I felt really good on Saturday and Sunday. It was like my body was saying, "We can go one more round!" So, the fanny pack and I bond once more and I'll probably be even closer to the couch for a while, but it's all good.

I'm scheduled to have a PET scan on April 14 to see what the cancer's looking like. The doctor said he wouldn't be shocked if the PET scan shows up hardly anything. (Another good and bold statement from the doc!) I meet with the surgeon on April 19, and we'll know a lot more after that.

In the meantime, my hope is that I will be able to attend church on Easter and enjoy a family gathering later that day.

Spring and summer are my favorite times of year. I just grit my teeth and get through winter. The cold, gray days make me go into a kind of hibernation. When the grass turns green, the sun shines and the flowers bloom, I feel like I'm blooming right along with them. The spring of 2010 was exceptionally encouraging because it reminded me that dark days are only for a season and that God is in control.

"Ah Lord God! Behold, Thou hast made the heavens and the earth by Thy great power and Thine outstretched arm! Nothing is too difficult for Thee." Jeremiah 32:17

⚓ Wednesday, March 31, 2010, 7:16 p.m.

Hallelujah! Today I finished my sixth and final (for now) round of chemo! With it being such a beautiful day and getting rid of the fanny pack for a while, I practically floated to the car when I left the doctor's office. Then, when I started the car, reggae artist Bob Marley came on singing, "Don't worry about a thing, cause every little thing is gonna be all right." I couldn't agree with him more. Every little thing is going to be all right!

Other good news: As a side effect of the chemo, my jaw hurt – badly – most of the time. The doctor lowered the dose of that particular chemo, and my jaw hasn't hurt since.

It's a good day. Thanks for celebrating with me!

I can't describe how good it felt to clear that final chemo hurdle. I still had far to go, but it was nice to stop and celebrate that victory. Sometimes we're so busy looking to the future – be it potential blessings or seemingly overwhelming obstacles – that we fail to stop and enjoy the present. Sometimes we're so focused on the past, be it good times or bad, that we miss what's right in front of us.

I also believe technology is taking too much of our focus away from the here and now. It drives me crazy to see parents talking away on mobile phones while their young children go unnoticed, or to see a family out to dinner and all of them busily texting away. We're so busy staying "connected" that we fail to connect with the people who are all around us; in the process, we let precious time slip away.

"This is the day that the Lord has made; Let us rejoice and be glad in it." Psalm 118:24

⚓ Monday, April 5, 2010, 7:51 p.m.

Early on in this battle I said that I decided there would be times when I would push through and do things I wanted to do even if I didn't particularly feel like it. Yesterday was one of those days.

I was up a lot Saturday night with my stomach killing me. Then, when I started to get ready for church I felt dizzy and ended up soaked with sweat. But I was determined to spend Easter at church. So, I sat down, cooled off, re-rolled my hair, and went to church. I'm so glad I did!

It was a beautiful service, and it was wonderful to see so many of my church friends and thank them for their prayers and support.

Then I got to spend a lovely Easter at my parents' house. It was a fun-filled family gathering, complete with an Easter egg hunt for the youngest of my nephews. They loved it, and it was so much fun to watch. They even found a baby bunny while searching for eggs! There was also lots of great food, and I had the appetite to enjoy it.

It was a terrific day, and for that I'm very thankful!

That was definitely a time when pushing through the pain was well worth the effort. I would have missed out on so much if I had given in and stayed home.

"When life knocks you to your knees, and it will, why, get up! If it knocks you to your knees again, as it will, well, isn't that the best position from which to pray?" – Ethel Barrymore

⚓ Monday, April 12, 2010, 11:21 a.m.

I haven't posted anything in a while because I really haven't had much to say. I'm pretty much in a holding pattern right now. I will say that I'm feeling pretty good, although I still battle fatigue and my jaw has started hurting again.

There are a few things on the horizon:

1. I have my PET scan on Wednesday and will have the results on Thursday. I'm very anxious to see how well the chemo worked. The doctor and I expect good results!
2. I meet with the surgeon on Monday. After that, I'll know a lot more about my next steps. My oncologist said that even if the PET scan shows nothing in my liver, he wants the surgeon to hold my liver in his hand to be sure nothing is there. I agree. I don't want to go through this again. Although it's a little odd to think about someone holding your liver...
3. This weekend my mother and I are going to a Wellness Retreat for cancer patients and survivors sponsored by Covenant Health and Thompson Cancer Survival Center. We are so looking forward to it! My sincere thanks to my friend Debby Saraceni for inviting us!

Stay tuned. I'll have much to report in the coming days. Thanks for your continued prayers and support!

I remember my appointment with Dr. Antonucci, how adamant he was that the surgeon be very certain about the condition of my liver and how strange it was to think about someone holding my liver. I believe that was one of the first times that I really stopped to consider the severity of my illness.

⚓ **Thursday, April 15, 2010, 1:44 p.m.**

Repeat after me... Hooray!

I just heard from the doctor's office. They said the PET scan reflected a "significant positive response to the chemotherapy." Nothing showed up in my liver, and the colorectal tumor has greatly reduced in size. Praise God!

I'll provide another update after I meet with the doctor on Monday. This news was just too good not to share now!

For cancer patients, a telephone call from the doctor's office is a tricky thing. It can be a swift kick to the gut or a bouquet of flowers. I have since learned from Dr. Antonucci that he generally delivers the kicks and lets the nurses call with flowers.

Before the scan, I thought the chemo was working because many of the symptoms caused by the size of the tumor were going away, suggesting it was shrinking. I had no idea, however, how much progress I had made. That was the first of many remarkable reports I was to get.

I later learned at the Wellness Retreat that the most extraordinary news was how well my liver responded to treatment. During one of our group sessions, I shared the good news about my latest scan. Afterward, a lady came to ask me more about what kind of treatment I had received. "They've tried all kinds of treatment on me," she said. "They still can't get the tumor in my liver to shrink." I have since heard many similar stories.

⚓ **Sunday, April 18, 2010, 4:53 p.m.**

I'm back from my weekend Wellness Retreat. Wow! It was a wonderful time of being together with ladies who have all been touched by cancer in some way – most have or have had cancer themselves; some were caregivers.

The retreat was founded 11 years ago by Debby Saraceni, an executive with Covenant Health, parent company of Thompson Cancer Survival Center. Debby created the retreat in honor of her sister, Shelley Ward, a cancer survivor. Both terrific ladies! They had about 20 women that first year. This weekend, we had (I think) about 120 women.

It was an eclectic group to say the least – some women were older, some middle aged, and some younger; some had hair, others didn't; some were long-time survivors, others of us were newly diagnosed. The differences didn't matter. We all bonded together beautifully. It reminded me of my Sunday school class, the Soul Sisters. We, too, are an eclectic group, but we are bound together by a common thread – the love of Christ.

And, while cancer was one thing bonding us together at the Wellness Retreat, it certainly wasn't the only thing. I noted that we all heavily relied on our faith. It's funny how we tend to look up when we're knocked down.

It was a fun-filled weekend with many highlights:

- Former Olympian and fitness expert Missy Kane spoke on Friday night about her battle with melanoma. Then we had a bonfire and many of us shared a little about our journeys.
- On Saturday night, we had a Disco party. I wore my old Cher Halloween costume. I got so many compliments, I'm wondering if Cher should come out more often!
- This morning, we had a worship service that included a speaker who was both hilarious and thought provoking.

On Saturday afternoon, I went to a meditation class that everyone said was a "must do." I have to confess, however, that it didn't do much for me. The facilitator said that meditation is a great way to help the body heal by allowing us to focus the mind, let go of our anger and get rid of the negative thoughts that plague us. I realized that I really don't have any anger, and my thoughts aren't negative. Maybe that's one of the reasons my body is healing so well!

I am refreshed, rejuvenated and ready for what lies ahead. I meet with the doctor tomorrow afternoon and will give another update after that visit.

My mother planned to attend the retreat with me, but last minute complications kept her from going. I believe her foiled plans were the result of divine intervention. I needed that time alone.

Following my cancer diagnosis, everyone treated me a little differently. My family became very protective and didn't want me to do much of anything; friends and coworkers cautioned me to abandon my normally active ways for a time of rest; and strangers and other acquaintances didn't quite know how to react.

At the retreat, I was no longer the exception but the rule. It felt good to be with people who had stood in my shoes, and it was encouraging to hear from longtime survivors who had beaten the beast. It was a perfect weekend.

⚓ **Monday, April 19, 2010, 5:31 p.m.**

Ready for more good news? The surgeon said that he was "amazed" at my progress and that he wouldn't have believed it if he hadn't seen it with his own eyes. The tumor, described as huge by everyone who saw it, is now almost completely gone!

I still need surgery, but it will be easier now that the tumor is so much smaller. I thought I'd have all kinds of details after my visit with the surgeon, but I really don't know much at this point.

My surgeon will spend more time reviewing the PET scan and talk to my oncologist before deciding what course of action to take. I'll keep you posted. In the meantime, join me in singing, "Praise God from whom all blessings flow!"

This was my first time to meet Dr. Gregory Midis, an exceptional and well respected surgeon. His enthusiasm during that first appointment further validated that my treatment was going extraordinarily well. I still had a long journey ahead, but my steps were considerably lighter.

⚓ **Friday, April 23, 2010, 9:50 a.m.**

You know how you feel when you're just getting over the flu or some other sickness? You feel like you're ready to take on the world, but if you do too much you end up sick again. That's where I am right now.

I'm feeling better than I was, and it's making me want to do more. I know that I'm not quite ready, though. I was given a strong reminder yesterday. I came home from work and thought I'd take a short nap and then take Henry for a walk, something I've been dying to do for some time now. Well, my "short" nap ended up being from 6:00 to 8:00! It's like God was saying, "Be still. It's not time yet."

I talked to the surgeon on Wednesday, and he had even more good news! They originally thought I would need two separate surgeries, but now they will be able to do everything in one surgery. Some of the surgery may even be laparoscopic. Yay!

Also, we now have a new plan:

I'll do four weeks of radiation and more chemotherapy prior to surgery. Unlike what I had before, the chemo will be very mild and shouldn't cause any side effects. Then, I wait for six weeks before surgery. This means my surgery should be in July.

I meet with my oncologist on Tuesday morning to discuss my treatment in further detail.

When I was in elementary school, I tended to put off projects until nearly the last minute. Inevitably, my mother and I would throw something together the night before the assignment was due. We typically managed to get not only a good grade, but also a good story to go along with it.

I remember one insect collection she and I assembled late one night. I have no idea why, but one of the bugs wasn't dead when we glued it to the poster. It kept crawling off the poster board and we kept sticking it back, laughing harder each time it crawled away. I now know how that bug felt. At this point of treatment, I was trying desperately to crawl off the couch, but I kept getting glued back down.

⚓ **Tuesday, April 27, 2010, 7:26 p.m.**

The song going through my head tonight is the theme to "Jaws." That's because my old nemesis, the fanny pack, is quickly heading my way. I met with my oncologist this morning, and he confirmed that I'll have radiation and chemotherapy prior to surgery and that I'll be wearing the pump – and along with it the lovely fanny pack – five days a week for six weeks. Ugh!!

In my head I completely understand that chemo and radiation are the right way to go. Otherwise, there is a real risk that the cancer will come back. However, I have to confess that I'm not thrilled at the prospect of strapping on the old albatross for such a long time.

When the doctor told me about the plan, he easily read my face (my eyes always give me away!) and knew I wasn't particularly happy. He smiled and said, "The surgeon was very pleased with your progress. You're so young and healthy and you've responded so well to treatment, we'd be crazy not to go after this as aggressively as possible." So, I give the doc points for calling me young and the pep talk. And, I'm sure it will go by quickly and won't be all that bad. Just for tonight, though, I'm going to whine about it.

Other news: It turns out the pain in my jaw may be from a cavity rather than side effects from the chemo. I have the cavity filled tomorrow. I'm a real chicken when it comes to the dentist, but this is one time I'll actually be glad for some dental work!

I love your posts, emails and cards, and I still feel your prayers. Thanks for sticking with me through this journey!

The prospect of radiation five days a week for six weeks – while also wearing the hated fanny pack – was daunting at best. It was truly a time that called for taking the first step and then another to get to the end of the journey, eating the elephant one bite at a time.

"To get through the hardest journey we need take only one step at a time, but we must keep on stepping." Chinese Proverb

⚓ Thursday, April 29, 2010, 7:31 a.m.

My trip to the dentist yesterday was nothing short of brutal. After the first two shots failed to numb me, the dentist pulled out something that looked like a tranquilizer gun for an elephant and proceeded to dig in my gums with it. The pain was excruciating. Even that shot failed to completely numb my tooth.

Every time he drilled or cold air or water hit my tooth, I writhed in pain. As sweat ran down my back, I tried to picture myself in a different place (as suggested by a friend), but it did no good.

The good news is that my jaw no longer hurts! And, even though I had to endure that awful pain to rid myself of the constant jaw pain, it was well worth it. It was also a good reminder that, while the chemo, radiation and surgery won't be a bed of roses, they'll be well worth it to rid my body of the cancer.

Today, I'm accompanying my dear friend Robyn Askew to a healing service at St. John's Episcopal Church. I've heard wonderful things about the service and look forward to it.

A side note: Earlier this week, Briana Bilbrey, the sister of my son's good friend died in her dorm room at U.T. My heart breaks for the family in their loss. Please keep the Bilbrey family in your thoughts and prayers in the days ahead.

I am a dental-phobe. My brother Phillip and I share the same dark memories of our childhood trips to the dentist. Remember the dentist who tortured Dustin Hoffman in the movie "Marathon Man"? He had nothing on the dentist of our youth.

Before starting his work, the seemingly kind and gentle dentist would smile and tell us to raise our hand if anything hurt. Then, Nurse Ratchet would grab onto our wrists and hold us to the chair until her boss was through drilling. I'm sure our hands would have gone up quickly and often if they weren't being held in a vice grip.

To add insult to injury, the dental work described in my post was the first of much dental work that was to come my way. Chemo did a number on my teeth. Fortunately, the dentist who caused so much pain isn't my regular dentist. I had to see someone who practiced in another office because of time constraints. My real dentist, Ann Trivette, has never hurt me.

I love the way that God reminded me that good can come out of pain. I honestly don't think I would have been as open to that message before cancer. By forcing me to slow down, my sickness has made me better able to hear God's voice.

⚓ **Monday, May 3, 2010, 4:53 p.m.**

Today I met with my radiologist, Dr. Daniel Scaperoth with Thompson Cancer Survival Center. I'm set to start radiation next Monday. That gives me one week of freedom. I feel really good and plan to enjoy it!

I've been thinking about why the fanny pack bothers me so, and I think I've figured it out. Other than the fact that it makes me look like a complete goob, which is reason enough in my book, I think it bothers me that it announces to everyone that I have cancer. I've said all along that I don't want cancer to define me and that I don't want to wave a flag saying, "Hey, everybody, I've got cancer."

However, this is where God has put me, and I will try to handle it with grace. Perhaps it will give me more opportunities to share how miraculously I am being healed and give glory to the One who is doing the healing. Or, perhaps this is to humble me. I said early on that vanity had to go out the window, but clearly I haven't allowed that to happen. Whatever the reason, I trust God for a good result.

So, we journey on. Thanks for going through this with me. I feel your prayers!

When I said that perhaps radiation would humble me, I truly had no idea how humbling the entire experience would be. As someone once said, "We live in bodies of humiliation, and they get more humiliating every day."

My cancer was rectal, meaning it was in the last 10 inches of my colon. It stands to reason that treating that area would be less than glamorous. To state the obvious, when administering radiation, precision is critical. To that end, before my first treatment, I was fitted with a mold that was shaped exactly to my body. Then, technicians applied tape and markers to my hindquarters to mark where the beams would be directed. You know how crews spray paint directional markings on a road before digging? My rear end looked like a road ready for a lot of work.

Then, five days a week, I would walk into the radiation room that included a flat screen monitor displaying a picture of my derriere. I would lie face down on the table in my little mold with said derriere displayed for the world to see while music played and lasers beamed.

I joked with the technicians that they should have a special radiation CD. It could include hits like "Disco Inferno" and "Fire." Joking was about the only way to survive. The technicians were very professional and pleasant to be around, and the doctor and nurse provided excellent care. Other than that, the only good thing I can say about the whole process is that it was over in a few minutes. It never got easier.

⚓ **Monday, May 10, 2010, 7:34 p.m.**

On a beach trip when I was about 16, my brother Kevin, our friends and I took a late night walk on the beach. Well, they walked... I was hyper from taking diet pills and would stroll with them for a while, run ahead, run back, and stroll some more.

I feel like I ran ahead of cancer this past week – and what a run it was!

- David, the boys and I went out for dinner on Tuesday. It was a wonderful outing and so good to spend time together.
- I started walking Henry again! Yes, he and I were both a little slower making it up the hill, but we made it. And, we got to see and visit with a lot of our neighbors. Something we both enjoy!
- On Saturday, Evan and I joined my parents at the pool on an absolutely gorgeous day.
- For the grand finale, I went to church on Mother's Day and later to a family gathering at my brother's house. It was a wonderful evening full of good food, laughter and fun. I simply love being with my family! To make it even better, Suzanne Eaton, a friend I haven't seen in years and who happens to live across the street from my brother, stopped by for a brief visit. It was good to reconnect.

It was a wonderful week, and I'm thankful to have had the opportunity to enjoy it so!

Now, I'm back walking with cancer and my old friend, the fanny pack. I started chemo today and had my first round of radiation. All went well, and I'll count this week and the weeks ahead a blessing, too.

Thanks for your continued prayers and support. They sustain me daily.

Celebrating victories, big and small, makes life a much more pleasant journey. I am reminded of my younger son, Evan, and his enthusiasm when learning to ride a bike. On his first solo attempt, Evan went barely a few feet before he toppled over and hit the pavement. Undaunted by what many would have deemed a quick failure, Evan jumped up and excitedly exclaimed, "I did it!"

⚓ Thursday, May 13, 2010, 7:39 p.m.

When I was a teenager, I kept a calendar of what I wore to school each day so that I wouldn't wear the same outfit twice in one month. When my mother discovered my practice, she admonished me and said that people would notice a lot more if I smiled at them and treated them well than they would what I was wearing. I took her advice to heart and remember it to this day.

However, there is no smile big enough or greeting warm enough to hide a giant, canvas fanny pack. The thing truly bothers me! The good news is that I have solved my fanny pack dilemma. Yesterday, I purchased a small leather purse that is just big enough to hold my chemo pump. It's not nearly as big or ugly, and it blends in much better with my work clothes. It's a big improvement!

Tomorrow marks the end of my first week of chemo/radiation, and all is going well. I'm still able to walk Henry, and I'm really not experiencing any side effects so far.

My hair continues to fall out, however. Walking downtown today the wind blew so hard it actually blew out some of my hair. When the wind can blow out your hair, you know you've got problems! For now, the worst of the hair loss is on top. Fortunately, I'm so tall most people don't see the top of my head, so I'm good for now. It's good to know, however, that I've got a wig on standby in case I need it.

If you're thinking I must have been a horrid teenager, you're right. I was particularly wretched in my junior high school years. When I think back on how I acted during that time, I can only say, "I'm sorry." I've thankfully shed a lot of the things that made me so dreadful during my teen years. I have, however, maintained a concern about my appearance.

I hated the fanny pack and felt self-conscious the entire time I wore it. As with all problems, I had choices: I could let it consume me and bring me down; I could learn to live with it; or I could find a way to solve the problem. I elected to find a solution.

The purse was a great compromise, and the radiation nurses thought my way of carrying around my chemo pump was ingenious. While I did go from looking like a goob to looking like I was afraid someone would steal my purse, I still thought it was a vast improvement.

As to the day of my hair disaster, downtown Knoxville is incredibly windy, particularly outside the tall office building where I worked. As I walked down the hill to the parking lot, the wind kicked up and had my hair flying everywhere. When I went to brush some of it out of my face, I came back with a handful of hair. What can you do at that point but laugh?

⚓ **Tuesday, May 25, 2010, 7:21 p.m.**

Since I got sick, I call my parents every day to let them know I'm "alive and kickin'." I consider this post my "call in" to let everyone else know the same.

Tomorrow marks day three of week three of my six weeks of chemo/radiation. All continues to go well. The doctor checked my blood work on Monday and said that everything looks very good. I also feel good – good enough, in fact, to walk Henry every day, which is a benefit not only for Henry and me but for everyone who has to share the house with Henry. He's much better behaved, albeit relatively speaking, when he gets his daily walk! He's still a notorious food thief with a penchant for getting in the trash. We love him anyway.

As we are about to enter the summer season, I hope you are enjoying these beautiful days as much as I am. I'm fortunate enough to even spend weekends by the pool. Life is good!

Henry, like most Basset Hounds, was obsessed with food. He spent the better part of each day devising ways to get to the food that his acute sense of smell made so maddeningly alluring.

One day I came downstairs and found Henry on top of the dining room table happily eating cookie crumbs left from the night before. After catching him in the act on another occasion, I realized he had gotten under a dining room chair, raised his back so it touched the bottom rungs of the chair and scooted the chair back. He then jumped on the chair and onto the table.

Another time, I came home to a yard littered with shiny bits of paper. Henry had helped himself to a huge box of candy delivered to our front porch while we were away. Henry, looking like a watermelon, was sprawled on the front porch with his last remaining piece of candy. He was too full to eat it, but that didn't stop him from growling when I tried to get the last piece.

We were afraid he would die from eating all that chocolate, but the vet told us that eating pure baking chocolate will kill a dog; eating milk chocolate will just make them sick. Henry went on to live a long and happy life.

The walks really were good for Henry and for me. The exercise made me feel better, and I enjoyed chatting with neighbors while I was out. We usually regret it when we find excuses to skip our exercise routine but almost never say we're sorry after finishing a workout.

⚓ Monday, May 31, 2010, 10:22 a.m.

Since today is Memorial Day, I get a break from chemo and radiation. Hooray! The break comes at a good time, as the radiation is starting to cause some side effects – skin irritation and upset stomach. I'm hoping to keep them under control so that my treatment schedule isn't interrupted. Needless to say, I want to finish treatment as soon as possible so that I can go ahead and have surgery and get on with my life.

I had a little wakeup call last week that reminded me I still need to take it easy. I was at a photo shoot at Richard Jolley's studio (he's the glass artist who does amazing work). It was a lot of fun being there and seeing his beautiful work, but it was really, really hot. I made myself kind of sick getting so overheated and had to leave the shoot early. It's good that I get these periodic reminders that I'm battling a serious disease and can't take it lightly.

I have to confess that up to that point my biggest concern was getting to my radiation appointment ahead of the "old lady" who always showed up early and got my timeslot, which meant I had to wait 10 or 15 minutes for my appointment. I met said "old lady" on Friday, and she's a delightful person who has known much adversity. I felt like a heel for only viewing her as someone who was slowing me down. And, I realize that slowing down should not be my biggest concern at the moment.

Anyway, I'm enjoying my lazy day sans fanny pack and am ready to face the second half of chemo/radiation starting tomorrow.

Hope you all have a happy Memorial Day!

My job at Moxley Carmichael public relations firm exposes me to many opportunities for unique and fun learning experiences. The trip to Richard Jolley's studio was one of the best. If you're unfamiliar with

Jolley's work, take a minute to look him up. He and his wife, Tommie Rush, are extraordinary, internationally recognized glass artists.

The day in the studio was so enjoyable I really didn't notice the heat was affecting me until it was almost too late. I felt horrible while driving back to the office, but it was worth it.

Around the same time, I also got to do a behind-the-scenes tour at the Knoxville Zoo. We spent time up close with the chimpanzees. What fun! These kinds of projects provided a great diversion from the reality of my treatment and couldn't have come at a better time.

On another note, reading the description of my attitude toward the "old lady" shames me. In an effort to eke as much as possible out of every day, I am prone to develop a schedule that works only if everything goes exactly as planned. One hiccup in the course of events causes a domino effect that makes the remaining plans topple. It's a bad system that leads to unnecessary stress and irritation, especially when others get in my way.

In getting mad at the lady who took my turn, I lumped her in with my stereotypical image of retirees who have nothing better to do than show up early for everything. It's so much easier to think negatively about people when we think of them as "they" instead of as individuals. Once I met this lady and knew her story, I never again considered her the time enemy. How could I?

"But you, why do you judge your brother? Or you again, why do you regard your brother with contempt? For we shall all stand before the judgment seat of God." Romans 14:10

⚓ **Saturday, June 5, 2010, 5:18 p.m.**

Four weeks down... two to go! Yesterday marked the end of week four of chemo/radiation, and I have to say that it feels good to be nearing the end. The doctor and staff seem pleasantly surprised at how well I'm handling treatment and that my side effects aren't worse than they are. When they comment on it, I just smile and say that there are a lot of people praying for me and that it's working. So, thanks for your continued prayers. They are working!

I'll most likely be having surgery in about six or eight weeks. Then I'll really feel like I'm making progress!

In the meantime, I am fortunate to be able to enjoy summer, perhaps my favorite season. I had another wonderful day by the pool today. The water feels perfect and, since the pool is at my parents' house, I get to spend some quality time with them. Pool time is always one of my favorite times!

Now that I've had my fun for the day, guess I better go clean house.

If my story were a horror movie, this post would have included the eerie sounding background music that has the audience yelling at the person on screen to take cover. I was still doing pretty well at this point; little did I know that things would be going considerably downhill in the not too distant future.

⚓ Monday, June 7, 2010, 7:58 a.m.

On Thursday, I heard a very good speaker at a conference I attended. She reminded us that life is all about choices. She said, "If you're not happy with your choice, make another choice." Well, I made a poor choice yesterday.

I mentioned before that the radiation is beginning to bother my stomach. Truth be told, my stomach is fine so long as I don't eat things I shouldn't. Unfortunately, sweets fall into the category of "shouldn't." Thanks to the pound cake and my attempts to keep my weight up during the winter, I've developed quite the sweet tooth.

My poor choice was deciding to take one bite of a cinnamon roll. That one bite ended up being half of a rather large cinnamon roll. It was a bad decision that I won't be making again! My stomach was messed up all evening.

Thankfully, I'm back to normal today and feel fine. And, I choose not to have any coffee (which also bothers my stomach) and certainly no cinnamon roll!

At the conference, I went up and thanked the speaker for her moving message. I showed her my chemo purse and told her a little bit about my story and how well my treatment was going. I said that I was making the choice every day to keep going and stay positive even in the midst of treatment. She gave me a big hug and thanked me for stopping by.

About two years later, I had the pleasure of running into the same lady at another function. This time, she came to me. She told me she had recently been diagnosed with breast cancer, but she thought of me and my story and it helped allay her fears. What a blessing!

Our lives and our words affect people more profoundly than we often realize. Every time I hear that my story has helped someone, it makes all I've gone through seem worthwhile.

⚓ Tuesday, June 8, 2010, 8:13 p.m.

Today, I had an interesting visit with the radiologist. He told me about a lady who had a very similar case to mine who has been cancer free and doing very well for about two or three years now. He then added, "We've come a long way in treating this kind of cancer. Five years ago, we would have only given you about six months to live." They were sobering words that made me even more aware of how fortunate I am to be responding so well to treatment. Praise God from whom all blessings flow!

On a related "note," I discovered a little treasure in my devotional last night. I'm reading *Streams in the Desert*, a very thoughtful gift my sister-in-law Pamela Ironside gave me when I was first diagnosed with cancer. Last night's devotional looks at Job 35:10, "... where is God my Maker, who gives songs in the night?" It talks about sleepless nights and how we can ask the Holy Spirit to fix our thoughts on God and believe that He can fill those lonely, dreary nights with song.

I was immediately reminded of the many nights this past winter when I was in too much pain to sleep and hymns would run through my mind over and over. God was filling my nights with song! What a blessing! The devotional closes by quoting Nathaniel William Taylor: "We must understand that for God to give songs in the night, He must first make it night."

I have to close by saying it again, Praise God from whom all blessings flow!

There were many dark nights to come, but God was faithful. I remember in particular a sleepless, pain-filled night in the hospital following surgery. One of the machines hooked up to my body seemed to be tapping out the hymn, "Great is Thy Faithfulness."

⚓ **Sunday, June 13, 2010, 3:12 p.m.**

Ugh, yuck, blcch. That's the only way to describe how I feel this weekend. I started feeling bad on Friday, and it's only gotten worse. I know I'm blessed to have done so well so far, but I have to admit that this is no fun.

When I started radiation, they said I might have to take a break from treatment at some point if the side effects became too bad. I'm beginning to think we may be at that point. Please pray that we'll make the right decisions as to how – and when – to proceed with my treatment. I only have one week to go and heaven knows I hate to admit defeat this late in the game, but I want to make the right choice and the one that will be the best in the long run.

Right now, I can barely eat anything because my stomach is so messed up. So, I'm becoming very weak. And, my skin irritation is worse than ever. Things aren't pretty.

Thanks for your continued prayers and encouragement.

I was, in a word, miserable. The radiation had burned my skin so badly that I would wince in pain every time I had to go to the bathroom, which was often. The radiation had done a number on my intestines, and diarrhea ruled the day. This was definitely one of the times that I had to throw in the towel and go to bed. There was no working through this pain.

⚓ Tuesday, June 15, 2010, 5:03 p.m.

I hoped to be able to report much progress by now, but it is not to be. I still feel dreadful. I did manage to eat a few pretzels, the only solid food I've had since Friday. The plan right now is for me to start radiation on Thursday and stay off the chemo until Monday. Assuming we stay on schedule, Wednesday will mark my last day of radiation (HOORAY!) and Thursday will be my last day of chemo (Another HOORAY!).

I do feel the prayers of so many, and for that I am very grateful. I know that this will soon pass and become only a bad memory. For now, my hope is that I'll feel good enough to attend the family Father's Day celebration on Sunday. I am so looking forward to it and really hope to be there.

Since my father is computer illiterate, I can write this with no worries. We're surprising him with a dog for Father's Day. She arrives on Saturday. She's an American Eskimo dog (a rescue) named Fergie, and she couldn't be cuter. We're very excited!

I've started new prescriptions. Please pray that they do the trick and that I can soon be off this blasted couch!

My love and appreciation to you all.

I've found that setting goals helps me get through tough times. In this instance, my goal was to get better in time to attend a family Father's Day celebration. That plan worked. My plan to get the dog, however, was ill-advised and a complete failure. You'll hear the rest of that story in a bit.

As to the new prescription for diarrhea, it worked wonders. To this day, I keep a bottle of Lomotil in my purse for emergencies.

⚓ Thursday, June 17, 2010, 4:10 p.m.

The good news is that I'm starting to feel a little better. The bad news is that I saw the doctor today and he said it will be at least another month before my skin problems improve. So, he and I agreed that I will just grit my teeth and plow on through the rest of my treatment. Got one down today, so only four more to go!

Since I've been a bit of a Debbie Downer the past couple of posts, I share this story purely for laughs (it's one of my favorites):

One morning after we dropped Drew off at school, a song on the radio finished playing. The radio announcer said, "And that was the Barenaked Ladies."

I hoped that Evan, who was about 3 at the time, didn't notice the name of the group.

About a minute later, however, up came a comment from the backseat. "That's a dumb name for a rock group," said Evan.

"Yes, it is," I agreed.

"All bears are naked," came the reply.

And that's my laugh for the day. Hope you enjoy!

I love my Evan stories. He took everything so literally as a young child. One day Drew said something sarcastic that Evan took at face value. Drew quickly corrected him. "Sarcasm, Evan. It's the Ironside way. You better get used to it."

⚓ Monday, June 21, 2010, 7:38 p.m.

In the last post, I was excitedly anticipating Father's Day weekend and the presentation of a dog to my father in celebration of the occasion. Well... things didn't exactly turn out as planned.

Mom and Dad picked up Fergie on Friday afternoon. By Friday night, she had bitten my husband, my brother and me. We jokingly changed her name to "Chomps-a-lot" and laughed it off. When Fergie snapped at my niece, however, it was no laughing matter. The surprisingly vicious ball of fluff was quickly loaded in the van and returned to her life as a rescue.

So, Dad's much anticipated gift was a "swing and a miss." We remain undaunted, however, and plan to get another dog. We're looking for one that is cute, gentle, housetrained and has no affinity for randomly attacking people.

We did have a wonderful Father's Day celebration at my brother Kevin's. Although his wife wasn't able to make it, my brother Phillip came in with his two kids, and we had a terrific time. Not many people make me laugh like Phillip can!

I started back on chemo today and had the first of three remaining radiation treatments. I'm feeling better, although I'm still not quite up to par. And, I can't eat much of anything. I just ate a small plate of rice and am quite proud to have accomplished the feat! Nonetheless, the doctor said my blood work looked good today, so my body continues to hang in there.

Thanks for your many emails, cards and prayers. You helped get me through a really rough patch. It's good to be back on the upswing!

The dog situation was hilarious. I made a Father's Day card for my dad that said on the outside, "What's fluffy and white and likes to bite?" On the inside appeared a picture of Fergie and the caption, "Your present."

Although my dad always had gotten a kick out of my homemade cards, he seemed confused by this one. Looking back, I now see that it was an early indicator that Alzheimer's was beginning to take a toll on his brain.

⚓ Wednesday, June 23, 2010, 5:46 p.m.

Everyone loves a happy ending, and today I have two!

First, I finished radiation today. Hooray! Dr. Scaperoth, my radiologist, said that technically everything went very, very well. Thanks to some high powered burn medication my skin irritation is beginning to ease up a bit, and I managed to eat a little bit for lunch today. Things are looking up. Tomorrow, I get the chemo pump off. Then I'll really be flying!

Second, my post about the beast of a dog we got my dad for Father's Day has paid off in a big way! A friend of the family who works at the *News Sentinel* came across an ad for a giveaway the day after my post. She thought the dog sounded perfect for my parents, connected them with the owners, and now my parents are the proud owners of a 2-year-old Maltipoo. He is adorable and has a great personality. As an added bonus – he doesn't randomly attack people!

Isn't it amazing how things work out? God is good!

Thanks for your continued prayers and support.

Another hurdle jumped, and it felt so good. I was happier to be finishing radiation than I had been to finish chemo in the spring.

Having been through traditional radiation treatment, I'm very encouraged to see that proton therapy, which is targeted radiation, has come to our area. Proton therapy is the most precise form of radiation treatment available today. It destroys the primary tumor site but doesn't harm the surrounding healthy tissue and organs.

Thanks to my radiation therapy, for the rest of my life, I will feel like I have a bruised tailbone. If you watch my face when I stand up, you'll see me wince in pain. When I asked Dr. Midis about it, he explained that the radiation permanently damaged my tailbone. But it was over, and that's good news.

Being shed of the chemo pump also was a big plus. While connected, the chemo pump stayed with me 24 hours. It made taking showers difficult. I had to tape a plastic baggie over the insertion point and place the pump itself outside the shower. It also made it difficult to sleep. It was in the way when I tried to turn over or change positions, and it made a constant chugging sound as it dispensed the medicine. Even after the pump came off, it felt like I was wearing it for days.

As to the new dog, where Fergie was a definite swing-and-a-miss, the Maltipoo was a home run. Baxter was a wonderful companion and source of comfort for my father while he battled Alzheimer's. Now that my father is gone, the little fellow is excellent company for my mom.

⚓ Tuesday, June 29, 2010, 6:24 p.m.

Remember the old plastic punching bag toys? You'd knock them down, and they'd bounce back up again. That's kind of what I feel like in this battle against cancer. I keep getting knocked down, but thankfully continue to bounce back.

The chemo/radiation hit me harder than anything has to date, but I'm starting to recover. My stomach seems to be settling, although I haven't really tested it to see what it can handle. These days, my diet consists largely of popsicles, pretzels and chicken noodle soup. I hope to expand my options soon!

My skin problems got really bad. And, despite my use of many different types of creams and ointments, nothing helped that much. The doctors say that it will just take time to heal.

Thankfully, Dr. Antonucci prescribed a pain patch for me yesterday, and it's just the ticket. It keeps pain medication in my system 24 hours a day with no side effects, so I can still work and drive. I feel much better today. Hooray!

I don't see the surgeon until July 19, so I won't have updated information about surgery for some time. However, I received encouraging news yesterday. Dr. Antonucci, my oncologist, said that if Dr. Midis is able to do the surgery by laparoscope (which he indicated is a possibility), I should be back on my feet within two weeks of surgery. Needless to say, it is my hope and prayer that is the case. Maybe the fact that radiation nearly burned my insides out will make it possible, which would definitely make my pain worth it.

Regardless of which route surgery takes, I trust that God has a plan for me and that He knows what's best.

On the dog front, Mom and Dad are thrilled with the new addition to the family. Baxter is an absolute delight and has already worked his way into all our hearts. I promise to post a picture of him soon!

Because chemotherapy follows a set schedule, you tend to see the same people over and over at the oncologist's office. After seeing me at a few visits, a lady asked, "Honey, are you on chemo?" When I told her that I was, she said, "You sure don't look like it."

On this latest visit, however, I felt terrible and it showed. The lady immediately recognized the change and said she was sorry I was feeling so sick.

Fortunately, the pain patch was a miracle worker. That's one of the things I really like about Dr. Antonucci. He plows forward with treatment that he knows will be tough because he recognizes that it's necessary to properly attack the cancer, but he still tries to make his patients feel better whenever possible. The patch didn't completely eradicate the pain, but it did make it much more tolerable.

⚓ Monday, July 5, 2010, 6:31 p.m.

Ahhh... Nothing like a beautiful holiday weekend to restore the soul! I feel rested, refreshed and relaxed.

I knew it was going to be a good weekend when I was able to eat an entire grilled tuna sandwich on Friday – the most food I've had in weeks. I felt like I could conquer the world after eating that sandwich! So far, everything I've tried eating has not bothered me, which is quite encouraging. I'm still taking it easy, however. I don't want another "cinnamon roll episode."

This has been a wonderful weekend! I've enjoyed several good days at the pool. Today, two of my nephews were there, and it was fun spending time with them. Last night, my sweet husband took me to see "Toy Story 3" to celebrate my completion of chemo/radiation. We've wanted to do it for a while, but were waiting until I felt good enough and for a time when we thought the theater wouldn't be too crowded so I wouldn't be around so many germs. All went well, and the movie was terrific!

Other good news – the hair situation is rapidly improving! My hair is starting to come back in, and I got it cut short on Thursday, so that as it comes back in it will do better. I'm very pleased and no longer feel like I need to explain why my hair looks so bad!

My pain patch continues to work wonders, and I feel like I regain a little more strength each day.

Things are definitely looking up!

As promised, I'm posting a picture of Baxter, the newest Ironside. He's even cuter than he looks in the picture!

Thanks for your continued prayers, cards, posts, emails and words of encouragement. They mean so much to me!

For weeks, my diet consisted almost entirely of pretzels and popsicles. I didn't realize how weak and rundown it was making me feel until I had that tuna sandwich. That experience reminded me what we put in our bodies is important; it's what makes them run. It also served as a reminder that crash diets do no good. As soon as I started to eat anything, the weight quickly returned.

⚓ **Wednesday, July 14, 2010, 7:43 p.m.**

At a lunch meeting yesterday, a friend and I were discussing the grand and exotic trips she often takes. She explained that she had some health problems of her own a few years ago. They made her realize that for far too long she had put off traveling to the places she longed to see. After the illness, she decided to "seize the day" and take some grand adventures. She then asked me if I have had a similar change of heart following my diagnosis.

It took only a few seconds for me to reply that, rather than making me want to change the course of my life, my illness has made me thankful that I have invested my time here on Earth the way that I have so far.

When I was pregnant with Drew, David and I decided that I would work part-time so that I could devote myself to motherhood. And I have. Until just a few years ago, I worked hours that allowed me to be home when the boys were home from school and to be involved in their school activities, at least when they were in elementary school and wanted me to be involved!

I am so thankful for all the time that I was able to spend with Drew and Evan, and I am so proud of the fine young men they are today.

I also look back at the almost 27 years I've been married, and I'm happy about that, too. David is a good husband, and he's good for me.

I am also happy with my jobs. My work at the Urban League gives me a real sense of purpose, Moxley Carmichael provides the perfect creative outlet, and Executive Women's Association affords me the opportunity to be around some amazing women.

I've tried to lead a balanced life that includes faith, family, friends and exercise, and it works well for me. Now that I put it in writing, I do realize that I don't spend enough time with my friends. I'll have to do something about that when I'm better!

I can honestly say that I am completely content and at peace with my life. For that, I am grateful.

On the health front, I continue to get a little better each day. I can't wait to see the surgeon on Monday so that I can get a little more direction on when I'll have surgery and what my recovery time will look like. I'll keep you posted.

I know that over the years I've left a lot of money on the table and missed opportunities because of my decision to work part-time, but it's truly a decision that I have never regretted. I am thankful my husband supported the decision even when we really could have used the extra money, and I'm grateful I now have the opportunity to stay home and write this book. My surgeon, Dr. Midis, said it well when he said no one ever gets to the end of life and says, "I wish I had worked more." How true.

Michelle Ironside Henry

"When you give someone your time, you are giving them a portion of your life that you'll never get back. Your time is your life. That is why the greatest gift you can give someone is your time." – Rick Warren

⚓ **Monday, July 19, 2010, 7:22 p.m.**

"Keep walking with Me along the path I have chosen for you ... The journey is arduous at times, and you are weak. Someday you will dance light footed on the high peaks; but for now, your walk is often plodding and heavy. All I require of you is to take the next step, clinging to My hand for strength and direction. Though the path is difficult and the scenery dull at the moment, there are sparkling surprises just around the bend."

This is an excerpt from a devotional I read the other day. It is so perfect for me!

And, while I know there are more "sparkling surprises ahead," I had some today that I'm delighted to share.

First, the surgery will be laparoscopic. As I mentioned before, this is huge. The doctor showed me what my incision would have been like with traditional surgery, and it was scary – about 10 inches straight down my midsection. Now, it will only be a two- to three-inch incision. My recovery time will be cut in half, the pain won't be nearly as bad, and laparoscopic surgery is much less risky. How great is this?!!

Second, because the chemo wiped out the cancer in my liver, the doctor's not even going to operate on my liver right now. Instead, he's going to thoroughly check it out with the laparoscope to be sure we don't need to do anything. He believes there's a good possibility that we won't.

Third, my surgery won't be until August 10 or 11. Typically, this wouldn't be good news for me because I would want to get it over with. However, Drew is working a Young Life camp until August 8. It

80

was really bothering him that he was going to be away while I had my surgery. Now, he'll be back for my surgery and freer to enjoy his camp without worrying about me.

So, my faithful friends and prayer warriors, know that your prayers are working. I am blown away at how well everything is going and has gone so far. I know that I am blessed beyond measure.

The devotional I quoted came from *Jesus Calling* by Sarah Young, a book that has truly blessed me. *Jesus Calling* contains a daily devotion, along with meaningful scripture references with each entry. It is written in first person, as if the words on the page come directly from Jesus. The result is messages that pierce the reader's heart. I have read completely through the book at least three times. My copy was a gift from a friend soon after my diagnosis. I now buy copies for people in my life I care about. Unless I specifically say otherwise, when I make reference in this book to something that came from my devotion, I am referring to a devotion from *Jesus Calling*.

Since starting my journal on CaringBridge, I've heard from people who say they have used my posts to teach Sunday school classes. Others have said they've directed acquaintances with cancer to my website in hopes they would draw comfort from my message. Stories like that warm my heart and make me see that flowers can bloom in the desert.

"He changes a wilderness into a pool of water, and a dry land into springs of water." Psalm 107:35

⚓ **Tuesday, July 27, 2010, 8:33 p.m.**

Testing. 1, 2, 3. Testing. 1, 2, 3.

Starting with my back-to-back colonoscopies way back in December and continuing until now, I've been poked and prodded quite a bit. I'm in for more of it on Thursday, August 5, when I'll have another CT scan and pre-op testing.

My surgery is scheduled for Tuesday, August 10. So, two weeks from now I will have jumped another big hurdle. I am quite ready to have it behind me and move on with this journey.

The doctor instructed me to eat "like a bear about to hibernate" while waiting for surgery. Fortunately, my appetite is good and my stomach seems able to handle about anything. I plan to enjoy my calories.

Tomorrow, we've got an Executive Women's Association meeting at Ruth's Chris Steak House where I get to dine on their world-famous filet. Friday, David and I celebrate our 27th wedding anniversary, which means I'll get to go out for another great meal. Looks like I'll be making up for having to eat all those pretzels and popsicles!

Henry and I are on the road again. We resumed our walks about a week ago. It feels good to be active.

I'm grateful that I can spend this time eating well and exercising so that I can build up my strength prior to surgery. The surgeon said I should plan on at least four weeks for recovery, but I'm hoping to bounce back quicker. We'll see.

Like a lot of women, thoughts of weight have occupied my mind most of my life. As a young girl, I was healthy and active, far from fat. Unfortunately, my older brother was so skinny a spaghetti noodle would have felt bloated in comparison. To make matters worse, we had our annual physicals together as young children because we were only a year apart. I always weighed more.

As I grew from childhood into adolescence, I carried at least an extra 15 pounds. Fortunately, my height of 5 feet, 9 inches made it fairly easy to hide the weight.

One summer when my cousin Tracy and I indulged in far too many milkshakes, my height could not hide the extra girth. We were nicknamed Tubsy and Wubsy. I don't remember which one I was, but the name hit its mark. I took the not-so-subtle hint and lost weight.

When I turned 16, I decided to strive for perfection, which to me meant good grades and being skinny. It took little effort to achieve straight As. Dieting became an obsession. Although the pounds fell off, I consumed fewer calories each day until I came perilously close to anorexia. With encouragement from my mother – "Start eating or we're going to send you for treatment!" – I managed to avoid full-blown anorexia and gained some weight.

Since then, I've never completely recovered from the feeling that my self-worth is somehow tied to my weight. It's completely wrong, but it's still a struggle. Having that short respite where it was doctor's orders to consume lots of calories was, for me, a fun diversion.

⚓ Friday, August 6, 2010, 3:50 p.m.

Yesterday was a fun-filled day of more probing and prodding than you can imagine. All went well, and I am now cleared for surgery.

Surgery will be Tuesday morning at around 8:30 or 9:00 and should last about three hours. The doctor will be removing about 8 inches or so of my colon. He said it is serious surgery, but that he fully expects everything to go well. I do, too.

In fact, when I was asking my mother to post an update on this site after my surgery, I found myself saying, "Tell them that the surgery went well and that I'm doing fine." And it didn't feel like wishful thinking. It seemed like a fact. I do believe that I'll do well, particularly in light of how well everything has gone so far. I know that I am blessed.

Expect an update sometime Tuesday afternoon or evening. Thanks again for your prayers, cards, emails and support. They uplift me, encourage me and carry me through these days.

I was not worried about my surgery. Just as Peter slept when he was in prison waiting to be executed, I slept soundly the night before my surgery, not because I was unaware of the dangers, but because I trusted God with the outcome.

The same God who saved Peter that night is the same God who protected Daniel when he was thrown in the lions' den and the same God who helped guide my surgeon's hands in surgery. As a Christian, did I have a guarantee that I would survive surgery? Or was it possible to believe it strongly enough to make it happen? Absolutely not.

Stephen was stoned to death. John the Baptist had his head delivered to King Herod on a platter. In talking about people of faith, Hebrews 11:37 says: "They were stoned, they were sawn in two, they were put to death with the sword; they went about in sheepskins, in goatskins, being destitute, afflicted, ill-treated."

Sometimes God delivers us from hardship and sometimes He delivers us through it; sometimes from pain, sometimes through pain; sometimes from the fire, sometimes through the fire; sometimes from death, sometimes through death. But God is faithful. He always delivers us.

"On God my salvation and my glory rest; the rock of my strength, my refuge is God. Trust in Him at all times, O people; pour out your heart before Him; God is a refuge for us." Psalm 62:7-8

⚓ **Tuesday, August 10, 2010, 3:36 p.m.**

Praise Him; Praise Him; Praise Him. We cannot praise God enough for continuing to pour out His love, mercy and grace on Michelle. She came through surgery beautifully, as we knew she would. She is in pain, but when told the hospital is quite full and she would be in recovery a little longer than usual, she responded "Good. Maybe that means they will let me go home sooner."

She asked that it be conveyed to each of you how very much she appreciates the love and concern you have shown her during her journey. Many have asked what they can do and the only thing she has asked for is a DEEP CLEANING for the house. A crew is coming tomorrow to clean windows, blinds, carpet, floors, bathrooms, baseboards, etc., etc. Let me know if you would like to contribute to that.

Thanks to each of you for loving our daughter.

Blessings to each of you,

Barbara Ironside

My mom is right. The first thing I talked about after waking up from surgery was how quickly I could go home. It's not always advisable, but I'm always in a hurry to get moving.

Asking to have the house deep-cleaned while I was away was one of the best things I could have done for myself. It was so much easier to rest and recover in a clean house.

⚓ Wednesday, August 11, 2010, 5:28 p.m.

Just arrived home from the hospital and am happy to report that Michelle is still doing great. It was a sleepless night last night with all the nurses checking on her but other than that it has been good. Maybe it will be better tonight.

The house is all cleaned and she will probably be seeing the results on Friday.

Thanks again and keep praying.

Barbara Ironside

That first night in the hospital was rough. I had a very chatty nurse who spent a lot of time in my room. Other than having had very little sleep the night before, the first day following surgery was not bad at all. I was up in a recliner most of the day and enjoyed visiting with relatives who stopped by to check on me.

⚓ Thursday, August 12, 2010, 4:30 p.m.

Michelle is still in the hospital, so if I confused anyone – sorry. She is in quite a bit of pain, but the surgeon says that is good because everything is working the way it should. She will probably be coming home on Saturday and cannot wait to read the guestbook. You all have been such an encouragement to her and to her family.

Continue praying.

Barbara

The second day following surgery was worse than the first but still tolerable. At the time, I was chomping at the bit to go home.

⚓ Friday, August 13, 2010, 4:04 p.m.

It looks like Monday will be the coming home day. It is not that she is not doing well; she decided not to ask when the departure date is to be and we were told later today just to sit tight through the weekend. I think this is a wonderful idea.

We have a tendency to forget how serious the surgery was and that it is going to take TIME. Michelle is being very patient.

The pathology report was very good and her red and white blood count reports were excellent. Dr. Midis said he felt VERY happy when he saw the tests reports.

Thanks again, everyone. Just keep praying. God is still answering.

Psalm 59:16 "But as for me, I will sing of Thy strength. Yes, I shall joyfully sing of Thy lovingkindness in the morning, for Thou hast been my stronghold and a refuge in the day of my distress."

I believe everyone recognized how much pain I was in when I finally stopped asking when I could go home. The good news, of course, is the pathology report was very good. The chemo and radiation, hard as they were at times to tolerate, had done their job very effectively. The surgery was an important safety measure, though, and well worth the pain.

The doctors told me that without surgery the likelihood of the cancer coming back was much greater. I am reminded of their words every time I hear a story about someone who had cancer similar to mine but didn't follow a treatment plan as rigorous as the one I endured. Inevitably, those stories do not end well.

⚓ **Sunday, August 15, 2010, 6:00 p.m.**

Michelle had another good day. If she can tolerate solids tomorrow she can go home. Pray God's will be done. We want her to go home but not too soon.

We have laughed a lot today – good therapy for patient and Mother.

Hopefully, Michelle will post tomorrow.

My mother and I did laugh a lot that day. As part of my surgery, I had a temporary ileostomy, defined in a medical dictionary as "an opening created in the small intestine to bypass the colon for stool elimination." Basically, I had a hole in the lower part of my abdomen with a bag attached to catch my waste. What had us laughing so hard were the sounds that came from that opening.

The nurses had me upright in a rocking chair to help release some of the gas that was trapped in my stomach. Every time I'd rock, air would come out of the hole. It sounded like I was sitting on a whoopee cushion. And every time that happened, my mother and I would laugh like a couple of adolescent boys.

We also joked about how I could explain these sounds when I returned to work. Fortunately, when the pastor came by to pray with me later that day I was back in bed with a pillow across my stomach. The pillow was intended to elevate a swollen hand (caused by a faulty IV), but it worked wonders at drowning out the obnoxious sounds emanating from my body.

As to going home, when the doctors said that I first had to eat solid foods, my appetite improved considerably. Up to that point, they had told me not to worry if I didn't have an appetite, to just take it slow and easy.

⚓ Monday, August 16, 2010, 6:51 p.m.

We have all been anxiously, but patiently, waiting for Michelle to be discharged. She called, and she is finally coming home. You will hear from her tomorrow as it will probably still be two hours or more before she arrives.

Thanks for all your prayers and encouragement.

Barbara

If there's one thing that cancer has taught me, it is patience. That last day in the hospital I was feeling fine and knew I was ready to go home. I also knew Dr. Midis was leaving the next day for a trip out of the country. Instead of anxiously watching the clock and worrying that in his haste to get out of town the doctor might forget to discharge me, I simply read a book and waited. I was quite relieved when Dr. Midis walked in the room late that evening.

Home! I can't say how good it felt to be headed there.

⚓ Wednesday, August 18, 2010, 7:14 p.m.

This is David, Michelle's husband. In an effort to keep Michelle resting, I am going to post tonight.

I am definitely not the writer in our family, but I must communicate to everyone that words alone cannot express the gratitude I have for your words of encouragement to Michelle. Also, your prayers have lifted the spirits of our entire family. I believe God has answered all of our prayers with a miracle.

Several people have communicated on CaringBridge how hymns get stuck in their head. There are two that have stuck with me: "A Mighty Fortress is Our God" and "Lift High the Cross" are two very old Lutheran hymns that are continually being played in my head.

As many of you know, I am extremely fortunate and blessed to be married to Michelle. She has been a loving Christian wife and mother through good times and bad (mostly good). We both have been blessed with our sons Drew and Evan, whom I am very proud of.

I must also say that I have been fortunate to have the greatest in-laws around in David and Barbara Ironside. I met them through my best friend from high school, Dean Craig. Dean's mom (Shirley Craig) and Barbara are sisters.

Dean and I used to occasionally go to the "Ironside Country Club" to work out with weights and swim. I was maybe 15 or 16 when I first met David and Barbara. David shook my hand, which is rare for a grownup to do to a teenager, and I was impressed with that. As many of you know, Barbara is a GREAT cook. I still remember a delicious hamburger she made me all those years ago. I am 51 and may someday even develop dementia, but I will never forget their love and kindness.

This is how I came to know Michelle and my life was forever changed for the good.

David Henry

P.S. Michelle continues to improve a little each day, although she still has no appetite and is having a hard time eating.

What a beautiful post from my sweet husband.

David is quick to say that he fell in love with my family as much as he did with me. It's a good thing. There is a six-year age difference between David and me, which is not much now that we're older but was considerable when we started dating.

In light of the age difference, my parents made us take my younger brother, Phillip, or my sister, Kristen, with us on dates. They admit now they hoped it would make David forget about me and date someone closer to his age. Their plan clearly, and thankfully, failed. Kristen and Phillip were on the couch with us when David proposed. They also spent a lot of weekends at our house after we were married.

We have now been married 30 years, and the Ironside family would not be complete without David.

⚓ **Saturday, August 21, 2010, 6:56 p.m.**

I've started twice now to update this journal, but haven't been able to collect my thoughts enough to capture them in this space. Much has been going through my head since the surgery.

First, I am so very grateful for your many, many prayers. The surgeon was extremely pleased with the surgery and said that it could not have gone better. He also said the pathology reports were excellent. No cancer in any organs or lymph nodes. There are a few remaining cells, but the cleanup chemo should take care of those.

Second, I have to admit that the surgery hit me much harder than I expected. At about day three in the hospital I thought to myself, "The Wonder Woman cape goes in the closet for now." I even stopped asking when I got to go home and just waited for them to tell me.

I actually felt pretty good right after surgery and the day after, but I took a turn for the worse after that. I felt pretty rough. Thankfully, I am now on the mend, although I still have a hard time eating and I get tired very easily.

My mom and David were a wonderful support team, with Mom staying with me during the day and David in the evenings. And, as you know, they were kind enough to keep this journal going while I couldn't. Drew and Evan have also been a big help.

I guess it's a good sign that I'm starting to get bored, although that also means I'll have to watch myself more closely so that I don't try to do things I shouldn't.

I'll close before this gets too long. Thanks again for all of your kindness and support.

Before surgery, Dr. Midis talked to me at length about the severity of the surgery and the fact it would take at least four weeks to recover. This was one of those things I had to experience firsthand to appreciate. It was a hard surgery, and it did knock the wind out of my sails.

Dr. Midis explained later that he removed about 12 inches of my colon and 14 lymph nodes. He also poked around quite a bit to make sure cancer wasn't hiding anywhere. All that rummaging around my internal organs on top of my already depleted physical state from chemo and radiation made the surgery tough to bear.

After writing the post I was encouraged that brighter days were ahead when I read a guestbook message that said, "Don't give that Wonder Woman cape to Goodwill because we hope to see you wearing it again soon!"

⚓ **Wednesday, August 25, 2010, 5:57 p.m.**

Looks like my road to recovery will be paved with chicken and green beans. I can eat again – hallelujah! – and chicken and green beans are the two things that seem to taste best to me.

Today, I had the pleasure of attending an Executive Women's Association meeting. Don't worry. I didn't do it by myself. My good friend Janice Bridges drove me to the meeting and helped carry in all of my meeting paraphernalia. It was great to see Janice and all the ladies of EWA. I really draw energy from being around good people. It was also great to be out of the house.

Other than tiring easily and getting dizzy if I jump up too fast (which, unfortunately, is a bad habit of mine), I'm doing really well. It feels good to be over the hump of surgery and ready to face the next challenge.

I see my oncologist on September 14, at which time I'll find out when the chemo starts again and for how long. Yes, that means the fanny pack will make one more appearance!

I see my surgeon on September 20. I'm hoping at that time to schedule my follow-up surgery, which will be sometime in November. After that surgery, I should be FINISHED!

In ways, it seems like this has been a very long journey. In others, it doesn't seem like it's been long at all since I was diagnosed. I am so grateful that things have gone as well as they have because I know it's made this much easier for me than it is for many people.

Thanks again for all of your prayers and support! I am continually overwhelmed at the outpouring of love coming my way.

Now that I think about it, going to that Executive Women's Association meeting two weeks after surgery was a bit ambitious. But

I still think it was the right choice for me. It was another time when I had to strike that balance of pushing myself hard enough to get better but not so hard as to drag myself down.

I'll also add that my friends have been a tremendous blessing. They've given me rides, cooked meals, sent cards and lifted me up in prayer. Soon after I was diagnosed, I made good on my promise to spend more time with friends and scheduled the first of what has become a regular Girls' Night Out. Those nights include lots of conversation and even more laughter. I always leave feeling energized and refreshed.

⚓ **Friday, August 27, 2010, 7:36 p.m.**

Dear Friends,

Michelle is in need of special prayer as she is back in the hospital. She has a bowel obstruction and they are hoping it will clear up with medicine. Otherwise she will have surgery. Pray the blockage will respond. She is fine other than lots of pain and of course she is hoping she will just have to stay one night. Thanks for your prayers.

Barbara

The small bowel obstruction was excruciating. At first, I thought my stomach was bothering me because I had eaten a hush puppy. I assumed that I would feel fine if I took it easy and rested for a while. After I gave him many assurances that I would be fine, David left to do some work.

While he was away, things went downhill fast. Within a few hours, I was feverish and throwing up, and my stomach was cramping terribly. When I finally broke down and called Dr. Midis' nurse, she said that I needed to go to the emergency room.

Poor David. I nearly scared him to death when he realized how sick I was. When we arrived at the emergency room – late on a Friday afternoon – it was crowded. We checked in and were told to wait.

Michelle Ironside Henry

The stomach cramps were a lot like being in labor, only worse. They were excruciating and came in waves every few minutes. I couldn't sit still because the pain was so intense, and I was still throwing up.

Despite my obvious discomfort, I remained in line behind people with seemingly far less immediate needs. David was about to blow a gasket. Finally, after a couple of hours in the waiting room, they took me back and gave me something for the pain.

When a nurse told me that surgery might be required to remove the obstruction, I was concerned. Dr. Midis was out of the country, and I didn't want another doctor operating on me. I was admitted, given IV medications and instructed to rest.

Because I was on the same floor as when I had surgery, a lot of the nurses recognized me when I rolled up. It was nice to see friendly faces. They had given me exceptional care before, and I was glad to know they were there for me again. Then *she* showed up. The only nurse who was ever rude to me just so happened to be the very nurse assigned to my room that night.

In talking to her, I learned that she worked a full-time job during the week and worked nights at the hospital on weekends. No wonder she was gruff. I was reminded again we never know what people are going through, and we need to treat them with kindness no matter what.

Thankfully, the obstruction finally cleared and no surgery was necessary. The episode did, however, set back my recovery.

⚓ **Saturday, August 28, 2010, 3:44 p.m.**

Happy Birthday to me! Thanks for all the well wishes!

I'll count this birthday as a good one, as I am writing this from home. I am doing much better, although not totally back to normal. I do thank God that no more surgery was required, and I thank you for your many prayers!

It was, once again, good to be home.

94

⚓ **Wednesday, September 1, 2010, 9:00 a.m.**

I must be getting better – I feel like writing!

Two things this journey is teaching me: patience and humility. In the humility department, I only thought I had it bad with the fanny pack.

I now have an ostomy bag until the doctor "puts me back together" in November. In explaining the need for the temporary ostomy, the surgeon said, "The ostomy gives your colon a chance to heal before you use it. Also, there's always a risk it could break apart while it's healing. If that happened with bowel in there, it could be lethal."

That's all the convincing I needed. The ostomy is hard to live with, but it is helping me live, so I'll deal with it.

I am sharing this for two reasons. First, I promised to share the good, the bad and the ugly. Since this is bad and ugly, I can't keep it to myself. The second reason is a good one that involves a story with my good – and crafty – friend, Mary Lee Keeler.

The ostomy bag is plastic and lies across my stomach. I hated the way the plastic felt across my skin and thought that Mary Lee could come up with some kind of cover. When I got home from the hospital, I called her up and presented my dilemma. She was more than happy to help. (You know you've got a true friend when she'll make covers for your ostomy bag!)

After our get-together, Mary Lee went straight to Walmart to purchase fabric. After struggling for a while to find someone to cut the fabric, she came across a random employee and asked for help. "I don't work in that department, but I can cut fabric," said the employee. While she was cutting the fabric, the lady asked, "So, what are you making?"

"Well..." said Mary Lee with a chuckle, before explaining what she was making and telling the story of my battle with cancer. When the story was finished, the Walmart lady was crying. "My brother was diagnosed with rectal cancer about a week ago," she said. "Our family has been devastated. Hearing this story makes me feel so much better."

After hearing that, I realized that if I had been too proud to tell my friend that I had an ostomy, this lady and her family would not have had the comfort that my story was able to provide. And I wouldn't have my lovely pouch covers!

So, that's my story. The good news is that the bag really doesn't show, and it's not causing too much trouble. The even better news is that it is coming off in November!

Thanks again for your prayers and support. The small bowel obstruction was rough. I pretty much got knocked back to square one on the digestion front and am pretty weak, but I am bouncing back and feeling better each day.

It was hard for me to talk publicly about the ostomy; it was embarrassing. But I'm so glad I didn't let pride get in the way. The covers that Mary Lee made were really nice. The much greater reward, though, was the knowledge that my story reached someone who needed it and that, because of me, a family facing a very scary diagnosis had hope.

"Do nothing from selfishness or empty conceit, but with humility of mind let each of you regard one another as more important than himself; do not merely look out for your own personal interests, but also for the interests of others." Philippians 2:3-4

⚓ **Tuesday, September 7, 2010, 12:06 p.m.**

It's hard to believe that nearly a week has passed since I last posted. I figured time would crawl by while I was recuperating, but it's going by quickly. Although I am still somewhat weak and considerably slower than normal, I am doing much better.

In fact, we had our "Henry Family Birthday Gathering" at my parents' house on Sunday night, and I was able to eat quite a bit. As usual, the meal was delicious, and it was a very fun and pleasant evening. Drew's girlfriend joined us, which made it even more special.

I am planning to go back to work tomorrow, and I'm looking forward to it. David and other family members keep asking, "Are you sure you're ready to go back to work?" To which I reply, "No, but I'm going to try."

I'm going to push myself a bit because I know it helped me when I was feeling rough before. There were days when I started to turn the car around and go back home because I felt so bad on my way to work, but once I got there I got distracted and forgot I felt bad at all.

I won't overdo it, however. I plan to cut my days short if necessary, and I'm sure my evening naps will be back on the calendar. But it will be good to be out of the house and back into a routine. I hate TV and have read about a thousand books, so I'm definitely ready for a change of pace.

The Henry Family Birthday Gathering is a much-anticipated annual affair. Because our four birthdays fall within a two-week time period, my mother cooks a special dinner and brings us together for a time of celebration. The girlfriend Drew brought, Sam (short for Samantha), is the same girl he ended up marrying.

Luckily for Drew, Sam's first introduction to my parents didn't hamper their budding relationship. Drew and Sam were talking about going to watch Boomsday, a huge Labor Day weekend fireworks show, after dinner. Boomsday is a longtime Knoxville tradition that draws a crowd of more than 100,000 people. Drew mentioned he was fortunate that Sam's apartment was in walking distance, and he could get a coveted parking space there.

My dad looked over at Sam without even a hint of a smile and said, "He's going to break up with you after it's over." We believe he meant to joke that Drew was using her for the parking space.

Sam was speechless; she just sat there with the most bewildered look. We all laughed it off and later told her to ignore anything my dad said. We explained that in his younger years he was really funny but lately his humor wasn't hitting its mark. Looking back, this was clearly another sign that Alzheimer's was taking a toll.

⚓ Saturday, September 11, 2010, 11:54 a.m.

Today's devotional, based on Philippians 4:4, talks about being content in all circumstances. It says that instead of wistfully thinking about a day when our troubles will be over and we can finally be happy, we should celebrate each moment and rejoice always. It closes by saying, "Now is the time to rejoice in My presence!"

How true those words are. The more we learn to rejoice in the moment – regardless of what that moment brings – the more content we become and better able to take what life throws at us.

Yesterday afternoon, I got a call from Evan. He told me in a very calm manner that he wasn't hurt but that he had been in a wreck. From the way he sounded, I assumed it was a minor fender bender. Upon talking to him further, I learned that his car was totaled and that he came very close to being hit head-on by a pickup truck. Thankfully, Evan was protected from injury and is fine. His already sad little Corolla wasn't so fortunate, but cars can be replaced!

My three days at work went very well. I was able to work my regular schedule, and I didn't get as tired as I feared I would. I'm able to eat more now, which is really helping me feel more normal.

Now, David may have to tie me down to keep me from doing things I shouldn't. Just this morning, I started to climb up on the kitchen counters to rearrange some things on top of the cabinets.

Fortunately, I remembered my propensity for dizziness and decided that was not a good idea.

Don't worry. I'll behave. I sure don't want to wind up back in the hospital.

Thanks again for your posts, cards and prayers! I've gotten some great cards lately that have had me laughing out loud.

Rejoicing in the moment seems far easier when you don't have cancer and your son didn't just total his car. But in Philippians 4:4 Paul exhorts, "Rejoice in the Lord always; again I will say, rejoice!" This is where it's necessary to make the distinction between joy and happiness.

Happiness is tied to circumstances. If things are going well, you're happy. If they're not going so well, you may not be so happy. Joy is much deeper than happiness. Joy springs up from within. Joy is our response to what God has done for us and our trust in Him.

I needed to move my focus from the negative, Evan just totaled his car, to the positive, Evan was just in a serious accident but God protected him from injury. Instead of focusing on the fact we were facing another financial burden so soon after incurring considerable medical expenses and lost income as a result of my sickness, I needed to be thankful I was able to return to work so soon after surgery.

Paul wrote Philippians while he was in prison, yet throughout the book he repeatedly talks about joy and finds reasons to be thankful. Paul doesn't whine about his predicament; he doesn't write and urge people to do everything possible to get him out. Instead, he finds reasons to be thankful.

In Philippians chapter 1, Paul says his imprisonment is good because it is helping to spread the gospel. He then goes on to say some people are preaching the gospel with the wrong motives, but he doesn't let that get him down either. In verse 18 he says, "What then? Only that in every way, whether in pretense or truth, Christ is proclaimed; and in this I rejoice, yes, and I will rejoice."

When you get down to it, joy is about making a choice. We can choose to be like Eeyore, the gloomy donkey in Winnie the Pooh, or we can choose to trust God and press on with joy.

"Life is 10 percent what happens to me and 90 percent how I react to it." – Charles Swindoll

⚓ Tuesday, September 14, 2010, 11:28 a.m.

In my last post, I talked about rejoicing. Today, I am REJOICING more than usual!

I got the most wonderful news from my oncologist this morning – I don't have to have any more chemo! As he looked at my reports from surgery, he said, "There's no reason for me to give you any chemo. There's no cancer." He went on to add, "Your results are phenomenal." He also commented that my surgeon, Dr. Gregory Midis, is amazing. I agree.

They will be keeping a close eye on me, with blood tests every three months and another PET scan in the spring, but for now all I have to do is stay well and wait for my final surgery in November. Hooray!!

For those of you wondering how I'm feeling, I am doing really well. Actually... I was doing really well until I ate a piece of barbecue chicken pizza last night. Bad choice! My stomach is killing me today. Other than that, though, I am doing just great!

Finally, I'm going to bring up something that has nothing to do with my medical condition but is a need nonetheless. Remember Evan's wreck? We found a car to purchase, but it won't be available until the end of October or early November. We are desperately trying to find something to drive until then. Right now, I'm sharing my vehicle with Evan. Poor David has to either schlep me to work at 8:30 or make the 50-mile round trip to take Evan to Hardin Valley Academy at 7:00 a.m. on days when I need my car. We're hoping to find someone with an extra vehicle we could use. (Renting is at least $600 a month.) If you have something but are worried about letting Evan drive it, no worries. I'm willing to drive the loaner vehicle and let Evan drive mine. We just need some temporary wheels!

Thanks again for all your prayers and support!

"Rejoice, rejoice, again I say rejoice!"

I loved that Dr. Antonucci used the word phenomenal to describe my progress. Hearing that I didn't need more chemo was definitely a mountaintop experience. I had made peace with the fact that having more chemo was a necessary evil. I was elated to learn that, this time around, the evil wasn't necessary.

This post also proved fruitful in our search for a loaner vehicle. As it turns out, a friend I went to church with years ago was following my CaringBridge journal. She and her husband had a Honda Odyssey van that was just in their way. I drove the van for a few months before my parents ended up buying it. After my father died, we bought the van as an extra vehicle for David. That van has been the gift that keeps on giving.

⚓ Monday, September 27, 2010, 5:54 p.m.

Greetings, all!

It has been a while since I've posted, simply because I haven't had anything to say.

I had an MRI of my liver last week and got the results today. (Yes, with all the CT scans, PET scans, X-rays and MRIs I should glow in the dark by now!) Anyway, I originally had two spots on my liver. Now, one 5mm spot shows up. The other one is completely gone.

When I talked to my surgeon, he said that he can't decide what to do. Because I've done so well and am so extremely healthy, he is tempted to go as aggressively as possible and remove a large portion of my liver just to be sure the cancer doesn't come back. On the other hand, he wonders if burning off the one spot will be sufficient.

He is meeting with his Tumor Board (who knew there was such a thing?) tomorrow morning to show them all my scans and X-rays and get their opinion on how to proceed.

Please pray that we make the right decision about how to go forward. I am game for whatever keeps the cancer at bay, but am also fond of keeping my insides as intact as possible!

On another note, my energy levels continue to increase and I feel better and better each day. I'm working full-time and still have energy to spare when I get home. I was able to go to Sunday school and church yesterday, and it was wonderful!

In hearing about the Tumor Board, I learned there are groups of physicians from various practices who regularly meet to share information and discuss some of their more challenging cases. When Dr. Midis met with the group to discuss my case, they all agreed taking the most aggressive route was the way to go.

It was good to see the camaraderie among the surgeons and to know that doctors are willing to admit they don't have all the answers. Even though the board concluded I should be treated as aggressively as possible, I am convinced it was the best way to proceed.

⚓ **Saturday, October 9, 2010, 10:22 a.m.**

I heard from the doctor yesterday, and I have to admit that at first I was a little bummed. I was happy to finally have news and to know that my surgery will take place sometime in early November. I was not thrilled to hear that it will entail another five-day hospital stay and four-week recovery time.

The reason for the long hospital stay and recovery time is that getting to the spot on my liver requires a rather large incision. No laparoscopic surgery this time around.

The surgeon said that he and his Tumor Board agreed that it is important to surgically remove the 5mm spot where the cancer was in order to keep the cancer from coming back. Getting to that spot won't be easy because of where it is located. He said it will be very painful. This time I believe him.

While the surgeon's in there, he'll look very closely at my liver to be sure he finds and removes any other spots that may be there but are not showing up on the scans.

I'm definitely on board with doing everything possible to keep the cancer from coming back, so my thoughts about surgery are turning more positive all the time. By November, I'll be turning cartwheels all the way to the hospital. (Figuratively, of course. I could barely do cartwheels as a child.)

On another note, I am continually reminded of the brevity of life. The week before last, Tim Wallace, the father of one of Evan's friends, died suddenly of a heart attack at the age of 49. Earlier this week, I learned that Jane Land, a friend of the family who is only 47, has lung cancer and the prognosis is not good.

Life is short. Love much.

Thanks to the surgery on my liver, I now have a rather large scar across my midsection. When I was teaching a Sunday school class about John 15 and God's heavenly pruning, I laughed when I told them I still have the marks of the pruning shears on my stomach.

While I laughed when I said it, there was truth in my statement. In John 15:1-2, Jesus says, "I am the true vine, and My Father is the vinedresser. Every branch in Me that does not bear fruit, He takes away; and every branch that bears fruit, He prunes it, that it may bear more fruit."

The message of the vinedresser was part of Christ's farewell address to His disciples; it was His "death bed" message. Jesus knew His time on earth was short, and He spent much of it talking about abiding in the Father and being fruitful. It stands to reason those are important truths that we all would do well to consider.

In *Secrets of the Vine: Breaking Through to Abundance* by Bruce Wilkinson, a book on which I relied heavily in preparing my lessons, Wilkinson says that grape plants grow vigorously, requiring a lot of wood to be cut away from the plant each year. Left to itself, he explains, a grape plant will always favor new growth over more grapes. The result of that growth is a plant that looks luxurious and impressive from a distance, but in reality doesn't produce much fruit.

He compares that rampant growth to the preoccupations and priorities that, while not wrong, keep Christians from more significant ministry for God. It goes back to what I was saying earlier, we often are so busy doing the good that we miss the best.

I am convinced my cancer has been a heavenly pruning. It has forced me to slow down, rethink my priorities and give up the idea that I'm in control. In the process, I've learned to trust God more and have gained a peace that can't be explained outside of God.

"Peace I leave with you; My peace I give to you; not as the world gives, do I give to you. Let not your heart be troubled, nor let it be fearful." John 14:27

⚓ **Thursday, October 14, 2010, 7:10 p.m.**

My surgery is scheduled for the morning of November 2. The surgeon says I should be in good shape for Thanksgiving and great shape for Christmas. I'll take that prognosis and run with it!

Considering that last Christmas I had just been diagnosed with cancer, this one should be much merrier!

And, if my hairdresser's forecast turns out to be correct, I'll recover more quickly than anticipated. When I had my hair cut yesterday, she marveled at how much it had grown and how healthy it is. She sees that as a sign of how healthy I must be.

I have to admit that I feel very healthy, and everyone I see comments on how healthy I look. Don't know if that's compared to how bad I looked before, but I'll take it all as a good sign and hope for a speedy recovery!

By this time, I was eager for surgery, not only because it meant crossing another important hurdle in my treatment plan but also because it meant having my colon reattached. Despite my fancy covers, life with the ostomy was not fun.

After surgery, the doctor and nurses told me that I couldn't eat things like nuts, corn or popcorn because they could block the stoma, the opening in my abdominal wall that allowed waste to escape my body. No one mentioned spinach. Yet, the day after I enjoyed a delicious lunch that consisted of scallops, rice and braised spinach, I realized I had a problem.

Be forewarned, this is gross. The spinach, which clearly had not been chewed thoroughly enough, was coming through the stoma. The pressure of that spinach moving through the stoma was making it impossible for the apparatus that held my bag in place to stay put. I ended up having to go back to the hospital to meet with the ostomy specialist. She and I both were amazed at the amount of spinach that bubbled through that hole.

I remember arriving at the hospital, dressed for work in a nice pantsuit and hoping we could get things under control before my suit was wrecked. As I walked through the hospital, I thought the people I encountered would never have guessed what was taking place just beneath my sharp outfit.

I again was reminded we just never know what may be going on in a person's life.

⚓ Sunday, October 24, 2010, 2:52 p.m.

I just got on the computer to do some work when I got sidetracked and started reading Jane Land's blog. (She's the friend who was recently diagnosed with lung cancer.) I wanted to write a post to her, but wanted the words to be just right. I was led to read today's devotional, and the words were not only for Jane but for me.

They read in part: "I have called you to walk with me down paths of peace. I want you to blaze a trail for others who desire to live in My peaceful presence. I have chosen you less for your strengths than for your weaknesses, which amplify your need for Me. Depend on Me more and more, and I will shower peace on all your paths."

Those words are so true. As I've traveled down this rough path for nearly a year now, I find that I am often much more at peace now than I was before. I know I can't fight cancer on my own, so I don't rely on my strength, but on God's. The way He intended it to be all along.

I know that jumping this final hurdle won't be easy, but I also know that the One who has sustained me thus far will stay with me through surgery on November 2 and beyond.

Thanks be to God.

Remember your child's first tenuous steps? Walking is so hard when we first learn how, but with enough time and practice it's one of the easiest things we do.

When I first started cooking, it was very difficult for me to figure out how to time everything so that it was all ready at the same time. For the tomboy who never spent a minute learning to be domestic, cooking a meal was a stressful and complicated task. After many years and enough practice, cooking became second nature. Remarkably, I'm even quite good at it.

I believe that's how it is in the Christian life. The more we practice living in God's peace and in His strength instead of our own, the easier it becomes.

⚓ Tuesday, November 2, 2010, 2:59 p.m.

Thank you for your prayers and thanks be to God who answered the way we were praying. Michelle came through surgery wonderfully well. Dr. Midis always uses the word miracle when he speaks of her. He cut a cherry sized cancer from the liver and said the rest of her liver looked very healthy. The gallbladder was removed and her colon was reattached.

She has a large incision but the pain is more manageable with this surgery as her internal organs are not so sore. Michelle explains it as a different pain than before. She is in very good spirits and wanted me to post her thanks to each of you.

Praise God who just keeps pouring out an abundance of blessings to us. We give Him all praise, honor and glory.

Barbara

Liver resection is very complex surgery with potentially serious complications. Before my surgery, a nurse inserted a catheter in an artery in my arm. He explained it would be used to monitor my internal blood pressure, a common safety measure during liver surgery. I now realize they do that because of the high risk of extensive blood loss during liver surgery and the need to have the most accurate blood pressure readings possible.

Thankfully, I came through the surgery with flying colors. I don't know if it was because I was expecting something far worse or perhaps my body was better able to take the second surgery since I was further removed from chemo and radiation. But the second surgery really was much easier than the first.

⚓ **Wednesday, November 3, 2010, 3:53 p.m.**

Michelle continues to amaze everyone who walks in the room. She looks great and sat up for an hour and decided not to overdo it as she did before.

Continue to pray that there will no setbacks and no infections. She is a "model patient." Thanks again. She is very anxious to read the entries.

Barbara

I've come to the conclusion that having a naturally dark complexion helps tremendously when you're fighting illness. Although this surgery took place in November, I still maintained some color from all my time spent poolside over the summer. That color did a lot to hide any post-surgery pallor. A tan, much like a good jacket, can hide a multitude of sins.

⚓ **Friday, November 5, 2010, 7:35 a.m.**

Hallelujah!!!!

Dr. Midis reported to Michelle this morning there was no cancer in the portion he removed from the liver. That is such wonderful news. She continues to feel a little better each day, but will need to stay until Sunday so that her system can tolerate a bit more food. Her diet is now liquids so maybe soft foods today or tomorrow.

Thanks again for the prayers, love and support. We appreciate each of you.

Blessings for today,

Barbara

Again, more great news. The chemo had done its job and destroyed the cancer. The portion of my liver that was removed merely had a footprint where the cancer had been. Even so, the surgery was necessary to help ensure the cancer didn't come right back.

When I think about all the steps we had to take to get rid of the cancer, I am reminded of how Christians have to deal with sin. It's not enough to clean things up until they look better; it is essential that we completely eradicate anything that is causing us to go astray. Problems with a sinful thought life? Then you had better take a long, hard look at the things you are feeding your brain and cast aside those things that are not glorifying to God. Tempted to stray on your spouse? Then you had better steer clear of people and situations that put temptation in your path, even if that means changing churches, getting different friends or finding a new job.

"No temptation has overtaken you but such as is common to man; and God is faithful, who will not allow you to be tempted beyond what you are able, but with the temptation will provide the way of escape also, that you may be able to endure it." 1 Corinthians 10:13

⚓ Sunday, November 7, 2010, 5:12 p.m.

Greetings, all!

I am writing this from HOME! Hooray!

Today's devotional says that our sense of security and well-being should not be dependent on our life circumstances but instead should spring out of our complete confidence in God. It talks about how God works in us to remove those things that clutter up our lives and distract us from Him.

As I find myself safely on the other side of surgery and the hospital stay, I feel there is a little less debris and clutter in me. Physically – no more gallbladder, a little less liver, and no more ostomy bag (hooray!). But also less of the other me – the one that wants things my way, on my schedule.

Everyone keeps telling me how great I look. My mom said that it's the beauty of Jesus shining through. I hope that's the case.

This last surgery wasn't nearly as painful as the first. My recovery time at the hospital went quickly. In fact, I enjoyed seeing all the nurses again, and it felt good that they seemed happy to see me.

I don't feel too bad – much better than I expected. I'm still taking pain meds, but I'm able to go up and down the stairs and move around fairly well. I'm slow, but I get there!

Thanks so much for all your prayers, posts and cards! You're helping to pull me through!

With much love,

Michelle

The nurses at Fort Sanders Regional Medical Center are fantastic, and I was glad they seemed happy to see me. One day, a student nurse was meeting all the patients on my floor. She later came back and asked if she could interview me about my cancer and surgeries. I was flattered when she said that she picked me out of all the other patients because she liked my smile and positive attitude.

I'll say it again. How we treat people matters.

"I've learned that people will forget what you said, people will forget what you did, but people will never forget how you made them feel." – Maya Angelou

⚓ Friday, November 12, 2010, 10:12 a.m.

Again, today's devotional hits the mark. It says in part, "Your cup runneth over with blessings. After plodding uphill for many weeks, you are now traipsing through lush meadows drenched in warm sunshine."

My cup indeed "runneth over" with blessings.

I saw the surgeon yesterday and got my staples out, and he was very pleased with my progress. His nurse said that she's amazed every time she sees me after surgery because I don't look like the typical post-surgery patient. I am thankful to bounce back so quickly.

And, I suppose my hairdresser was right when she said I'd do even better with this surgery than the last. I feel quite good – no dizziness, fatigue or weakness this time around. The hardest part is trying to not overdo it.

With that in mind, I think I'll go sit on our back deck and enjoy the sunshine!

Have a great weekend, everybody!

When I was about 5, our family visited an amusement park. This was in the late 1960s, before many safety measures were in place. Despite my young age, I rode what at the time was one of the tallest and fastest roller coasters in America. I also rode the bumper cars all by myself and managed to hit one man so hard he disgustedly walked me out to my parents and suggested they do a better job of controlling me.

It's fair to say I've always enjoyed wild rides, which is a good thing. My battle with cancer has had more ups and downs than any roller coaster. Obviously, I much prefer the highs like those in this post, but my goal is to be like Paul, content whatever my circumstances.

"Not that I speak from want; for I have learned to be content in whatever circumstances I am. I know how to get along with humble means, and I also know how to live in prosperity; I have learned the secret of being filled and going hungry, both of having abundance and suffering need. I can do all things through Christ who strengthens me." Philippians 4:11-13

⚓ **Thursday, November 18, 2010, 9:35 a.m.**

As I've admitted before, I'm not so great at this whole "rest and relaxation" thing. I'm much more content being active. I am happy to report that, thanks to the wonderful folks at Gallaher Spa, yesterday I experienced relaxation at a level I've never achieved short of anesthesia.

For more than a year now, I've been carrying around a certificate for a free facial. I always thought about using it, but never took the time. As I was sitting around bored the other day, I thought about that certificate and figured using it would be the perfect way to divert boredom and follow my doctor's orders to rest.

The facial was amazing! I was so relaxed after that hour of pampering I nearly melted off the table. My skin looks good, too!

For nearly a year now, I've had people "messing with me" all the time. Most of it has been painful. I think that's what made the facial even better – I realized how nice it was to have something done to me that didn't involve pain, needles or that blasted adhesive tape.

As I stay home recovering, it is dawning on me – that part of my life is nearly over. Sure, I'll be seeing the oncologist fairly often and the surgeon periodically. There will be more scans and lots more blood work, but I've crossed the finish line on the worst of it. For that, I am immensely thankful! And, I can honestly say that it wasn't nearly as bad as I thought it would be.

Thanks again for your prayers, posts, cards and support. They sustain me daily.

Before I was diagnosed, I watched a documentary about Farrah Fawcett's battle with cancer. I'm not much of one to watch television and normally wouldn't have been inclined to watch the documentary. Something, divine providence perhaps, made me watch the presentation in its entirety. I remember thinking how horrid the treatment must have been and wondering if I could be as brave as Farrah if I were facing cancer. I believe this was one more way that God was preparing me for the diagnosis that was to come my way months later.

Having been through it myself, I can say there is a lot of pain associated with treating cancer. Following chemo, radiation and two major surgeries, I had gotten to the point that I just expected pain; it was just part and parcel of my new life, the life after my cancer diagnosis.

I believe the facial was particularly soothing because it helped reach a place inside of me that was beginning to scar. As someone with a choleric temperament, I'm not the touchy-feely type anyway, but I was beginning to associate touch only with discomfort. The facial reminded me not every touch would hurt. You still won't catch me running around giving lots of hugs, but you won't see me flinching when someone reaches out.

⚓ Monday, November 22, 2010, 12:44 p.m.

The good news continues to pour in!

I saw my oncologist, Dr. Antonucci, this morning. As he looked at my latest surgery and pathology reports, he said, "We're in uncharted territory. We just don't have patients who go from Stage IV to complete remission like you have. There aren't even any case studies on it."

I'm happy to travel these "uncharted waters." And, if you ever find yourself wondering if miracles still happen in this day and age, think of me and know that they do. I am both humbled and honored to have been chosen as a vessel of such tremendous blessings.

Hope you all have a very happy Thanksgiving! I know that our family has much to be thankful for this year!

While I was recovering from surgery, my cousin recommended I read *Same Kind of Different as Me*, a wonderful book that tells the true story of how one woman's faith and determination helped forge a life-changing friendship between her husband and a homeless man. The inspirational story demonstrates how God works through us to change lives.

As I was reading, I noted Deborah, the woman about whom the book was written, had the same kind of cancer as mine. "Oh, look. She had colorectal cancer, too," I thought. "And her cancer spread to her liver, just like mine." I assumed Tracy recommended the book so I could read an amazing story of survival.

Imagine my surprise when I got to the part of the book where Deborah dies. I was reminded once again that there are no guarantees, particularly when you're dealing with cancer. Lest you think badly of Tracy for recommending the book, she had forgotten about the death because it wasn't the central story of the book.

Talking about Deborah's death makes me think of Al Wright, a dear neighbor who was battling lung cancer. When Al's cancer was in remission, I walked by and saw him and his wife working in the yard. After saying how good it was to see Al outside and doing well, I said, "God is good." Al's wife, Suzanne, replied with a smile, "No matter what."

Al's story ended the same as Deborah's, with cancer eventually ravaging his body and taking his life. Al's sweet wife still thinks God is good. I agree.

An interesting footnote, David and I were so impressed with Al's funeral service at Sevier Heights Baptist Church that we later started visiting the church. We are now members. We see Suzanne's beaming face up in the choir every Sunday. To this day, when I hear the choir sing a particularly moving hymn, I'll catch myself thinking, "I want them to sing that one at my funeral service."

For the record, the latest song on my hit parade is "I Will Rise." I love all the lyrics, but the chorus particularly resonates with me. It says in part: "And I will rise when He calls my name. No more sorrow, no more pain. I will rise on eagle's wings. Before my God, fall on my knees."

⚓ Friday, November 26, 2010, 11:06 a.m.

I knew this Thanksgiving would be special. What I didn't know was that my sister-in-law, Pamela, would ask me to select a hymn that the family would sing before our Thanksgiving meal. I commend her bravery in taking up the challenge to get the Ironsides to sing. To say that we are not the von Trapp family is to put it mildly. Singers we are not.

Nevertheless, I selected the hymn, "Give Thanks." It's one of my favorites, and our family has much to give thanks for this year. Of course, there's my miraculous recovery. Also, Kevin and Pamela successfully adopted a son from Uganda, overcoming many obstacles to do so, and my father is doing much, much better health wise. There are many other things to be thankful for, but those were the biggies.

At any rate, we rallied the troops and sang the song. It was good for us to step outside our comfort zone to thank God for everything He has done and is doing for us.

And, even as we have so much to celebrate, I know there are so many others who are hurting.

Just yesterday, Evan learned his friend Josh has leukemia, and it is apparently very advanced. As Evan said this morning, "It's been a tough year." He's had a mother face cancer, one friend lose a sister, one friend lose a father, and now this. I'm glad to see his faith growing, and trust that God will not only help him but help him support his friends who are hurting.

I pray that I, too, can be a help to those who are hurting, just as so many have helped me this past year.

Once again, a hymn takes a prominent place in my walk. If you ever hear me sing, you'll understand how surprising it is that I can be so touched through music. There isn't a musical bone in my body. And, for those who know my family, I'm sure the picture of us holding hands and singing a song is not one that comes to mind without a few chuckles. I do, however, appreciate Pamela's faithfulness in following what God called her to do. I'm sure it wasn't easy.

When I wrote about Evan's friend, I optimistically said Evan's faith was growing. I was, unfortunately, very much mistaken. As a kid, Evan displayed spiritual insight that was uncanny. I remember a conversation he and my nephew had about whether or not the boy who cried wolf would go to heaven.

"He would go to heaven if he prayed the prayer of salvation," Christian said.

"Not if he didn't mean it in his heart when he prayed the prayer," replied the very young but very spiritually aware Evan.

Evan also was unfazed when I took him on hospital and nursing home visits. With his upbeat disposition and outgoing personality, Evan was a ray of sunshine in those sometimes gloomy places. I wondered if he might end up being a pastor.

Imagine my shock one night when Evan said he didn't believe in God. "If there's a God, how do *you* get cancer? You've never done anything to hurt anybody," he said with emotion. "And what about Granddad? Greatest guy in the whole world, and now he can't do anything."

It breaks my heart to think about it and to know how much my cancer, in particular, has affected Evan. He has endured a lot of pain these past few years, and he is clearly hurting.

At church yesterday, the sermon was on prayer. We were provided with cards and encouraged to write our biggest prayer request and lay it on the altar. I didn't list my cancer; it probably wouldn't have even made my top five. Evan is at the top of my prayer list.

⚓ Tuesday, December 7, 2010, 4:53 p.m.

When I was sick, I almost never talked about my cancer. Except, of course, on this website. Now that I'm better, I find myself wanting to tell everyone that I had Stage IV cancer that is now in complete remission. There's good and bad to that.

The good is that I get to share with everyone the miracle that has happened, and my story offers encouragement to others who are facing cancer or have loved ones battling the disease.

The bad is that by sharing my story I am more apt to hear horror stories about people whose struggle with cancer resulted in a recurrence and very unpleasant results.

I just read a book about a lady who had about exactly the same kind of cancer as mine. She died. And I just heard about a guy whose colon cancer went away but is now back and worse than before.

It kind of reminds me of the war stories you hear when you're pregnant. You know the kind – "I was in labor for 28 hours before I finally had a C-section." "I was in so much pain I wanted to die."

I didn't listen to war stories when I was pregnant, and I won't listen to them now. I was fortunate enough to deliver Drew and Evan in only 30 minutes after arriving at the hospital with very little pain.

My cancer experience so far has been far from ordinary, so I'm not going to compare notes with others. I'm going to treat my remission the same as my pregnancies. Plow ahead and stay positive. I'm also going to keep telling my story even if it means I'll hear some bad ones. God has blessed me with a miracle. I have to shout it out to the world!

Today's devotion talks about how we need to keep our focus on God, not on all the worldly things that cry out for our attention. It says that God is always focused on us but that our focus on him wavers; when that happens, it is easy for us to be discouraged and feel miserable. It's true. When we focus on God, the one constant in our lives, we're able to experience peace even in the midst of trouble, just as a spinning ballerina is able to prevent dizziness by focusing on one stationary object.

I'm choosing to focus on God instead of the horror stories that regularly assault me and the potential medical setbacks that are statistically viable. God has helped me travel this road safely thus far, and I have every confidence He'll be with me from here on out.

My love to all. Enjoy this Christmas season!

It's like Paul said, "We look not at the things which are seen, but at the things which are not seen; for the things which are seen are temporal, but the things which are not seen are eternal." 2 Corinthians 4:18

I think of Mary and Martha, how Martha was so busy with her dinner preparations while Mary sat at Jesus' feet. When Martha complained to Jesus about having to do all the work, He replied, "Martha, Martha, you are worried and bothered about so many things; but only a few things are necessary, really only one, for Mary has chosen the good part, which shall not be taken away from her." Luke 10:41-42

Later, Mary anointed Jesus with an alabaster of costly perfume, valued at 300 denarii, equal to a year's salary for a rural worker. The disciples were furious, thinking the perfume should have been sold and given to the poor.

"But Jesus, aware of this, said to them, 'Why do you bother the woman? For she has done a good deed to Me. For the poor you have with you always; but you do not always have Me.'" Matthew 26:10-11

We can get so caught up in the world that parades in front of us that we miss the things of eternal value. When you get down to it, it's hard for us to comprehend the meaning of eternity. In something I recently wrote for work, I used the following examples to demonstrate the difference between billions and trillions:

One billion is a **thousand** millions.
One trillion is a **million** millions.
One billion seconds is about **31.5 years**.
One trillion seconds is more than **31,000 years**.

It's hard enough to wrap your head around those comparisons. How do we begin to compare the difference between our brief lives on Earth and eternity?

Remember how it felt to be a teenager? How monumentally important everything seemed? Looking back, we feel foolish to have wasted so much energy and emotion on things that mattered very little, if at all. Having endured a major illness, I now realize how trivial it makes most concerns of daily living. At the same time, I realize my suffering on Earth will be nothing but a blip on the radar compared to the eternal glories of heaven. It's all about perspective and our need to keep it eternal.

⚓ **Wednesday, December 29, 2010, 10:27 a.m.**

What a difference a year makes.

This time last year I was preparing to deal with the unknown – hoping for the best, but assuming that my battle with cancer would be a long, tough battle that would put me on the sidelines for the better part of a year.

Now, I'm on the other side of the fight. Yes, it was a long, tough battle, but I am so thankful that I wasn't completely out of commission for most of it. Being able to continue to work and take care of my family – albeit with a messier house and much less home cooking – really helped.

In one of my early posts I promised to take it easy and behave. I also promised my tranquil lifestyle would only last as long as I was sick. Staying true to my word, I'm going skydiving with Drew and Evan and two of their friends as soon as we have a weekend when it's warm enough to do so.

Although David is deathly afraid of heights, he really wanted to do it. I talked him out of it for fear of killing him in the process. I prefer to keep my husband alive.

After my surgeon, Dr. Midis, and I discussed how long I needed to wait before skydiving, he laughed and said, "If you go and get yourself killed, Antonucci (my oncologist) and I won't even feel sorry for you. We get you through all this ..."

It is funny to think how ironic it would be to get killed skydiving after surviving what I've gone through, but what I really think about is we only have one life, and we need to live it to the fullest.

I plan to spend more time with friends and family and less time cleaning floors; take a few chances here and there to experience things I'll remember a lifetime; and live my life with purpose so when I'm gone I will leave the world a better place than I found it.

I see both the surgeon and oncologist next week for follow-up visits, which will be a regular part of the coming year. I'll be sure to post any news. Other than that, I imagine I won't be posting much in the coming year, but I will take time to share things when I have something to say.

Again, thank you so very much for your prayers, cards, posts and support. Words will never be enough to let you know what they mean to me.

I did eventually get to go skydiving and lived to tell the tale. It was fun, but I still contend scuba diving and horseback riding are more fun.

As you may have guessed by now, I'm a bit of a daredevil; I have been since I was a young child. When I recently brought up the possibility of hang gliding, David put his foot down. "That's where I draw the line," he said. I figure I've given him enough scares lately, so I let the hang gliding idea drop.

When I wrote that post in December 2010, I believed it would be one of my last. Had I known then that I'd still be posting – and battling cancer – more than three years later, I would have been discouraged. It's a good thing we can't see into the future.

"Therefore do not be anxious for tomorrow; for tomorrow will care for itself. Each day has enough trouble of its own." Matthew 6:34

⚓ Wednesday, January 5, 2011, 5:08 p.m.

No big news to report, which is a good thing.

I saw Dr. Midis on Monday, and he is pleased with my progress. He said it's a very good sign that I'm feeling good and that my digestion is working well.

My only problem has been a nagging pain at the incision site. Dr. Midis said it is because he had to cut through nerves. The good news is that they are already beginning to fuse back together, and the pain is not nearly as intense. It will take a while, but eventually that pain should completely go away.

I am also cleared to exercise and do whatever I want. Hooray!

When I asked about exercising, Dr. Midis warned that it will probably be painful because I have a lot of scar tissue. As he so eloquently put it, "Ease off if it hurts, and it will hurt. You have a ton of scar tissue. We poked you all full of holes."

I don't know why, but I find it terribly amusing how blunt all of my doctors are with me. Perhaps it's because I'm getting a dose of my own medicine. I have been called blunt a time or two.

I went to the oncologist today, but only had blood work done and my port flushed, so there's no news from that visit. I will only hear back if there's bad news from my blood work, so I'm hoping for no news.

It's a snowy night here in Knoxville. Think I'll go curl up with a good book!

I still have some pain from those surgeries. It flares up at the oddest times, a stabbing, sharp pain that comes out of nowhere. Based on my experience, I would recommend people who have other treatment options available think long and hard before opting for surgery. While surgery is often necessary, and was vital in my case, it isn't the quick fix so many mistakenly believe it is.

⚓ **Saturday, January 22, 2011, 10:03 a.m.**

You know how you feel when you've just gotten over being sick? It feels so good to have energy again that you want to run laps around the house? Or maybe that's just me. Anyway, that's how I feel right now.

My energy levels are pretty much back to normal, and it feels great! I knew I wasn't myself, but didn't realize how low my energy levels were until I compare how I felt only a week or two ago to how I feel now.

On Wednesday evening, I exercised for the first time in ages, and it felt wonderful. Mom (who has amazing energy for a lady her age) and I did a walking tape that includes various exercises over the course of a two-mile walk. It's the perfect way for me to start back. And, it didn't even make me sore!

On Thursday evening, I attended a Celebration Event for Purses with Purpose, the women's philanthropy group in which I participate. It was so good to feel like doing something after work, and it was wonderful to see so many friends.

Now, I'm going to do the exercise tape again before coming home to clean house. It's good to be back!

The walking tape has been such a blessing for Mom and me. We're up to four miles now, and we do the workout three times a week. We talk the whole time, so it's a great way to catch up and share whatever is in our hearts. We solve a lot of the world's problems in those four miles.

God clearly had a plan when he prompted us to start that exercise routine. We use bands, so in addition to aerobic exercise, we also get strength training. All that training came in quite handy last year when my mom had to do a tremendous amount of lifting and carrying while taking care of my father at the end stage of his illness. I don't believe she could possibly have done it all without having built her strength and stamina to such a high degree.

In addition to just being fun to do the workouts with my mom, having a training partner makes me go ahead and exercise even when I may not feel like it at the time. Mom says she feels the same way. If you're not getting regular exercise, I encourage you to find a well-suited exercise plan and enlist a buddy to join you.

"Two are better than one because they have a good return for their labor. For if either of them falls, the one will lift up his companion. But woe to the one who falls when there is not another to lift him up." Ecclesiastes 4:9-10

⚓ Sunday, January 30, 2011, 3:24 p.m.

Today is beautiful – blue skies and 60-degree weather. A much needed break from the dreary winter we've been suffering through. As soon as I saw the excellent forecast, I scheduled the skydiving outing that I've been waiting to take with Drew and Evan and their friends. We were so excited.

As I walked out of church, I thought rather smugly how smart I was to schedule us in advance, and how I couldn't wait to "fly the friendly skies." Unfortunately, it was not to be. While I was gone, the skydiving company had cancelled our adventure because the runway was still too wet. We'll have to do it another day.

As it turns out, this is the second time I've tried to plan something fun, only to have my plans canceled at the last minute. On Dr. Martin Luther King Jr. Day, my mother, Drew's girlfriend, my aunt and her friend were supposed to go to Liza Moz' Pottery Studio to select and paint our own pottery piece. Unfortunately, Mom was sick with the stomach virus that's been going around. We're trying to reschedule, but this time I think I'll let someone else pick the day.

The good news is that I actually am working at having fun and spending more time with family and friends. I'm even succeeding at times.

I'll be sure to post whenever we finally get to jump from a plane. In the meantime, I'll have to manage with my feet on the ground.

It's easy to become frustrated when we're forced to change our plans. It's much less frustrating when we stop to think that wrecked plans just might have saved our lives.

After 9/11, there were many stories of people who had problems with transportation, or were sick, or for a variety of other reasons were saved that day because of complications with their schedules. There were many similar stories regarding the Titanic.

Grammy Award-winning singer Patti Austin was booked on United Flight 93, the plane that was hijacked by Al-Qaeda as part of the 9/11 attacks. Because her mother had a stroke, Austin was forced to move a performance and change the flight to another day.

The Reverend J. Stuart Holden, vicar of St. Paul's Church in London, had planned to sail to America aboard the Titanic to speak at a Christian conference at Carnegie Hall. When his wife was struck with a sudden illness, Holden canceled his trip to stay by her side.

Austin and Holden likely were a bit upset with their situations. Not only did they have loved ones suffering from health problems but they also had to change plans that involved their careers because of those problems. They both had a much different view when they realized those setbacks saved their lives.

When I stop to remember those kinds of stories, I'm much less likely to be frustrated when my plans are changed or delayed due to unforeseen circumstances. We'll probably be shocked someday to discover how many times we were spared disaster by seemingly incongruous events.

⚓ Monday, February 21, 2011, 1:52 p.m.

I had intended for this post to include updates about my skydiving adventure and my appointment with my oncologist this morning. Unfortunately, the sky dive was cancelled due to extremely windy conditions, making this the third time we've tried to schedule but have had weather problems change our plans. We'll get there eventually.

I did, however, have a good visit with Dr. Antonucci, my oncologist. He walked in the exam room just as I was taking the phone call telling me that the sky dive was canceled. Like Dr. Midis, Dr. Antonucci laughed at me for wanting to jump out of a perfectly good airplane. I know lots of people share his amusement, but I still think it's a good idea. Drew and his friend Chris went yesterday and loved it.

I couldn't go yesterday because David and I went to see "The Color Purple." It was a very good musical, and I'm glad we went.

Anyway, back to the doctor. He said that everything looks great, my blood counts are excellent, and he's very pleased that I'm feeling so good. And he enjoyed another good laugh at my expense when I asked if I could postpone having my port removed until fall so that I won't miss any pool time this summer. He went along with my request.

Next up is a PET scan in April, followed by a colonoscopy later that month. I've been told that if the PET scan comes back with good results, it will be very good news and means that the cancer is much less likely to come back.

So, I'm looking forward to the scan. The colonoscopy, not so much.

And one of these days I'm going to post about my sky dive experience.

By this time, a lot of people were pleading with me to give up the whole skydiving experience. They thought all the failed attempts to jump meant I shouldn't go at all. I felt differently because I knew we were pushing our luck by trying to go skydiving during the winter. If it had been the middle of summer and our plans kept getting foiled, I might have reconsidered.

⚓ **Tuesday, March 8, 2011, 6:06 p.m.**

I've said many times that, despite my complete lack of talent in the musical department, hymns speak to me in a special way. Even more so since I've been sick. On Sunday, we sang "In Christ Alone," one of my new favorites. Its lyrics tell the beautiful story of how our hope is found only in Jesus Christ. The words really spoke to me, particularly those in the fourth stanza, which talks about how we can live a life free of guilt and without fear of death; it closes by saying: "'Til He returns or calls me home; Here in the power of Christ I'll stand."

I've heard so many stories lately about people who had the same kind of cancer as me, were declared cancer free, and are now "eaten up" with cancer. Last week, I wrote some articles for work that said the five-year survival rate for Stage IV colorectal cancer is about 6 percent.

Nevertheless, I haven't felt afraid. I started wondering, "Am I being oblivious and ignoring the obvious dangers that surround me?" As we sang that hymn, I realized that's not the case at all. I believe, like the song says, that Jesus controls my destiny and that 'til He returns or calls me home, I'll be standing in His power.

I don't think of God as a magic Genie who will bring me luck and good fortune if I believe it enough. I'm standing on the belief that He alone knows what's best for me, and I'm at peace – whether that means I'll continue with my miraculous recovery or become another grim statistic. In the meantime, I'll keep this wonderful hymn rolling around in my head.

It is impossible for me to hear this hymn and not be moved. They sang it at the funeral service for our neighbor, Al Wright, and it touched me deeply. After my father died, I asked that it be one of the hymns for his funeral service. As my sweet and talented friend Lynn Bennett sang that song, David reached over to hold my hand. I nearly lost it. I get emotional now just writing about it.

The words to that hymn say it all. When we place our hope and trust in the Lord, we can stand firm even when tremendous storms surround us.

"Trust in the Lord forever, for in God the Lord, we have an everlasting Rock." Isaiah 26:4

⚓ Sunday, April 3, 2011, 6:32 p.m.

"The best laid plans of mice and men ..."

If there's one thing cancer has taught me it is that I better not count on anything going according to plan. I was supposed to have a PET scan tomorrow morning. Supposed to. I got a call late last week telling me that my insurance company won't cover a PET scan unless there are "active signs of disease."

I clearly had active signs of disease the last time I had a PET scan, and I'm sure glad that's not the case now. Nevertheless, I was looking forward to having the scan because my doctors indicated that a clean scan would really go a long way to showing that my cancer isn't coming back.

Dr. Antonucci is out of town this week, so I'll have to wait until he gets back to see what course of action he recommends. In the meantime, I'll just enjoy the fact that I feel really good and hope that means I really am still disease free.

Notice a theme here? There is a definite pattern of my plans being waylaid.

In one of his sermons, Brother Bob – the pastor of my youth – said that the opposite of patience is pride. His message stepped on my toes a bit. With my choleric temperament I am, by nature, impatient.

In describing the choleric, Florence Littauer says, "He is the easiest temperament to understand and get along with, as long as you live by his golden rule: Do it my way NOW!"

Ecclesiastes 7:8 says plainly, "Patience of spirit is better than haughtiness of spirit." Some translations say, "Patience is better than pride." There's no getting around the fact that impatience is equivalent to pride, and pride is a sin.

All of these changes in plans forced me to let go of my sense of control and learn how to roll with the flow. In short, I've had to learn to give up the prideful feeling that I deserve to have things go a certain way, on my terms and on my timetable.

In the process of learning to let go, I've gained much more of the formerly elusive virtue – patience.

"[May you] walk in a manner worthy of the Lord, to please Him in all respects, bearing fruit in every good work and increasing in the knowledge of God; strengthened with all power, according to His glorious might, for the attaining of all steadfastness and patience … " Colossians 1:10-11

As a footnote, it occurs to me that I often quote things that Brother Bob said in sermons I heard more than 30 years ago. I would have missed out on his words that impact me still today if I had not been at church. I am thankful that my parents faithfully took us to church, even though there were many times when I fervently wished they didn't.

In talking about putting on the full armor of God, someone once said that our shield of faith gets a little larger every time we hear the Word of God. As an adult, I can honestly say that not once have I regretted forcing myself to go to church even when I didn't feel like going at the time. And when I'm tempted to hit the snooze button and blow off church, I think of my shield and how I want it to be as large as possible.

⚓ **Friday, April 22, 2011, 7:27 p.m.**

I've got good news and bad news. The bad news: I never got approval for a PET scan. The good news: the insurance company won't approve a PET scan because nothing indicates I have cancer.

My most recent blood work indicated a CEA count of 0.2. A CEA count higher than 5.0 suggests the presence of certain types of cancer, particularly colorectal. When I was first diagnosed, the count was 28. So, a count of 0.2 is really good.

And, despite the insurance company's reluctance to approve a PET scan, they did approve a CT scan, which I had this morning. I should have the results in a few days.

It's funny. When the nurse was preparing to insert the IV needle, I presented her with my "good" vein, the one in my left arm that everyone loves. When she had trouble getting the IV to go in she asked, "Have you been poked in this vein a lot?" I laughed and said, "You have no idea." Turns out I probably have scar tissue in that vein. I'm glad that the days of brutalizing my veins are becoming few and far between.

As I prepare to celebrate this Easter, I can't help but think back to the last one. I had only recently finished chemo and still had so much ahead of me. But I felt pretty good and full of hope for good things to come and was enjoying the beauty of the spring season. I have to say, this spring seems even more beautiful, and I'm glad that I feel better than pretty good. I feel great!

In the words of Charles Wesley:

> Christ the Lord is ris'n today, Alleluia!
> Sons of men and angels say, Alleluia!
> Raise your joys and triumphs high, Alleluia!
> Sing, ye heav'ns, and earth reply, Alleluia!

Wishing you and yours a wonderful Easter!

Satan must be delighted with how we've tarnished Easter. At a time set aside to celebrate the death and resurrection of Christ, the very cornerstone of our faith, we far too often get sidetracked with the Easter Bunny, what clothes we're going to wear and where we're going for lunch after the service.

Christ's resurrection assures us of life after death and makes it possible to live joyfully today regardless of our circumstances. That bears celebrating!

"And if Christ has not been raised, your faith is worthless; you are still in your sins. Then those also who have fallen asleep in Christ have perished. If we have hoped in Christ in this life only, we are of all men most to be pitied." I Corinthians 15:17-18

⚓ **Thursday, April 28, 2011, 8:10 p.m.**

When I first told people about my cancer diagnosis, I often opened with the phrase, "I'm afraid I have some not so pleasant news to share ..."

Tonight I'm happy to say, "I have some very pleasant news to share." The results of my CT scan were excellent. No signs of cancer! Hooray!

I am continually amazed and thankful for how great everything has gone. When I was at the GI doctor's office the other day, they took me around the office like a show pony telling everyone, "This lady had Stage IV colorectal cancer! Can you believe it?"

I love to share my story. I know it gives many people hope to see how far I've come and how there are no visible signs that I was ever sick. To God be the glory!

Now, for a funny follow-up story. At work today, I was going through some old interview notes looking for information about a project I had worked on about a year ago. I came across something I had written down following a phone call around the same time. The notes read: "Six years old. Miniature Eskimo Dog. Fergie. Very nice." Remember Fergie? She was the beast of a dog we got for my father. My parents had to give her away because she bit everyone!

Now, they have Baxter. The greatest dog ever.

Sometimes it's like that. We have to go through the bad to get to the good. It only makes the good that much sweeter!

That dog story has given us a lot of laughs. It's like that, isn't it? I assume that most families are like ours, laughing the hardest and talking the most about things that didn't work out quite right.

There's the story of Toby, our practically feral cat, for example. Toby preferred to avoid humans whenever possible and was much happier outdoors than inside. He would come in the garage to eat, but if anyone happened to enter while he was there, the skittish cat would jump through a place in the side door where a small pane of glass was missing.

On one of his late night jaunts, Toby got in a catfight that left him with a nasty looking sore on his tail. As the injury worsened, we knew a trip to the vet was necessary; we just weren't sure how we could catch the cat to get him there.

My father came up with a plan. He assigned me, his 10-year-old daughter, with the task of holding a pillowcase over the opening in the door. Dad took the job of encouraging the cat to jump through the hole. Yes, I know. His job was far better.

The next time Toby came in to eat, the plan was put into action. I was posted outside the side door with my trusty pillowcase, while Dad came in through the back door to coax the feline my way. Instead of just opening the door, which is all that would have been required, my father stormed into the garage clapping his hands and making all kinds of racket.

The cat was terrified. The next thing I knew I was staring down a storm of claws and teeth flying in my direction. I'm not ashamed to say I dropped the pillowcase and ran.

Did any good come out of that cat? Well, he did give us a good story that's generated a lot of laughs. That experience also helped toughen me up, and I know that being tough throughout this experience has definitely been a plus.

⚓ **Wednesday, May 4, 2011, 3:02 p.m.**

More good news! I had my colonoscopy today and everything was perfect – not even any polyps! Hooray!! This was the final hurdle for me to jump for now, and I'm so happy that I got more good news.

Thanks so much for all of your prayers and support!

The clean colonoscopy was excellent news. I knew there was a very real possibility that I would at the very least have polyps, which would have meant annual colonoscopies and an even greater risk the cancer would return. It was very reassuring to see Dr. Edmunds with a big smile when I awoke from the procedure.

⚓ **Monday, August 29, 2011, 8:07 p.m.**

Yesterday was my birthday, and I have to say 47 was much more fun than 46. Last year, I was in the hospital with a small bowel obstruction. It was dreadful! This year, my son Evan and I FINALLY got to go on our long awaited skydiving adventure.

Skydiving was a lot of fun, although surprisingly it was more relaxing than scary. In fact, I was never scared the entire time. Of course, I've never been scared of much and am even harder to faze after all I've been through.

It's been a long time since I've posted anything. Since then, I've been to see doctors... and have more lab work... and more scans. If you see a glow coming from the Fountain City area, that'd be me!

Anyway, the good news is that every report has come back perfect. The plan is to take out my chemo port in November. With the port gone I'll really feel like I've moved to the other side of this fight.

Again, I can't say enough how much everyone's prayers and support have meant to me along the way. I couldn't have done this alone!

Love to all,

Michelle

Although we jumped from a height of more than 11,000 feet and accelerated to 120 miles per hour in our freefall, I really didn't find skydiving the least bit frightening. The freefall was exciting, and the ride down once the parachute deployed was very serene. The experience was not at all what I expected. While I wouldn't discourage anyone from going skydiving, it's not something I would put in the "must do" category.

⚓ **Thursday, January 12, 2012, 7:03 p.m.**

Since it's been quite some time since I've posted anything, I'll start by saying that all news is good.

I had a CT scan the Tuesday after Christmas. It was needed because the previous scan had shown two spots on my lung. Yes, my lung. I learned about the lung when a nurse called and said, "Dr. Antonucci is a little worried about the spots on your lung."

To which I replied, "Lung? I've never had anything on my lungs. Do you mean liver?"

Clickety, click on the computer. "No," she said. "Your lung. You had two spots on your lung in April, and they showed up again on this last scan. Dr. Antonucci wants to do another scan at the end of the year to make sure everything's OK."

She went on to explain that the doctor felt like the spots were probably nothing because if they were cancer they would have gotten much bigger since the scan in April. She finished the call by saying I needed to have another scan at the end of the year and that having my port removed would have to wait.

When she apologized for giving me bad news, I laughed and said that I'd had more than my share of good news and couldn't be greedy. We scheduled the scan for the 27th and a follow-up visit with the doctor a week later, on January 3.

I went in for my scan and assumed I wouldn't hear the results until I saw the doctor. When the nurse called at 11:15 the next day with a message saying I needed to call the office, I was a little alarmed. When I called back around 12:15, the office was closed for lunch. So, I waited and called in about an hour. After staying on hold for a while, I was told that the nurse was putting in an IV and would have to call me back.

So, I waited. And started taking down the Christmas tree. And watching the phone. And the clock.

At 2:30 I couldn't wait any longer and called the office again. After being kept on hold a few minutes, I was told, "Angie is the only nurse here today, and she's really busy. She said she promises she'll call you back."

After that, I got a little worried. I started thinking, "If she's the only nurse there, AND she called me at 11:15 the day after my scan, the news must be bad."

But almost as quickly as those thoughts entered my mind, they were replaced with Philippians 4:13: "I can do all things through Christ who strengthens me."

I made my peace with the fact that I might have cancer again and that this time it might be in my lungs.

Then, I got a call from the nurse telling me that my scan was perfect and that the spots must be scar tissue. I have to say, the scare made me appreciate my clear scan all the more! I believe I had started taking for granted that all of my reports would be good.

I ended up not seeing the doctor until this past Tuesday. He said that everything looks "perfect" and that he couldn't be more pleased with my progress. The plan now is to do another scan in June and pull the port in August when I hit the two-year mark of being cancer free. Works for me!

On a non-medical note, David and I enjoyed a Caribbean cruise the week before Christmas. It was the first trip we've been able to take since I got sick, and it was WONDERFUL!

As I start 2012, I am so very thankful to be sitting here healthy and well, and I wish you and yours a Happy New Year!

That little scare made me appreciate the news of a clear scan all the more. It also was good to experience moving so quickly from a place of fear to a place of confidence in Christ. At that point, I knew that if cancer did come back I could handle it because I wouldn't be fighting the battle alone.

I'm so thankful that David and I were able to go on that cruise. Spending time in the warm Caribbean sun and just enjoying time together was exactly what we needed after a long, hard uphill climb. We enjoyed another cruise just before Christmas 2013, and we hope to make a wintertime cruise an annual event.

Section Two

Remission

January 13 – September 9, 2012

"Thy rod and Thy staff, they comfort me." Psalm 23:4

There was an eight-month break in my journal entries following the January 12, 2012, post. The lack of posts, however, didn't mean there was nothing going on in my life.

In April, David's mother, Bobbi, was diagnosed with breast and colorectal cancer. I am sad to say we had a strained relationship with David's parents at that time. We didn't even know about her diagnosis until after her surgery and hospitalization.

After we got the news, David and I immediately took the boys and went to see her. We had a good visit with her and David's father that evening and enjoyed several more visits over the course of her hospital stay. I gave Bobbi some tips for success after colon surgery, provided my cell phone number with instructions to call with any questions, and made plans to cook meals that I believed her stomach would tolerate.

I thought cancer could be the bridge to bring our lives back together. If that had been the only reason for my cancer, that would have been reason enough.

Unfortunately, a renewed relationship with Bobbi outside the hospital was not to be. She developed one complication after the other. Despite the doctors' repeated assurances that she would be okay, on May 5, 2012, she lost her life to this ugly disease.

One good thing that came out of that very difficult loss is that we are back in communication with David's father, grandmother and other family members. It was wonderful to have them in the audience for Drew's wedding.

During this same time period, my father's health continued its downward spiral. His Alzheimer's got much worse, and other health problems kept him sick most of the time. He had spells where he would freeze like a statue for about 20 minutes or so; he suffered nearly constant diarrhea; and he was rail thin.

Before his illness, Dad was a tall, handsome, athletic man who faithfully worked out with weights and looked much younger than his years. By spring 2012, however, Dad looked and seemed at least 20 years older than my mom, who was only one year younger. He spent the entire day on the couch watching television, mostly war movies and "Downton Abbey," the award-winning British television series that follows the lives of the aristocratic Crawley family and their servants from 1912 through the early 1920s. Thank you, Crawley family, for keeping my father entertained!

In June, Dad was hospitalized when he developed shingles and strep throat. The pain from the shingles and his disorientation at being away from home drastically affected my father's mind. He believed his hospital stay was an elaborate hoax and that everything taking place in his room was being videotaped. We finally hung a drape over the dry erase board, which he believed to be the camera.

Meanwhile, Drew headed off for basic training with the U.S. Army Reserves.

I gave my dad and Drew cards that included the same verse: "Be strong and courageous! Do not tremble or be dismayed, for the Lord your God is with you wherever you go." Joshua 1:9.

As I reflected on the verse, a still, small voice inside me said the verse was as much for me as it was for them. It was then that I started to think my cancer probably was coming back.

In basic training Drew wound up hospitalized with pneumonia. Despite the illness, he managed to complete the rigorous training. I told him that in the future whenever he faces a difficult challenge he could remind himself, "I did basic training with pneumonia. I can get through anything." I, of course, gave him that advice based on my own experience.

Not long after my father came home from the hospital, he fell and broke his hip. Thankfully, I was at my parents' house when it happened. My mom and I managed to get him in the van and take him to the hospital. Despite the fact he sat for hours in a wheelchair with a broken hip, we never heard a word of complaint out of my father. He managed to survive surgery and was later moved to a nursing home for rehabilitation.

In June, I had a follow-up scan as planned. It showed the spots on my lungs had gotten a little bit larger, meaning they were not simply scar tissue. This time, when Dr. Antonucci ordered a PET scan, the insurance company agreed to cover it.

David and I decided to keep the possibility of cancer recurrence to ourselves until we were sure. While waiting for a diagnosis, we spent the weekend at the lake with the entire Ironside clan. My mom, who at the time almost was constantly with my dad at the nursing home, even came out for a few hours that Saturday. It was a wonderful weekend filled with lots of laughter and good times.

I remember one evening when David and my brother-in-law were smoking cigars on the back deck. When some of the smoke blew in my direction, I went into a coughing fit. We were all laughing that a little smoke could cause such a violent reaction. I stopped myself just before saying, "Yeah, and I'm the one who ends up with lung cancer."

When my suspicions were confirmed and I learned the spots on my lungs were cancer, I told only my immediate family and a few close friends because I wanted to give the news to Drew in person and didn't want my father to know about it at all. It was hard for me to keep it secret. As is probably clear from my posts, I'm not one to hold things back. I tend to share whatever is on my mind or in my heart. The fact I refuse to tell a lie made things all the more difficult. If someone directly asked me if my cancer was still gone, I told the truth but asked them to keep it quiet until I had time to tell Drew.

My father did remarkably well with his rehabilitation. In fact, it was amazing to see the transformation during his nursing home stay. He gained weight, regained some of his sense of humor and was even reading books. With his pleasant disposition, Dad was a staff favorite. On his birthday not long before he was discharged, all of his caregivers and other staff signed a giant poster wishing him well.

My father's rebound was, unfortunately, short lived. His health declined after he returned home.

In August, David and I, along with Drew's girlfriend, Sam, and his best friend, Chris, traveled to South Carolina for Drew's basic training graduation ceremony. It was so good to see Drew and to spend time with him and his closest friends. Seeing him light up the moment he saw Sam was touching. At lunch, I shared the news about the cancer. I now know otherwise, but at the time when I said it wasn't a big deal, I believed it.

Following graduation, Drew departed for advanced training in Virginia.

Also in August, my sister, Kristen, was diagnosed with thyroid cancer. When she told me, I said I was sorry but then happily added, "I've written lots of stuff about thyroid cancer. If you're going to get cancer, thyroid cancer is the one to get. It's very treatable."

Later that day she told my brother Kevin, who has suffered thyroid problems of his own. Kevin said, "Thyroid cancer is actually better than thyroid disease. With cancer they just remove the thyroid and you're fine."

At that point Kristen wondered what it takes to get a little sympathy from the Ironsides. Apparently more than thyroid cancer.

All kidding aside, this was a trying time for our family. My poor mother, in particular, was facing struggles at every turn. She was being pulled in a thousand different directions between taking care of my dad, and having two of her daughters fighting cancer. She handled it all with grace, however, and trusted God throughout. Never one to worry, Mom modeled a strong faith and strength that made it easier for us to follow suit.

"Worry does not empty tomorrow of its sorrow, it empties today of its strength." - Corrie ten Boom

At about age 6, pictured on the back patio with my brothers, Kevin, 7, and Phillip, 3. My sister, Kristen, didn't come along for another six years. I like this picture because it captures a true snapshot of our younger years.

The Ironside family gathers for a family photo at my brother Kevin's wedding in 1991. My father and Kevin are front center. I am pictured front left, with Kristen behind me. My mother is front right, and my brother Phillip is behind her.

David and I enjoy dinner on our honeymoon in St. Thomas in 1983. We have been blessed with a long and happy marriage.

My sons, Evan, 7, and Drew, 10, pose for a shot with our Basset Hound, Henry, in 2000. I've heard that the longer a basset's ears, the more stubborn they are. Henry's ears were quite long.

The Henry family celebrates Drew and Sam's wedding on May 18, 2013. For a while, we were concerned I might not be released from the hospital in time to attend the wedding. Thankfully, that was not the case.

My brother Kevin and his family pose for their annual Christmas photo in 2011. Pamela and Kevin are front center; with them are their sons, from left, Collin, Kai, Christian, Blake, Mugisha and Addison. They have since adopted another son from Uganda, Asiimwe, who is not pictured here.

My brother Phillip and his wife, Tashia, with their children, Elijah and Tejah. This photo was taken in 2007 when Phillip and my sister, Kristen, along with their families, joined us for a Hilton Head vacation.

My sister, Kristen Vandergriff, and her husband, Tommy, with, from left, Lindsey and Lauren Vandergriff and Kristen's son, Parker Gentry. This photo also was taken on our Hilton Head vacation.

It wasn't easy, but we managed to corral the family for a photo at Drew and Sam's wedding. We were happy to have David's grandmother, Ruth Burchell (third from left wearing black pants and a white top), and his father, Guy (behind her), join us at the wedding.

Enjoying a night out with my girlfriends, Joni Oliver to my right, Mary Lee Keeler, back left, and Janice Bridges, back right, in 2014. Lisa Hurst, who usually joins us for our regular get-togethers, was unable to attend that night.

My cousin, Tracy Craig Satterfield, and I (center) enjoy a
moment with our sisters-in-law at a wedding shower in May
2011. Far left is Lisha Craig, far right is Pamela Ironside.

Section Three

"About those spots on your lungs . . ."

September 9, 2012 – December 11, 2013

"Surely goodness and lovingkindness will follow me all the days of my life, and I will dwell in the house of the Lord forever." Psalm 23:6

⚓ **Sunday, September 9, 2012, 9:28 p.m.**

My plan for some time now has been to take the journal entries I made on this website and turn them into a devotional, looking back on my journey from the safety of the other side. I still hope to do that someday. However, I always thought my ending was going to be my miraculous healing and that all was well. All is still well, and I still consider my journey miraculous, but I have hit a small bump in the road.

In my journal entry before this one, I talked about having a scan in June before pulling the port in August. Well... when they did the scan in June, it showed three spots on my lungs that had gotten a tiny bit bigger. A subsequent PET scan confirmed that they're cancer. The good news is it's not lung cancer; it's colorectal cancer that spread to my lungs. That's why the spots are still so small. It's also why the cancer diagnosis isn't as scary as it was before. Dr. Antonucci, who is always quite candid with me, said that we caught it so early that it should be very easy to treat. Our hope is that chemo will take care of the small spots and that I'll just continue to be watched after that. Worst case scenario is that I'll have to have some minor surgery to "pop out the spots" if the chemo doesn't work.

I waited to share this news for two reasons:

1. Drew, my older son, is away for Army Reserves training. I wanted to tell him in person at his basic training graduation on August 23, when he could see that I'm doing fine.
2. My father has been struggling with serious health issues since the spring. We're not telling him because we don't want him to worry. (So, if you happen to talk to my dad, mum's the word!)

I've already completed three of the four prescribed rounds of chemo and am doing well. I feel pretty rough for a couple of days after the infusion and a little bad for about 10 days after. Then I'm pretty good until the next round. The good news is I don't have to wear the hated fanny pack chemo pump this time. Instead, I take six pills a day for two weeks. Much better!

My fourth and final infusion is this Friday, which is why I decided to go ahead and post. I'll be honest -- I really want your prayers! They carried me through last time, and I know they will again. Of course, my hope is that this chemo will do the trick and that no surgery will be needed. However, I know that if surgery is needed – or whatever comes my way – God will carry me through.

I remarked before that what I found so miraculous was not that my cancer went into remission, although that was wonderful, but how God was there with me through the entire journey. You were there, too, and I need you now.

With much love and thanks for your continued support,

Michelle

At this point, my doctor and I still considered the cancer in my lungs to be a minor problem. I really thought the chemo would take care of the cancer, we'd finally remove the port, and that would be the end of it. How wrong I was.

As I think about the cancer in my lungs, I am reminded of my comment earlier about inappropriate things people say. One of my all-time favorites is, "Did you smoke?" As if that would somehow make it okay. For the record, I never smoked and mine isn't true lung cancer; it is colorectal cancer that spread to my lungs. But it doesn't really matter; I wouldn't wish cancer on anybody, even if they chain-smoked cigarettes two at a time from the day they were 10. And I sure wouldn't try to make them feel like they deserved it.

It occurs to me I never fully explained my chemo port. It is a device implanted beneath the skin, usually in the upper chest. It includes a catheter that is inserted into a large central vein that delivers blood to your heart. The port makes it possible for technicians to deliver chemotherapy or other IV medications without having to stick a needle in your vein.

The port is not pretty. In fact, it looks a bit like an alien lurking beneath my chest. Nevertheless, I have a great appreciation for my port because it saves me from a lot of unnecessary and painful needle sticks. Ugly as it is, I am happy to keep my port as long as necessary.

⚓ **Saturday, September 15, 2012, 2:33 p.m.**

I had my fourth and final infusion yesterday afternoon. Hooray!

I feel a little flu-like, but not dreadful. Mostly I'm just very weak and tired, which may be a good thing. The chemo pills I take affect my feet, making them very tender and prone to blister and crack. When I showed my feet to the nurse yesterday, she said that I need to delay starting the pills until my feet look better. I had admitted to her that I'm not always easy on my feet – walking from one end of downtown to the other in dress shoes, going barefoot all the time at home, playing in the pool with my nephew... I didn't tell her about the four-mile workouts I do three times a week. Nonetheless, she sent me home with orders to keep my feet drenched in lotion and to behave. I told her I'd feel too bad to misbehave anyway.

The plan now is for me to complete this round of chemo and do another CT scan on October 5. If the scan comes back clear, I'll take two more rounds of the chemo pills – no more injections – and then they'll just keep a close eye on me like before. If the scan's not clear, we'll have to talk about surgery.

During my infusion yesterday I struck up a conversation with the lady next to me – "What are you in for?" Turns out she had colorectal cancer and the same colon resection surgery that I had. I told her that since the surgery I can't eat sugar or fat without getting very sick and asked if she had similar problems. She can't eat fiber or seafood. As we talked, I thought about the delicious salmon salad I ate right before going to the doctor. I'd much prefer a salmon salad to fats or sweets, so I feel blessed.

I'm blessed in so many other ways, too. I thank God for my dear friends and family who support and pray for me, a husband who is always by my side, for my sons – Evan who cleaned the house for me yesterday while I was at the doctor, and Drew who is thriving through his Army Reserve training.

Many of you have said you're praying for my father. Thank you for that, too. He and Mom need your prayers. It's a tough season right now.

Love,

Michelle

The lady who couldn't eat fiber or seafood also admitted she made the mistake of insisting that the doctor pull her port immediately following her colon surgery. When her cancer later came back, she had to undergo another procedure for a new port to be implanted. I was glad I listened to my doctors and left mine in place.

I still can't digest anything that contains a high amount of fat or sugar, which is expected to be a lifelong problem. Usually, I can tell the minute I put a bite in my mouth if it's something I shouldn't eat. Sometimes, though, I'll accidentally consume the wrong thing and pay for it dearly with stomach problems that can last for days.

My dietary restrictions are not so bad, though. It really comes down to choice. I can choose to eat right and feel good, or I can choose to eat wrong and feel lousy. At least I have a choice.

⚓ **Tuesday, October 9, 2012, 7:24 p.m.**

I should know by now that the main thing to know about cancer is that you just don't know. I still make the mistake of thinking I have a handle on the disease. That the doctors and I can develop a plan, follow the plan, and things will go the way we expect. I learned again today that's just not the way it operates.

I finally got the results from the scan I had on Friday. The good news is that the cancer hasn't spread anywhere else and the spots on my lungs have gotten a tiny bit smaller. The bad news is they haven't gone away. I eventually will think it's good news that we're going to try two rounds of very aggressive chemo in an attempt to do away with the pesky spots without the need for surgery.

As I type this, I have to be honest and say that I'm not thrilled about more chemo – especially Avastin, the kind that makes my hair fall out and trashes my teeth. However, it's that very chemo that annihilated the much, much larger tumors before, so I'm hopeful that it will reap similar results this time around.

I see Dr. Antonucci on October 16 to discuss my treatment in more detail. I go in on Friday, October 19, for an infusion. After that, I'll continue to take the chemo pills for two weeks. Then I'll wait a week and do it all one more time.

I know it could be far worse, and I'm truly grateful for how well I'm able to tolerate the treatment. I'm also grateful for all the love, prayers and support that help carry me through.

Keeping the faith,

Michelle

Who would have guessed that some tumors the size of pencil erasers could have caused so many problems?

In this post, like so many before it, I notice a theme. Almost all of my posts end on a bright note, even if they don't start out that way. I believe part of the reason is because writing, for me, is very therapeutic. Once I put my thoughts into words, they become something to be explored and reasoned with instead of something that torments me. Also, when I admit what I'm feeling, God is freer to work in my heart.

King David must have been the same way. There are many Psalms where he begins writing from a place of despair but ends by praising God. Psalm 69 is a good example.

"Save me, O God, for the waters have threatened my life." v. 1

"I am weary with my crying; my throat is parched;" v. 2

"Those who hate me without a cause are more than the hairs of my head." v. 4

"I will praise the name of God with song, and shall magnify Him with thanksgiving." v. 30

"Let heaven and earth praise him, the seas and everything that moves in them." v. 34

⚓ Saturday, October 13, 2012, 7:45 p.m.

People often tell me that I inspire them. I just had to stop and say how much all the guestbook posts inspire and encourage me. I was just looking through old posts trying to find one where a neighbor was bragging on Drew. I plan to use her quote on his resume – he returns from basic training in November and is beginning a job search. He's also getting married in July. She's a wonderful young lady, and we're thrilled!

Anyway, as I looked back through all the old guestbook posts, I cried tears of joy. Yes, it takes a lot to make me cry, but it happened. I believe God led me back through those posts so that I could remember again how He pulled me through the toughest chemo and two surgeries before. I know He'll pull me through again.

Thank you all for caring, for posting, for praying, and for loving me. It helps more than you'll ever know.

Feeling better prepared for Friday,

Michelle

CaringBridge has been a tremendous asset throughout my illness. Without it, I doubt I would have had the discipline to so diligently maintain journal entries, and I certainly wouldn't have been able to tap into such a remarkable network of support. The guestbook posts bring joy to my heart every time I read them, and so many times they have included the very words I needed for the moment.

"A man has joy in an apt answer, and how delightful is a timely word!" Proverbs 15:23

⚓ **Tuesday, October 16, 2012, 5:23 p.m.**

If this website had a window, you'd see my big smile right now. I haven't stopped smiling since I saw Dr. Antonucci this afternoon. I got a one-week reprieve from my infusion, and I couldn't be happier.

I know work has to take a backseat to my treatment, but treatment was REALLY getting in the way of my responsibilities this time around. The Urban League has a huge Gala on the 25th, and I was concerned about missing work for an infusion and then feeling terrible up to and at the Gala.

So, I asked Dr. Antonucci if we could put it off for a week. In asking, I said, "If it affects my treatment in any way at all, I want to go forward with the infusion. But, if it doesn't matter, I'd much prefer to wait."

His response was, "Those spots aren't going anywhere and they're not hurting anything. We just need to get rid of them. It won't matter a bit for you to wait a week." His nonchalant attitude gave me further comfort that we're not dealing with the big, hairy beast we battled last time around. It's just something to deal with, which is much better than something that could kill me quickly.

The other good thing about waiting is that my feet will have more time to recover from the pills. Dr. Antonucci couldn't believe how bad my feet still look after being off the pills as long as I have. When I start treatment, we're going to reduce the number of pills I take from six a day down to four and see if that helps. And, he thinks the

Avastin may not bother me as much as it did last time because we're spacing out treatments more.

After finding out I needed more chemo, I commented that it felt like I had just finished running a marathon and they moved the finish line by 20 miles. This extra week gives me the opportunity to "get my running shoes back on." I already feel much better mentally prepared than I did before.

All in all, a wonderful visit to the doctor. I love sharing good news!

Thanks for your continued prayers and support,

Michelle

While you may feel like chastising me for changing my treatment plan to accommodate work, it was absolutely the right decision. The Gala is the Urban League's only fundraiser throughout the year. It is a first-class event that draws about 900 people. I handled a lot of the event details and taking care of my responsibilities was important to me. Once I had the Gala completed, it was much easier for me to sit still for another infusion.

The night of the event, it was obvious how badly my feet hurt when I was willing to wear ballet slippers with my formal outfit. Once again, vanity had to take a backseat to cancer.

In addition to helping with work, moving back the infusion allowed time to recapture the level of motivation required to successfully manage my remaining infusions. Being a very goal-oriented individual, it was deflating to have worked toward a goal only to find that when I got to the "end," I wasn't there after all. I believe a history of pushing hard in exercise helped me dig deep and find more energy when I needed it most.

"There isn't a person anywhere who isn't capable of doing more than he thinks he can." – Henry Ford

⚓ **Friday, October 26, 2012, 4:43 p.m.**

Just a short and sweet message to say that I had my infusion today, and it wasn't as bad as I feared it would be. I don't feel great, but right now I feel no worse than I usually do after an infusion.

Thanks for your prayers and support!

Love,

Michelle

Inevitably, so long as I was well prepared to face the worst, things turned out better than I expected. When obstacles loomed large, I was much more likely to rely on God's strength instead of my own. It was the times when I thought I could handle things on my own that I was more likely to be knocked down a notch or two.

⚓ **Saturday, November 3, 2012, 5:09 p.m.**

I haven't updated my journal this past week for a couple of reasons: 1) I don't want to bombard everyone with updates when there's not much to tell; and 2) there's not much to tell.

I am very pleasantly surprised at how well I tolerated the last infusion. I felt pretty lousy all last weekend, but the blessing was that I was also able to sleep the better part of it. By Monday, I was not only able to get back to work, but managed to work like crazy the whole day and meet some scary tight deadlines.

On Wednesday, I was able to get out at lunchtime on a gorgeous fall day and visit some gardens where we plan to hold Drew's wedding. The gardens are amazing, and Drew's fiancé is the most easy to get along with bride-to-be you'll ever meet. It was great! I also pulled out an old Halloween mask and had fun taunting my coworkers. It was a fun and uplifting day!

By Thursday, I was able to put in my four-mile workout and today I've cleaned house all day. So, surprisingly, I'm actually faring better this time around than I typically do after an infusion. It's a blessing I can't explain – your prayers, perhaps? – but one that I certainly celebrate.

My feet may be getting a little better; they're definitely not getting worse. My hair is falling out at a rapid pace, but because it came back so thick it's not very noticeable yet. I always have the wig that Mom bought me last time if I need it.

I'm due to see Dr. Antonucci week after next and have another infusion on November 16. That's supposed to be the last infusion, but something in my gut tells me it won't be. I'm guessing when the doctor sees how well I'm doing he may want to do another round to be safe. We'll see...

As always, I am grateful and humbled by all the prayers and support coming my way. Thank you, thank you!

- Michelle

The gardens Sam and I so enjoyed exploring are not ordinary gardens. Terracing all the way to the Tennessee River, they are so spectacular they garnered a feature in *Southern Living* magazine.

The gardens came into play when Drew contacted me from basic training with an urgent request: "Sam and I want to get married somewhere beautiful and outdoors, but we don't have much money. Can you help us find a place?"

After discussing several possibilities with my mother, I came up with the idea to ask Sharon Pryse about using her gardens. Sharon is a member of the executive women's group for which I work; she is a lovely lady who has been very supportive during my illness. Sharon's husband,

Joe, was one of Drew's favorite customers at Cherokee Country Club golf course where Drew worked for several years.

When Sharon said yes, I was thrilled. Sam and I had a great time wandering through the gardens and dreaming of the wedding. A rental company sales manager I had often worked with during my days as an event planner was kind enough to come give us advice. He and Joe both warned of potential downsides to an outdoor wedding, most notably heat and inclement weather.

Sam and I plowed fearlessly ahead with no concerns. We both had eyes only for the spectacular wedding and reception that could take place in such breathtakingly beautiful surroundings.

Thankfully, Drew was not so starry-eyed. He insisted we develop a bad weather backup plan. After many phone calls, we found the Laurel Theater. It's fortunate that Drew was so levelheaded. The rainfall levels in 2013 came very close to breaking a 100-year record, and it rained on the day of the wedding.

⚓ Tuesday, November 13, 2012, 8:22 p.m.

When I was pregnant, I often went barefoot at the office. Not because I needed to – my feet never swelled – but because I could. These days I often sport slippers at the office not because I want to, but because I need to.

After seeing Dr. Antonucci today, I told my coworkers I hoped they liked seeing me in house shoes because I'd be wearing them for the rest of the year. In my last post I mentioned that I had a feeling the doctor would suggest an extra round when he saw how well I was tolerating the chemo. Well, I must look better than I thought. He prescribed not one, but two, extra rounds. My next round is this Friday; the other two are December 7 and December 28. I close out the year on the 31st with a CT scan. Nothing like toasting in the new year by drinking a little dye!

After looking at the calendar, I realize that the timing works out well. I should feel fine for Thanksgiving and Christmas. And, as I told the ladies at the doctor's office, I couldn't care less about New Year's anyway.

If the scan shows that the tumors are gone, I won't have to endure any more chemotherapy at the beginning of 2013. If they're still hanging around … We'll have to cross that bridge when we get there. I'm very optimistic, though. These tumors are the size of a pencil eraser. The last tumor was the size of an orange. If Avastin can knock out an orange, surely it can take on a couple of erasers.

I'll close with a couple of updates to my last post. Drew is back in town and officially engaged. He surprised Sam with a dramatic proposal on Friday night. They are so happy, and so are we!

And, in the last post I talked about how thankful I am to be so active. Talking about all that I'm doing had some people concerned that I'm not getting enough rest. No worries. I usually take a power nap for about 30 minutes or an hour when I get home from work, and I have a great warning sign if I'm pushing myself too hard. My voice always goes when I've done too much. It's my body's way of waving the white flag. I always listen when it's time to stop. And David does a good job of keeping an eye on me to make sure I don't overdo it. All in all, I really think I'm striking a good balance right now.

As always, I thank you for your prayers and support. I could not do this alone.

Marching on,

Michelle

A good Southern girl, I have always been most comfortable in my bare feet. Before chemo, I typically kicked off my shoes as soon as I walked in the door. Unfortunately, going barefoot no longer holds the same appeal now that the skin on the soles of my feet is so badly damaged. When I had my first post-chemo pedicure about six months after ending treatment, the manicurist said she could tell my feet had been burned from the inside out because of how the skin was peeling off.

As to the problem with my voice, it's a great barometer of my well-being. I still catch my voice giving out if I get too tired. Surprisingly, I'm much more likely to lose my voice when I'm mentally exhausted than when I've overdone it physically. I always lost my voice at work on days when I pushed myself really hard to meet a grant deadline. Thinking back, while I was on chemo I typically headed home with a voice not much more than a whisper. I finally gave up the practice of calling Mom on my way home from work because I couldn't speak loudly enough for her to hear me on the mobile phone.

⚓ **Sunday, November 18, 2012, 6:43 p.m.**

Worse than Rotten Ralph, a book I used to read to Drew and Evan when they were little, has come to mind more than once this weekend. I believe the reason that book keeps coming to mind is because it describes how I've felt – worse than rotten. Even my eyelids hurt.

I'm not sure if it hit me so hard this time because the toxicity levels are building up or if they gave me a certain kind of chemo too fast. I'm definitely going to ask to get it slower next time and hope it helps.

I have managed to read a little bit, which was a help. The book, *Almost Heaven*, is a fictional tale of a humble boy in West Virginia and the guardian angel assigned to protect him. The angel at times feels like he could have more important work to do but stays to his assigned task. A big point of the book is that God often uses the weak things to bring glory to His name.

The story of the guardian angel reminded me of a time when I believe my angel stepped in and saved my life. I slipped and fell on a street beside the downtown post office. Just as I fell, an elderly man in a huge, old car was backing into a parking spot. The back tire of the car was mere inches from my head when the car suddenly stopped. The man said he thought he heard something hit his car, although nothing had. Someone standing nearby said that I should thank my guardian angel. I did.

I believe God intervened and saved me that day because He still had a purpose for me here on earth. And I know that He can use the weakness of my illness to His glory. I will strive to fulfill my purpose, and I believe that part of it has to do with my ability to write. I will do my best to use my words – written and spoken – to bring glory and honor to Him. I'll be honest, written is easier. My mouth has always gotten me in trouble.

I will close by thanking "Dr. David" for giving me good advice that helped me feel a little better and able to write this post. I was feeling dreadful this afternoon when he gave his always useful advice to go to bed. I slept soundly for a couple of hours and now feel much better. Not good, but not worse than rotten.

Thanks for your prayers and support. I'll close with the verse that keeps popping in my mind: "Though He slay me, I will hope in Him..." Job 13:15

With thanks,

Michelle

After this post, God gave me a glowing example of how He can use my words to bless others. Prompted by my post to read *Almost Heaven*, a friend of my mother's was able to get peace about a problem that had plagued her most of her life. The friend, a strong Christian, had for years been struggling with hurt and anger. Her words went something like this: "My father committed suicide when I was a child. Since then, I've struggled with anger at him for taking his life; I've also wondered if he could be in heaven even after killing himself. That book helped me get past all that. I now feel a peace and freedom that I haven't known for years."

In the book, a faithful Christian takes his own life. The fictional tale does a good job of portraying the inner struggles that man faced, and it helps the reader better understand how someone could come to make such a tragic decision. I never thought about the suicide part because I was focused on the guardian angel. But God had something else in mind when he nudged Mom's friend to read that book.

I'll also add I strongly believe there is a spiritual world all around us. There are angels protecting and helping us, and there are demonic forces working to trip up Christians and minimize God's ability to work through us.

Also, I believe one of the greatest victories for Satan is the person who regularly attends church but never truly turns his life over to God. It's much easier for a drug addict, murderer or thief to realize their need for salvation than the person who lives a mostly moral life and goes through the motions of Christianity.

"Many will say to Me on that day, 'Lord, Lord, did we not prophesy in Your name, and in Your name cast out demons, and in Your name perform many miracles? And then I will declare to them, 'I never knew you; depart from Me, you who practiced lawlessness.'" Matthew 6:22-23

⚓ Wednesday, November 21, 2012, 3:15 p.m.

Thanks so much for your many kind words, thoughts and prayers. Just a quick update to let you know that I am doing much, much better. I'm looking forward to spending Thanksgiving with my family and praying that my father will feel up to joining the celebration.

Wishing you and yours a happy Thanksgiving!

Love,

Michelle

> Make a joyful noise to the LORD, all the earth!
>
> Serve the LORD with gladness! Come into his presence with singing!

Know that the LORD, he is God! It is he who made us, and we are his; we are his people, and the sheep of his pasture.

Enter his gates with thanksgiving, and his courts with praise!

Give thanks to him; bless his name! For the LORD is good; his steadfast love endures forever, and his faithfulness to all generations.

Psalm 100, ESV

There's not much more to say here. Psalm 100 says it all.

⚓ Thursday, December 6, 2012, 7:46 p.m.

I've always said I'm not a big fan of "Hallmark events." I want people to be nice to me because they want to be nice to me, not because the calendar urges them to do so. Lately, I've had several pleasant surprises.

My friend Mary Lee Keeler dropped off a delicious casserole a couple of weeks ago. It kind of stunned me when she called to say she was bringing something over. I forget that I'm sick and that someone would feel the need to help out. While we certainly didn't need the casserole – the guys are very self-sufficient and I do still manage to cook from time to time – it was really nice having good food at the ready.

Last Saturday a florist called to say they were delivering flowers. I again forgot that I'm sick and wondered who in our family was getting flowers and for what reason. When the flowers arrived with a note from my Aunt Betty, I was even more shocked. She's going through some serious health issues of her own, and I was really touched that she would think about me with all she's facing. As an added bonus, the flowers are not only beautiful but smell wonderful. One of the side effects of the chemo is that I now have a hound dog sense of smell. It can be a real pain. Believe me when I say there are a lot of smells out there that we're better off doing without. With the flowers, however, I catch a whiff of a wonderful fragrance every time I walk in the room.

On Sunday I requested that the guys bring up the Christmas tree from the garage and move a giant plant out of the spot where the tree would go. I offered to assemble and decorate the tree, knowing that they really don't care whether or not we have a tree. Evan surprised me by bringing up the tree by himself and fluffing the branches, despite my assurance that he didn't need to do it. We now have the house decorated and the tree assembled. Putting on lights and decorating the tree will have to come later.

Last night David treated me to a back rub with warm lotion. He knows that after an infusion I hurt all over but can't stand to be touched. The massage was a nice calm before the storm.

As I sit here tonight, I am so thankful for these and so many other acts of kindness. I also have to admit that I feel a little bit like I'm walking the plank. I feel fine tonight but know that with tomorrow's infusion I'm probably in for a rough few days. I saw Dr. Antonucci on Tuesday, and he agreed that we'll try slowing down the Oxaliplatin to see if that will help minimize side effects. I'll be stuck at the doctor's office for four hours, but the extra time will be well worth it if it helps reduce the pain.

After tomorrow, I'll have seven infusions down and only one to go! It feels good to be nearing the finish line. I just hope they don't move the tape again.

Walking the plank but keeping the faith,

- Michelle

Before I was diagnosed, I attended a luncheon where an excellent speaker shared her story about the sudden death of her husband and her subsequent fight with cancer. "Beth" had been through a lot, but her message was one of hope and was very inspirational. One thing that stuck with me was her story about roses.

"My husband always made sure I had three beautiful yellow roses by my bedside. They were meant to signify our marriage and the lives of our two sons. It was something we barely even talked about, but the simple gesture meant a lot to me."

After her husband died in an accident at a relatively young age, she thought about those roses and began to feel a little sorry for herself. She asked God, "Now who will give me roses?"

Imagine Beth's surprise when a friend, without recognizing the significance of her gift, stopped by with three yellow roses. "I know this isn't much, but for some reason I just felt led to get these for you." Beth's friend didn't know anything about the history of the yellow roses. She just obeyed God's nudging in her heart and in the process greatly blessed someone who was hurting.

More than 30 years ago, a pastor's wife shared with me a very personal story about her family's financial struggles. "We literally had no food in the pantry," she admitted. "When the kids looked to me for answers I told them that God had promised to give us our daily bread and that we could trust Him to provide. Minutes later, a church member came by with a freshly baked loaf of bread."

When we obey God and do whatever He calls us to do, the result is miraculous even if the thing that we are called to do seems mundane.

"For we are His workmanship, created in Christ Jesus for good works, which God prepared beforehand, that we should walk in them." Ephesians 2:10

⚓ **Monday, December 10, 2012, 10:56 a.m.**

I'm afraid that "Rotten Ralph" once again reared his ugly head. I said I felt worse than rotten last time around, so I'm not sure what to say about this time. Despite my grand plan to slow down the chemo in an attempt to minimize side effects, I feel worse this time than last.

The good news is that I do seem to be rallying a bit today, so maybe I'm coming out of it. I'm also sleeping a lot, which really helps.

I'm taking today off, and I couldn't have picked a better day to stay inside and be lazy. What a nasty day – rainy and bleak!

There was one good thing about Friday's infusion. I overhead a nurse talking to a new patient about the potential side effects of the chemo. In hearing the warnings, I assumed the patient was getting much the same treatment as me. I ran into the patient and her mother on my way to the bathroom and struck up a conversation. Turns out she has Stage IV colorectal cancer that spread to her liver and had just finished her first treatment. I could tell by the look on her face that she was feeling completely overwhelmed. When I shared about my treatment and how well it had gone, I could see relief wash over them. It was such a good feeling to be an encouragement. I hope I have more opportunities in the future to help encourage others.

On another note, my father continues to struggle greatly with his health. It is so hard to watch. Please keep him and my mother in your prayers.

With thanks for your support,

Michelle

That last infusion was brutal, but being able to offer encouragement to the cancer-stricken lady and her mother helped take the sting out of it. Those two were in a tough place. Facing what they feared was an almost certain death sentence, the thing they needed most was even a glimmer of hope that survival was possible. Seeing that I not only survived but also thrived helped give them that hope.

"Blessed be the God and Father of our Lord Jesus Christ, the Father of mercies and God of all comfort; who comforts us in all our affliction so that we may be able to comfort those who are in any affliction with the comfort with which we ourselves are comforted by God." 2 Corinthians 1:3-4

⚓ Monday, December 17, 2012, 8:51 p.m.

What a difference a week makes! This time last week I wasn't feeling so hot, but now I'm feeling much better.

The chemo is beginning to take its toll, but there are still many bright spots:

Even though I feel terrible after the infusions, at least I always know it is relatively short lived and that I'll be back to normal soon enough. I know there are a lot of people (my father, for example) who have no idea when or if "normal" will ever be back.

I'm getting chemo brain and can tell that my brain doesn't always work the way it should, and my energy levels are still much lower than normal. When Brenda, a coworker, was teasing me today, I laughed, "Just wait until I'm smart again and I have my energy back. You'll be sorry." Again, it's good to know that this is only temporary. It's also good to be able to share a laugh at work.

My hair is falling out pretty quickly, but my hairdresser says that, amazingly, new hair is growing in as fast as the old is falling out.

It seemed to take forever to get the Christmas decorations up, but they are up and I'm really enjoying them. And my next infusion is not until December 28, so I'll be able to enjoy celebrating Christmas with my family.

I could go on and on, but I'll stop by saying that God is good, and there's so much to be thankful for. Even if my brain occasionally misfires and I leave a trail of hair behind with every shampoo and blow dry.

Wishing you and yours a very Merry Christmas!

- Michelle

Chemo brain is a funny thing. I could still function and perform job duties, but my thoughts were muddled. At work we later jokingly referred to my time on chemo as the dark period because my memory was very nearly erased. Before chemo, I had a knack for remembering even the smallest details of work projects, such as grants. I still wrote grants while on chemo but later couldn't even remember having written them. My penchant for organization made it easy to follow the trail of work I had done, but it was odd to revisit big projects I had completed and feel like I was seeing the work for the first time.

I'm glad I was still able to see bright spots in the midst of treatment. As we liked to say at St. John's Lutheran Church, where David and I were members for many years, "God is good all the time. All the time God is good."

⚓ **Tuesday, January 1, 2013, 1:50 p.m.**

I had planned to write an entry last night, but just didn't feel up to the task. I am happy to report that I am feeling much better today.

For those who worry that I don't get enough rest, you'll be glad to know that I've been quite the sloth since Friday. After getting my eighth – and hopefully final – infusion, which included what the nurses refer to as "Happy Juice," I went to bed at 5:30 p.m. and didn't get up until about 11:00 a.m. the next day. Since then, I've done more than my fair share of napping.

I had my CT scan yesterday but won't have the results until tomorrow. I'm definitely hoping for a clear scan which means I'll be through with treatment! Whatever the results of the scan, I trust God.

When I have CT scans, there's a dye I have to drink about an hour beforehand. Yesterday when they asked what flavor I wanted, I said the flavor didn't matter but that the dye needed to be served room temperature instead of cold. In making the request, I explained that because of chemo side effects I can't have anything cold to drink. (It feels like glass going down my throat. Very unpleasant!)

An older gentleman, also a colon cancer survivor, overheard my request and struck up a conversation about battling the disease. I admitted I was feeling pretty rotten from my last infusion. He said, "Not much fun, is it?" I agreed but then felt like I was being too negative. So, I said, "Yes, but God is good." He smiled a knowing smile and said, "Yes, it's like that verse in Habakkuk." I knew just what he was talking about, because it's come to my mind more than once lately:

> Though the fig tree should not blossom, And there be no fruit on the vines,
>
> Though the yield of the olive should fail, And the fields produce no food,
>
> Though the flock should be cut off from the fold, And there be no cattle in the stalls,
>
> Yet I will exult in the Lord, I will rejoice in the God of my salvation.
>
> Habakkuk 3: 17-18

I'll share results of my scan when I have them.

Happy New Year!

- Michelle

To someone looking from the outside in, those verses from Habakkuk must seem like the ravings of a lunatic. It's hard to understand until you've experienced it for yourself. Having been there, I can say there is real peace when you learn to trust God more than your circumstances.

Of Habakkuk 3:17-19, Billy Graham said: "We will never be free from discouragement and despondency until we know and walk with the very fountainhead of joy... No matter what the climate is, what the troubles are, what the difficulties are, there is joy for the child of God, because joy is produced supernaturally by the Holy Spirit in us."

⚓ Wednesday, January 2, 2013, 7:33 p.m.

First it was the verse in Habakkuk, then this morning the hymn "It Is Well with My Soul" kept going through my mind. I kind of knew the news from my scan might not be what I wanted to hear. It's like when I got the cancer diagnosis. Bible verses and various things had prepared me for the news beforehand.

So, here it is. First the bad news. Not only are the tumors still there, they've gotten a tiny bit larger. I'd be lying if I said I'm not disappointed. Going through all that chemo for nothing. Ugh!

Now the good news. There are only two tumors showing up on the CT scan, they're both still very small, they're both on the same lung, and even in the same lobe. This will really help facilitate surgery. The PET scan shows up a third tumor on the other lung, which could still be there but too small to show up on the CT scan. That remains to be seen.

I have not yet talked to Dr. Antonucci, but he already said I'd be looking at surgery if this last round of chemo didn't take care of the tumors. I know I'll have to wait some amount of time before having surgery because Avastin, one of my chemo drugs, causes bleeding problems.

I want to have the surgery as soon as I can so that I can get it over with and be in great shape to enjoy Drew's wedding. I don't know what kind of recovery will be required, but Dr. Antonucci said this surgery won't be nearly as extensive as those I've already gone through. He described it as "going in and popping out the tumors."

I'm guessing Dr. Antonucci will call me tomorrow and I'll have more information. What I'm reporting now I learned from a nurse who was careful to say, "The news isn't official because the doctor hasn't seen the report."

While the news isn't "official," I am rather certain it is accurate. I am also certain that all will be well.

Faithfully,

Michelle

> *When peace, like a river, attendeth my way, When sorrows like sea billows roll;*
>
> *Whatever my lot, Thou has taught me to say, It is well, it is well, with my soul.*
>
> *Though Satan should buffet, though trials should come, Let this blest assurance control,*
>
> *That Christ has regarded my helpless estate, And hath shed His own blood for my soul.*
>
> *My sin, oh, the bliss of this glorious thought! My sin, not in part but the whole,*
>
> *Is nailed to the cross, and I bear it no more, Praise the Lord, praise the Lord, O my soul!*
>
> *For me, be it Christ, be it Christ hence to live: If Jordan above me shall roll,*
>
> *No pang shall be mine, for in death as in life, Thou wilt whisper Thy peace to my soul.*
>
> *But, Lord, 'tis for Thee, for Thy coming we wait, The sky, not the grave, is our goal;*

Oh, trump of the angel! Oh, voice of the Lord! Blessed hope, blessed rest of my soul!

And Lord, haste the day when my faith shall be sight, The clouds be rolled back as a scroll;

The trump shall resound, and the Lord shall descend, Even so, it is well with my soul.

Lyrics by Horatio Spafford.

The prosperity gospel is a theology that equates the Christian life to a winning slot machine. Put in some coins of belief and you're guaranteed a bonanza of blessings. On its surface, the idea of a religion that guarantees an immediate return on investment sounds like a great thing. Give $5 to the poor and see the amount multiplied and returned to your bank account. Trust God and get a big house, new car and great health. There's only one problem with that philosophy: it's simply not true.

There are plenty of examples in the Bible where faithful people suffer. Take Job, for instance. He was described as "blameless, upright, fearing God, and turning away from evil," yet he lost his wealth, health and family. The Lord ultimately blessed Job with more than he had in the beginning, but there were some long, dark days before the blessings came.

Throughout the Bible we read stories of faithful followers of the Lord who are mistreated, imprisoned, beaten or killed. Across the world today there are many faithful Christians facing persecution or dying for their beliefs. And what about those who are facing terminal illness, long-term unemployment or foreclosure? Would all of their problems be solved if only they believed strongly enough?

Although God certainly blesses us this side of heaven, He doesn't guarantee it. What He does guarantee is so much more. God's promise to us is that He will never leave us or forsake us, and His free gift to us is eternal life through Jesus Christ His Son.

Here on earth we can be certain that we're not fighting our battles alone and that God is in control. When this life ends, we have assurance we will spend eternity in the presence of our Lord in a place far more spectacular than our minds can begin to imagine.

> Therefore having been justified by faith, we have peace with God through our Lord Jesus Christ, through whom also we have obtained our introduction by faith into this grace in which we stand; and we exult in hope of the glory of God.
>
> And not only this, but we exult in our tribulations, knowing that tribulation brings about perseverance; and perseverance, proven character; and proven character, hope; and hope does not disappoint because the love of God has been poured out within our hearts through the Holy Spirit who was given to us.
> Romans 5:1-5

⚓ Thursday, January 3, 2013, 6:40 p.m.

Just a quick update. I talked to Dr. Antonucci this afternoon. He wants to do another PET scan before doing surgery. I see him on January 15, at which time we'll schedule the scan and discuss in more detail what surgery will look like.

I laughed when I found out I have to undergo yet another scan. In the "serves me right" category, back before all this started, I was trying to worm my way out of the scan that identified the tumors. Since going through with the scan I didn't want in the first place, I've had an MRI, a PET scan and two CT scans – and there's another PET scan on the way!

It reminds me of what I was just laughing about last week. When I was in the hospital after my first surgery, I complained to my daytime nurse that the night nurse kept me up all night (the first night following my surgery) with inane chatter. He promised to fix the problem and put a "Do Not Disturb" sign on my door before switching shifts with the night nurse.

Having insisted that I was fine and sending David and my mother home for the night, I settled down to sleep. It wasn't long before I was throwing up. I somehow managed to knock the nurse call device in the floor and couldn't find it in the dark room. I pulled on several cords, all of which were connected to me, before finally deciding to place a call with the cell phone I had been trying to use as a flashlight. Rather than scaring David to death, I called my mom and asked her to call the nurse's station and send someone in.

The lesson of the story is – just get the scan when they tell you to, and never, ever put a "Do Not Disturb" sign on your hospital room door!

Thanks for all your prayers and support! I feel really good today, and I know it's because of your outpouring of love.

- Michelle

I remember trying to get out of having the scan that first identified the cancerous tumors in my lungs. I had a high deductible on my health insurance and knew the entire cost of the rather expensive scan would come straight out of my pocket. David and I were planning a cruise, and I thought I'd much rather go on a cruise than have another scan.

"If you're just doing it for my peace of mind, I'd rather just skip this scan," I said with all sincerity.

"I'm doing it for *my* peace of mind," Dr. Antonucci said.

I told him later how grateful I was he insisted I have the scan. Unlike the original GI doctor who didn't even recommend I have a colonoscopy when protocol would have called for one, Dr. Antonucci wasn't about to let me do anything to put my health at risk.

⚓ **Tuesday, January 15, 2013, 6:55 p.m.**

I saw Dr. Antonucci today, and overall the visit was positive. We scheduled a PET scan, a highly sensitive scan that detects cancer, for Monday. After that, we'll have a good idea of what I'm looking at in terms of surgery. For now, the doctor presented the following possible scenarios:

1. The PET scan doesn't detect cancer and we're through with treatment for now. (I list this option first because it's obviously the one I'm hoping for.)
2. The PET scan shows only the two spots that showed up on the CT scan. In this case, the surgery should be minimally invasive. It would require one or two days in the hospital and about a week of recovery. (Still, not a bad option.)
3. The PET scan shows more spots than showed up on the CT scan. Not a great scenario. As Dr. Antonucci so bluntly put it, "If they have to crack your chest open, your hospital stay and recovery time will be a whole different story."

If I do have surgery, it likely will be late February or early March.

Today, my cousin shared Joshua 1:9 with me: "Have I not commanded you? Be strong and courageous. Do not be terrified; do not be discouraged, for the Lord your God will be with you wherever you go."

As I told her, I sent this verse to my father and son back in the summer before I was diagnosed. As soon as I sent it, a little voice told me the verse was for me, not for them. I thought, "Oh, no. Here we go again." But, again, I can say that the Lord has been with me through this entire experience, and I am not terrified or discouraged. Thanks be to God.

I'll be sure to give an update after I get the results from Monday's scan, which will likely be Tuesday or Wednesday. In the meantime, I'll be praying – and hope you will too – for a clear scan, but more than that I'm trusting God regardless of the results. Please also pray for my sister, Kristen, who has a huge dose of radiation on Thursday to finish treating thyroid cancer she was diagnosed with this summer. (Yes, our family is having FUN these days!)

As always, I am humbled by and appreciative of all the prayers and support coming my way.

Much love,

Michelle

Kristen came through her radiation treatment just fine, although she did have to spend nearly a week isolated in her bedroom after the procedure so she wouldn't expose others to radiation. The risk for exposure was so great that she couldn't even use household items such as glassware, dishes or silverware.

When I dropped off a meal for her one day, I just had to leave the Styrofoam container on the counter and run. I later realized I forgot to leave a disposable knife and fork. When I called to let her know, she assured me it was fine. "I'll just eat it with my hands," she said. "I'm living like an animal back here anyway."

More of that quirky Ironside humor. We got a good laugh out of it.

⚓ Tuesday, January 22, 2013, 8:31 p.m.

I had my PET scan yesterday and heard the results late this evening. Dr. Antonucci once told me that if the nurses call, it's good news; if he calls, the news isn't as good. He called.

The good news is that the scan still only shows the same tumors that have been there all along. The bad news is the scan still shows the tumors that have been there all along. More bad news is that the cancer counts they check when they do my blood work are also up. This means I'll definitely need surgery, probably the sooner the better. Dr. Antonucci wants to get me in to see the surgeon as quickly as possible, and I am happy with that line of action. It still looks like we'll be able to go the minimally invasive route, which would be a huge blessing. Of course, I'll know much more after I see the surgeon.

I've often quoted passages from my devotional, *Jesus Calling* by Sarah Young. My son Drew got me her newer devotional, *Jesus Today: Experience Hope Through His Presence*, and it also speaks to me every time I read it.

An excerpt from today's devotion:

"I am the Lord of peace. I give you peace at all times and in every way. There is a deep gaping hole within you that can be filled only by My peaceful presence."

...

"I made it clear that this is a gift: something I provide freely and lovingly. So your responsibility is to receive this gift, acknowledging to Me not only your need but also your desire. Then wait expectantly in My presence, ready to receive My peace in full measure."

I can honestly say that I am at perfect peace. Not because I'm anything special but because it is a gift from God. For that, I am so, so thankful.

Marching on,

Michelle

Going back to the prosperity gospel, another fundamental problem with that philosophy is the fact there is an empty place in us that can't be filled with anything other than God's peaceful presence. If we could fill that gaping hole with success, money, power or fame, then explain how so many celebrities and politicians are so miserable. If we try to fill that hole with anything other than God, we will never be satisfied.

I'd much rather have the gift of peace – even when it is accompanied by the prospect of serious surgery – than all the material things the world can offer.

⚓ **Monday, January 28, 2013, 7:42 p.m.**

Remember the old television game show, "Let's Make a Deal"? In it, contestants were given the option of taking a cash prize or choosing a prize hidden behind one of three doors. Choose the right door and they may win a car; choose wrongly and they might win a pig or a donkey. It looks like I'm picking what's behind door number three, even though I know what's back there and don't really want it.

I met with my new surgeon, Dr. Lacy Harville, this afternoon. He spent a lot of time showing me the results of my scan and explaining why the surgery won't be as simple as going in and popping out the tumors. It looks very likely that I'll need to have the upper lobe of my left lung removed. Sounds dreadful, doesn't it? He assures me that I will fully recover and not even notice the difference once I bounce back from surgery.

I won't know for sure until late tomorrow or early Wednesday after he's had a chance to meet with his Tumor Board. I believe this is the third time my case has been part of a Tumor Board discussion!

Despite this less than glowing report, there is good news. Like Dr. Midis, my other surgeon, Dr. Harville has an excellent reputation as a surgeon and a wonderful bedside manner. I feel very confident knowing he'll be handling my surgery. He's even friends with Dr. Midis, and they regularly operate together. Also, he won't be "cracking my chest open," as so graphically described by Dr. Antonucci. Instead, there will be about a four-inch incision on my left side.

The surgery will be major, similar in scope to the other two surgeries I had. Probably five to six days in the hospital and at least a few weeks of recovery time.

Again, I won't know for sure until after he meets with a bunch of other doctors. Please pray that they – and we – will have wisdom on how best to proceed.

Still marching on and singing my song. "It Is Well with My Soul,"

- Michelle

My first appointment with Dr. Harville was a good one. He did an excellent job of explaining everything in full detail and spent so much time with me it seemed like he had no other patients.

We looked at the X-rays, and he pointed out that my tumors were located so deeply within my lung that it would be impossible to just go in and pop them out like we had hoped. Among the many possible complications of surgery, he included death.

When Dr. Harville was trying to decide how to surgically address my lung cancer, he, too, said he wanted to bring my case before a Tumor Board. While I was still in his office, Dr. Harville called his good friend Dr. Midis to be sure he would be there for the meeting. As it turns out, Drs. Harville and Midis routinely work together; both are considered the best in their field. It was comforting to know these two incredibly skilled surgeons would be working together to decide how best to proceed.

When we talked about recovery time, I told Dr. Harville how well I bounced back from my other surgeries. "If you came back from those surgeries that quickly, you should do the same with this one," he said. "Quicker, actually. I'm a better surgeon that Dr. Midis." We laughed, and I said I'd be sure to tell Dr. Midis what he said.

I guess Dr. Midis got the last laugh on that one. I spent more time in the hospital following my lung surgery than I spent at home recovering from both my colon and liver resections.

⚓ **Tuesday, January 29, 2013, 5:16 p.m.**

This will be very brief. The doctors on the Tumor Board agreed that surgery looks like the appropriate course of action for me. We have the date set for Tuesday, March 5.

Please know that when I say I'm fine with this, I truly mean it. I'm not excited about the surgery, but I'm not worried or fearful. Thanks, no doubt, in large part to the many prayers going up on my behalf.

Thank you so much for your beautiful posts, sweet notes, emails and calls of encouragement. I am blessed to be supported by so many wonderful people!

Gratefully,

Michelle

There was a lot going on in our lives at this time. I was facing very serious surgery, and my father's health continued to decline.

To add insult to injury, a few of our neighbors started stirring up problems with our Homeowners Association. They made a lot of false and hurtful accusations against David, who had served as the HOA president for many years. We were shocked and hurt that neighbors would do such a thing, particularly knowing what we were enduring. They continue to take jabs to this day.

Thankfully, the overwhelming majority of our neighbors are wonderful, and many called to tell David they stand firmly behind him and are sorry for the abuse he's absorbed at the hands of a few callous people.

I share this because it's the thing that most readily comes to mind as I think about the time before surgery. Not fear, not worry, but hurt perpetuated by people who called themselves friends. David and I have had to turn this over to the Lord and trust Him. We are commanded to forgive others as we have been forgiven, so with God's grace that is what we will do.

"The tongue is a small part of the body, and yet it boasts of great things. Behold, how great a forest is set aflame by such a small fire!" James 3:5

⚓ Monday, February 18, 2013, 7:37 p.m.

I've heard from people who are worried because I haven't posted in a while. This is to let everyone know that I'm doing very well. I feel better each day as the chemo works its way out of my system.

When people asked if I felt bad when I was on chemo, I assured them I was fine. Now that I'm getting back to normal, however, I realize that I felt fairly bad a lot of the time. I am so grateful to be getting back to normal and so very thankful that ordinarily I have an abundance of energy and good health. I know there are so many people who don't enjoy those luxuries.

I know, I know. I do have cancer so my health isn't all that great. But I have managed to make it through cold and flu season without getting sick, and my blood work has stayed good except for the cancer. Yes, it is a bit like saying "Other than that, how was the play, Mrs. Lincoln?" but I'll stick with my positives anyway.

I am also happy to report that I'm battling my chemo brain by playing brain training games on Lumosity, a website that has games specifically designed to strengthen different areas of your brain. I'm rather addicted. I can already see improvement, and it's very encouraging to feel like I'm heading back to normal in that area, too.

I continue to be humbled and amazed at all the support that comes my way. There are so many people praying for me every day. I know that's the difference and how I'm managing as well as I am.

Gratefully yours,

Michelle

One day at work, a coworker offered to help move tables and chairs to set the room for a board meeting. In accepting the offer, I commented that I hated for him to do it because I knew his hip was giving him problems.

"I'm fine," he said. "I just have trouble walking."

I laughed and said, "That's as bad as me. I say I'm fine except I can't breathe. Breathing and walking are both kind of important."

I think my coworker and I had it right, though. You're better off to just keep going when at all possible. The minute you give in to pain or problems, you're putting them in the driver's seat. I'd much rather keep them in the back.

⚓ Wednesday, February 27, 2013, 6:46 p.m.

"I am training you to hold in your heart a dual focus: My continual presence and the hope of heaven." From *Jesus Calling*.

I was trying to think of something to capture what I'm feeling right now, and I believe the above quote does a good job. I was telling someone today that I have felt God's presence every step of the way through this difficult journey, and that it's the thing that has been most remarkable to me. I also realize that I have no fear of dying because of my hope of heaven.

Honestly, when I think of the possibility of dying, the only sad thoughts that come to mind are of family members and friends I'd be leaving behind. Don't misunderstand. I'm not saying I think I'm going to die, but simply saying that for me there is no fear in death because I know it's not the end. I also know that my finite mind cannot begin to fathom what glories await in heaven. Nonetheless, I am quite content to stay here on Earth a while longer.

I went to the hospital on Monday for my preadmission tests. The only thing that showed up wrong was that my blood oxygen levels were low. The nurse kept adjusting the device and saying, "This can't be right." I've been complaining that I'm getting short of breath, and I suppose I was right. I guess that's what cancerous tumors in your lungs will do to you.

Now I'm just counting down to surgery, scheduled for Tuesday morning at 7:30. That's the good thing about having complicated surgeries. You get to go to the head of the line. No waiting for this girl!

I have to say that I continue to be amazed and touched by all the support flowing my way. The prayers and well wishes are my constant companions and help carry me through each day. Someone recently referred to me as "trudging along," but I truly don't feel like I'm trudging at all. Though my feet still throb at times from chemo side effects, my step is light. And there are arms much stronger than mine carrying me through when my own strength fails me.

Counting down to surgery and counting my blessings. Love to all,

Michelle

As Christians, we hold dual citizenship. We're citizens on Earth, but we're also citizens of heaven. To us, death shouldn't be seen as dark and scary but rather as the means of transportation to our permanent home.

I knew there was a chance I would die in that surgery. I know there's still a chance that cancer will claim my life at a relatively early age. Yet, I am not afraid. Feeling such a huge sense of urgency to write this book, the thought has occurred to me that perhaps once I finish the book, my time here will be over. That thought doesn't make me type any slower. I know God is in control and nothing can take my life until He decides it is time for me to go.

"For to me, to live is Christ, and to die is gain." Philippians 1:21

⚓ **Tuesday, March 5, 2013, 4:12 a.m.**

"Instead of the thorn bush the cypress will come up; and it will be a memorial to the Lord, for an everlasting sign which will not be cut off." Isaiah 55:13

Not your typical verse of hope, but this verse came to me soon after I first started back to chemotherapy. I felt so strongly that it was meant for me that tears came to my eyes. Back then, my eyes hurt when they watered, yet another lovely side effect of the chemo. Luckily, as my family knows, it's not often that I get teary eyed.

Thankfully, there will be no more chemo and no more hurting when my eyes tear up. I still think this verse is speaking to me, and I'm confident that God is using all of this to His glory and for good. I praise Him for that!

David and I are preparing to leave for surgery. As we do so, I am completely calm and without fear. I slept all night. That kind of peace is only possible with and through God and with a lot of help from so many people who are praying for me.

I have received so many kind notes, calls and emails. Each one was special. I wish I could give a personal thank-you to everyone who sent something, but there's no way. Do know that your efforts have not gone unnoticed or unappreciated.

Thank you, thank you!

David will post something on here as soon as he can when I'm out of surgery.

With much love and gratefulness,

Michelle

Cypress trees are described as majestic, durable, hearty and extremely resistant to harsh conditions. Cypress is some of the world's most prized wood because it is lightweight and durable, making it an ideal building material.

While my cancer at first glance would seem to be a thorn bush, God took the curse out of the cancer and instead made it something beautiful and useful.

I also note that cypress trees are tall, something I've been called more than once.

⚓ **Tuesday, March 5, 2013, 11:02 a.m.**

First, let me express to everyone how grateful and humbled I am for your continual prayers and uplifting words for Michelle and our family. As most of you know I am one lucky guy to have such a beautiful wife and best friend. On July 30th we will celebrate our 30-year wedding anniversary.

Dr. Harville said that Michelle's surgery went great. As expected he removed the top half of her lung due to the tumors being too deep to remove individually. She will be in ICU tonight and maybe tomorrow. Her hospital stay will be a week even though she will be ready to leave tomorrow. I will keep everyone posted on her recovery. Again, thank you for your love, prayers and support. We have truly felt it.

Sincerely,

David

I should have turned the keyboard over to David more often. His posts were always so sweet.

I don't remember a whole lot about the surgery, but I do remember waking up in quite a bit of pain. One of the nurses commented it looked like I was trying to run away from the pain because I kept scooting farther and farther down the bed.

⚓ Wednesday, March 6, 2013, 5:43 p.m.

Good news. Michelle has moved to a step down version of ICU where she will be until she goes home. She is doing just fine and sat up most of the day but is requiring a lot of pain medication. She made the comment today that this has been the hardest surgery yet, or she has just forgotten how bad the other ones were.

It may be a few days before she can have visitors because the medications are causing her to sleep quite a bit. I will keep everyone posted.

Thanks again,

David

I have a very high tolerance for pain. I delivered both babies naturally 30 minutes after arriving at the hospital. With the first birth, I spent the afternoon in the pool while continuing to have contractions five minutes apart. When I spoke with the doctor on call, she insisted I must be in false labor because I talked to her through a contraction and didn't sound like I was in any pain. I even drove myself home to get David and go to the hospital.

I say all that to explain that it is easy to understand how no one realized how badly I was hurting when I said I was in pain.

⚓ Friday, March 8, 2013, 3:24 p.m.

I saw a bumper sticker while driving yesterday that said, "Prayer Changes Things." Simple, yet so true. The Father listens to his children and he has heard the prayers of so many people. Thank you!!!

Michelle had a dream several nights before surgery that someone was poking and prodding her while asking, "Does this hurt?" It has been a challenge getting her pain under control so they called in an anesthesiologist who began poking her while asking, "Does this hurt?" Apparently dreams can come true. She was in continual pain and should not have been able to feel anything, so he changed the pain medication in her epidural and that worked.

They started walking her yesterday but this has been the first day she has been awake for a long period of time and feeling closer to normal.

Humbled and amazed,

David

One morning they placed a board behind my back to take an X-ray, and it felt like someone plunged a dagger in my back. Later, a nurse tried to help me get up to walk a little. When I stood up, my blood pressure and heart rate went crazy, and I nearly passed out. That's when they finally realized the extent of my pain.

It was so odd to have that doctor poking me and saying the same words from my dream, but I sure was glad he came to help. I had an epidural, which should have rendered my entire torso completely numb, but that wasn't the case. The morphine they were giving me was not working, and I felt everything. The pain was incredible.

After experimenting with a few different kinds of pain medicine, they found something that would work. Thanks to Dilaudid, I was like a new woman. I was able to get up and move around and felt so much better. The nurses remarked it was good to see me smiling.

Later, my cousin Tracy came to visit. As we talked and laughed, I developed an irritating itch. Then, we noticed big welts were developing on my arms and legs, and my face began to swell.

The nurse explained it was either the result of so many medications in my system or an allergic reaction to the Dilaudid. She gave me a shot of Benadryl. The nurse seemed quite calm at the time but later admitted it kind of freaked her out to see me in such a state. I knew if the problem persisted I would have to stop taking the only pain medication that helped. Fortunately, the Benadryl did the trick, and I had no other allergy attacks.

⚓ Sunday, March 10, 2013, 5:11 p.m.

WARNING: The post you are about to read has been written by a highly-drugged individual. Please ignore any typos or misspellings.

First, many thanks to David for keeping up my posts while I wasn't able to and for faithfully staying by my side in this dreadful hospital room. Hospitals are the worst. However, I have to say that my nurses have all been wonderful and have taken very good care of me.

As David mentioned, the first few days after surgery were pretty rough. I went through the most pain I've ever felt, which is saying a lot with all I've been through. Thankfully, we now have the meds where they need to be to regulate my pain. Also, the doctors have removed all the tubes. Now we're just waiting for me to lose enough fluid to make it safe to go home. If all goes according to plan that will be tomorrow.

In other good news, my blood oxygen levels are already much better than they were pre-surgery. So half a lung with no cancer really is better than a whole lung with cancer!

Many thanks for all the prayers that have gone up on my behalf!

I'll close with a quote sent by my sweet friend Joni Oliver:

"The nicest place to be is in someone's thoughts... The safest place to be is in someone's prayers... And the very best place to be is in the hands of God. May you always be there!"

Today is March 9, 2014, almost a year to the day since I wrote that post-surgery journal entry. This morning I got an email from my boss, Cynthia Moxley, saying that our coworker and friend Bob Wilson passed away quite unexpectedly yesterday while out working in his yard. We later learned the death was probably related to heart problems. Bob was a few years younger than me; thin and fit, he seemed so healthy and full of life. Bob was a great guy. His contribution to my Moxley Carmichael gift basket was *Amazing Grace*, a book that includes inspirational stories about some of our most treasured hymns.

Getting the news about Bob kind of sucked the life out of me. I lazed around all day not wanting to do much of anything. I realized a little while ago that this same feeling came over me when we heard about the death of Briana Bilbrey, the college student who died from an epileptic seizure (the sister of Evan's good friend), later when Tim Wallace (the father of Evan's friend) died of a heart attack and again at the passing of Josh Moore, Evan's friend who died of cancer. I know my passing wouldn't have had any impact on these deaths, but I can't help feeling a little guilty that I'm still here against all odds and these people are gone.

As I look to the words from the poem in the post, I realize I am in the hands of God. I know that He is in control and that if I'm still alive it means there's a reason for me to be here. I believe part of that purpose is writing this book, which is why I felt compelled to add this post on the eve of receiving such devastating news. As I thank God for my life and ask that all that I do bring glory to His name, I pray for those families who have faced such tremendous loss.

⚓ Tuesday, March 12, 2013, 11:59 a.m.

I now live my life in four-hour increments – "I took my pain pills at 11, which means I can take them again at 3." I am managing to keep the pain mostly under control, but it's always there. The doctor said he was able to work through a four-inch incision but had to dig through a lot of muscle to get to the tumors, so it's normal that I'm in a lot of pain.

I was on the cardiac/thoracic surgery floor, and one of the nurses said that my surgery is 10 times more painful than open heart surgery. So I feel very grateful that I'm doing as well as I am.

I am at home, and it's wonderful to be here! I'm doing fine, although I do get short of breath very easily. Climbing our rather steep staircase about does me in, but I'm trying to take the stairs more slowly, and I sit down to catch my breath once I reach the chair in our bedroom. Who would have thought that climbing 16 stairs could feel like climbing Mt. LeConte?

The cards and well wishes continue to pour in daily, and I so appreciate them! Challenges are much easier to tackle when you're not facing them alone.

Marching on, albeit at a slower pace,

Michelle

P.S. Still on major medication, so the disclaimer from my prior post continues for this one.

Coming home from the hospital was, as always, a time for celebration. I just never could completely get a handle on the pain.

⚓ Thursday, March 14, 2013, 1:10 p.m.

"Remember that I, the Mighty One, am in your midst, and I am greater than all the trouble in the world. My right hand will save you! Hold tightly to my hand and you can walk confidently through your toughest times."

When I saw this in my devotional, *Jesus Today*, it really struck me. The other night I plopped down on the couch too quickly and got in an uncomfortable position. Unable to move without causing a lot of pain, I lay there like a turtle on its back. Finally, I yelled for David. He held out his right hand and I was easily able to pull myself up and get in a better spot.

I now use David's right hand readily and often. Why risk hurting myself when I can do it so much easier with his assistance?

I think it's that way in life. Things work out much better when I shed some of my fierce independence and seek help.

As for my walk with God, it's so easy to think I can handle the little things by myself when that's not what He intends at all. "Hold tightly to my hand..." I believe that means in good times and bad, through big struggles and small. The minute I try to go it alone is the very minute I'm at risk for failure.

Each time I reach out for David's helping hand, I'm reminding myself that I can't do everything alone and that I'm not supposed to. And I'm thanking God for all the love and care I'm surrounded with.

I am doing better each day, far better than I expected to be at this point. The main struggle I have is with pain, but the pain pills are keeping it mostly under control.

Thanks for extending your "right hand" through continued prayers, cards and support. They carry me through the days.

Looking forward to brighter days ahead,

Michelle

This whole reaching out for help thing has been a difficult lesson to learn. I'd much rather take care of something myself than ask for assistance. And, while I was willing to accept help when my body demanded that I do so, it wasn't long before I would fall back into old habits of self-sufficiency. In fact, I believe that on the very day I wrote that post, I pulled something loose on my lung when I got up by myself.

⚓ **Monday, March 18, 2013, 3:34 p.m.**

I've been taking baby steps forward up until now, and I've been very pleased with my progress. Unfortunately, yesterday I started hurting very badly and struggled to breathe.

Earlier today I went in for an X-ray and to see the doctor. The good news is that the X-ray looks good, as do my vital signs. The doctor remains pleased with my progress. The bad news is I'm still hurting. A lot.

The doctor added a steroid pack, which he hopes will help. He thinks I may have some pleurisy, which could be causing a lot of the pain. Or I could have pulled a muscle getting out of bed. Or it could just be pain associated with the surgery...

Bottom line, we're not sure why I'm hurting so much, but it doesn't seem to be caused by anything too serious.

I've been told to give this new regimen until Wednesday or Thursday. If it doesn't help by then, we'll have to look at doing something else. One option offered up was to go back in the hospital, which I definitely see as the last choice. You never know, though. If I'm still hurting like crazy by Thursday I'll probably be begging to be admitted.

I'd be remiss if I didn't say once again what a huge help David has been. As I listened to him advocate with the doctor's office on my behalf, I felt protected and safe. The doctor is concerned about overprescribing pain medicine, but I've never had any kind of problem with stopping the pain meds when it's time. In fact, I'm more likely to try to stop them too soon rather than too late. If we can just find something that works!!

Thanks for your continued prayers and support.

Pressing on,

Michelle

Notice a recurring theme in these posts? Pain was a serious problem. Following my colon and liver surgeries the pain was managed with medication, and I was able to quickly and easily wean myself off all medication soon after going home. That just wasn't the case following this surgery, and it frustrated me to no end.

Dr. Harville didn't know me as well as my other doctors did, so I think it's the same kind of situation that occurred when the obstetrician thought I was having false labor pains when I actually was about to give birth. Since I don't carry on with a lot of dramatics, it's easy to miss my signs of distress. David knew me, though, and realized I was suffering. I appreciate his willingness to advocate on my behalf.

⚓ **Tuesday, March 19, 2013, 6:49 p.m.**

I've been waiting to post, hoping to have news of a miraculous recovery or at least significant improvement. I have improved somewhat today, although only slightly. I still have a lot of pain, which gets much worse when I stand. Because of the pain, I can barely breathe when I walk. Not the best situation in the world.

I did manage to take a shower today which made me feel a lot better. The mere fact that I was willing to go to the hospital and the doctor yesterday looking so dreadful tells a lot about how bad I felt. If things don't improve tomorrow, we'll be back in touch with the doctor. Currently, I'm scheduled for another X-ray on Friday and to see the doctor on Monday.

Hoping for some relief,

Michelle

Being raised by a mother who always looked immaculate made an impression on me. While I'm not as well-coiffed as Barbara Ironside, I do care about my appearance and typically won't go out in public without looking presentable. I felt so poorly that day when I went to the hospital and doctor that getting cleaned up just wasn't possible. I had to look away when I saw my reflection in the elevator mirror.

⚓ Wednesday, March 20, 2013, 2:20 p.m.

After a very frustrating call with my surgeon's nurse, I finally broke down and called my oncologist's office. The surgeon's nurse offered great advice like, "Picture yourself at the beach." Hard to think of yourself at the beach when you're in so much pain you can't breathe. Last night my back went into spasms that lasted about 15 minutes each. It was very scary. I was in tremendous pain and could not get my breath.

When I talked to the oncologist's nurse, she said, "You're not getting anywhere near enough pain medication." Fortunately, Dr. Antonucci knows me well enough to realize that I don't complain lightly. He's prescribed something that should deaden the nerve pain, which is causing the spasms.

Here's hoping that the new scrip works. It's a shame that doctors are so scared of patients becoming addicted that they won't write prescriptions for the drug that works the best. Anyway, I am hopeful that this additional medication will do the trick. Dr. Antonucci has always taken good care of me, and I trust him.

Thanks for your continued prayers and support,

Michelle

Those spasms were horrendous. I was writhing in pain and felt like I was suffocating. In *I'll Watch the Moon*, a wonderful book by Ann Tatlock, a boy with polio talks about being weaned off the iron lung. When I read the passage, I couldn't believe how perfectly it described how I felt the night of my spasms:

> *I felt like I was choking. The room started filling up*
> *with black spots, and I couldn't even get enough air to*
> *scream. I wanted to scream and beg the therapist, Miss*

> *Snyder, to turn the lung back on, but I couldn't. I couldn't
> do anything but hope she'd turn it back on before I died,
> because that's what I was doing.*

While there was no Miss Snyder to turn on a lung, I was pleading with God to give me breath. It's easy to take breathing for granted until the air stops flowing. Then, you can't possibly think about anything else.

When I talked to Dr. Harville's nurse the next day, she just didn't appreciate the intense level of pain I felt. When she said, "Try picturing yourself at the beach," I wanted to come through the phone line and strangle her.

The medication Dr. Antonucci prescribed – Elavil – helps with nerve pain. I still take it to this day. The problems I was having at the time of my post, however, were related to much more than nerve pain.

⚓ **Thursday, March 21, 2013, 9:17 a.m.**

"You, O LORD, keep my lamp burning; my God turns my darkness into light." Psalm 18:28, NIV

The past few days have been a bit dark. I was hurting and could not find relief. It was exhausting and frustrating.

I am happy to report that today things look much brighter. I'm feeling quite a bit better. Still not great, but much improved. I'm hoping I've turned a corner. I plan to take it very slow and easy through the weekend to try to avoid a relapse. My goal is to keep moving forward.

Today's devotional in *Jesus Today* was very timely. Below is a brief excerpt:

> When your path takes you through a dark valley and
> you are struggling, look to Me for help. Follow me
> obediently, trusting Me in the midst of darkness and
> confusion. As you stay close to Me, I show you the way
> forward. Little by little, I turn your darkness into light.

It feels good to be seeing a little light.

I try not to post unless there's actual news to share so that I don't drive everyone crazy with updates. I'll post an update after I see the doctor on Monday. Otherwise, assume that no news is good news.

Pressing forward,

Michelle

I was trying so hard to be positive and get better, but this rally, like those before it, was short lived.

⚓ Monday, March 25, 2013, 4:24 p.m.

Just to keep everyone updated I must let you know that Michelle has been readmitted to Fort Sanders Hospital. When she saw Dr. Harville today, she learned that she has some fluid buildup in her lungs. She is still experiencing pain and muscle spasms, and for these reasons he put her back in the hospital.

Most of us know how Michelle feels about the hospital. For her to be in complete agreement to be readmitted is very revealing as to how bad she is feeling. This is as bad as I have ever seen her feel ever. Please continue to pray for her recovery.

Sincerely,

David

I somehow managed to shower and dry my hair before this appointment, but those futile attempts at improving my appearance did nothing to disguise the fact I was not doing well. My friend Ruthie, who drove me to this appointment, recognized something was horribly wrong the minute she saw me. As we made the 30-minute drive to the doctor's office, Ruthie politely made small talk and asked a few questions. Each time I tried to answer, I would collapse into a coughing fit. I still could barely breathe.

When I saw the doctor, he said the X-ray showed some fluid around my lung. He didn't seem particularly worried about it, though, and still thought I would be able to work through any problems. At some point during that visit, however, Dr. Harville realized how terrible I felt. I surprised myself when I eagerly agreed to his suggestion that I go back to the hospital.

Despite having devoted her morning to my doctor's visit, Ruthie offered to take me to the hospital for admission. At first I accepted, but then I started to feel guilty about taking up so much more of her time. I kept insisting she should drive me home, and David could take me to the hospital later that day. Thankfully, Ruthie paid no attention and drove me straight to the hospital.

My friend Joni joined us, and my two friends valiantly fought on my behalf. It took many hours and several complaints from my friends before I finally received medication at a level needed to ease the pain. It was around this time that my brother sent the text about biting down on a stick. Even though I thought it was hilarious, I can appreciate how it didn't seem funny to anyone else.

⚓ **Tuesday, March 26, 2013, 9:04 a.m.**

Just a quick note to let you know that I'm doing much better today. They have upped my pain meds (finally!), and Dr. Harville put in a chest tube to help vacuum out the excess fluid and air, which were above and below my lung and pushing on it. That's what was causing a lot of the pain.

If you're thinking that a vacuum cleaner inside your chest doesn't sound particularly comfortable, you'd be right. It also wasn't any fun having the tube inserted. However, I was glad to do it and willing to do about anything to make the pain stop.

I'll be in the hospital for at least a few days, which is fine by me. I want to be well again.

I have to say again that David and I have been deeply touched by all the acts of kindness and support coming our way. Thank you, thank you!

With restored hope for healing,

Michelle

After I was admitted to the hospital, Dr. Harville ordered a CT scan to see what was really going on with my lung. CT scans are more advanced than X-rays and offer images with greater detail and clarity. The CT scan revealed my lung had collapsed and was surrounded by fluid and air.

I believe Dr. Harville was shocked to see how badly my condition had deteriorated. That evening he performed a procedure in my room to insert a chest tube. To numb me, he had to administer a shot just beneath the pleural lining of my lung. It was incredibly painful, but I gritted my teeth and thought about the fact the temporary pain would ultimately bring much needed relief. During the procedure, one of the nurses said something about my trusting Dr. Harville. The doctor replied, "She's not going to trust me until I make her stop hurting." I believe that was his way of saying he was sorry he hadn't listened to me when I said I was hurting.

To be clear, I do trust Dr. Harville and know he's an excellent surgeon. My case just happened to be bizarre, and I don't behave like a typical patient. I still think my problems may go back to the day I got up by myself and felt something pull. Thankfully, the chest tube helped tremendously.

⚓ **Thursday, March 28, 2013, 9:44 a.m.**

The first miracle Jesus performed was turning water into wine, perhaps to show us that God cares about even the smallest details of our lives.

This morning, I was chatting with my respiratory therapist and mentioned that I couldn't get Internet access yesterday and it was driving me crazy. I then said, "If I had Internet connection and a clean head of hair, I'd be one happy lady." The therapist immediately went and got "real" shampoo – the stuff they use at the hospital actually makes your hair look worse instead of better – and washed my hair. And, as you can see by the fact that I'm posting, the Internet came back up.

On a larger scale, someone close to me recently said that God laid it on her heart to send David and me a $500 check. David went to the dentist on Monday and needed a crown. The cost of the crown after insurance? $500!

I believe those events transpired to let me know that God hasn't forgotten me and that He'll take care of all my needs. That said, the need right now is for my lung to stop leaking air and fluid. The machine that is suctioning out the leaking air and fluid sounds a bit like Niagara Falls, and no one is sure why.

The doctor gave me two huge doses of antibiotics last night in case there's undetected infection. I'm also doing physical therapy twice a day, which seems to be helping.

If the leak doesn't stop by Friday, the doctor plans to do a bronchoscopy (a procedure that lets the doctor look at your lungs' airways) so that he can get a good look at everything and hopefully determine what's going on.

The good news is that my pain is largely under control. Now the only problem is that I'm stuck here for a while. But truthfully I'd rather be here not in pain than at home in misery.

Serving a faithful God,

Michelle

Sometimes we make the mistake of imposing our limitations on God. When we do that, we can't imagine how He possibly could care about something as insignificant as shampooed hair or Internet access. But God is omniscient and omnipresent; He knows everything, and He can be everywhere at once. He also is omnipotent. Nothing is too great or too small for God.

The $500 gift came at a time when we sorely needed it. The most significant thing about the gift was it exactly equaled the amount we needed to cover our most recent and unexpected expense. It was as if God came down to personally deliver the check and let us know we were not forgotten.

When we follow the leading of the Holy Spirit, whether that means giving someone three yellow roses, a loaf of freshly baked bread or a $500 check, there are no limits to the blessings we can bring others.

The respiratory therapist, Wendy, was another way God showed me His love during that hospital stay. Soon after she and I met, we discovered we both go to Sevier Heights Baptist Church. After that, she seemed to almost miraculously appear every time I needed her most. She blessed me with her sweet spirit, as well as her considerable medical knowledge.

⚓ Friday, March 29, 2013, 1:05 p.m.

Good news! I finished my bronchoscopy earlier today, and it looked really good. All the bad things the doctor searched for were not there. So, other than the leak, my lung is in good shape. Hooray! I'm going to stay here at the hospital as long as it takes. I don't expect to go home any time before late weekend or early next week.

With much courage thanks to so many prayers, I am

Gratefully yours,

Michelle

When I finally got home from the hospital, a mountain of mail from my health insurance carrier awaited. Almost all of it related to extensions of my hospital stay. Everyone kept thinking I'd be going home any day, but the days stretched on and on.

⚓ **Monday, April 1, 2013, 7:41 p.m.**

As I write this post, I do so with enough medication in my system to put down an elephant. Please forgive any typos or misspellings. I continue to do better every day, and the pain is almost completely under control. Although at the moment my back is in spasm and killing me. I'm hoping that writing this post will help keep my mind off the pain until the pain pills kick in.

The doctor still isn't positive what's going on so I just had another CT scan. Interesting tidbit: When they remove half of the lung, the other half expands to fill the space. He thinks mine may not have expanded all the way to the top which could be allowing fluid to build up there.

I can't go home until the air leak stops for one full day. It has slowed down dramatically, but it just won't stop. Through God's grace and lots of prayer (and medication), I am surprisingly content here. I'm just doing what they tell me to do so that I can heal and go home. I also feel like there must be some purpose for my being here for such a long time. I've had some wonderful conversations with the nurses, and I've recently heard of examples where this blog has touched someone in a special way. If I'm able to help even one person, all this extra time will be well worth it.

I had a nice treat earlier today. My friend Gwen stopped by with a wonderfully soft, bright yellow prayer blanket that she and some ladies in her church choir made. The entire choir prayed over the blanket, especially for me. It's a great reminder that I am blanketed in prayer.

I should hear back about the scan sometime tomorrow, so I'll give another update.

Behaving and following doctor's orders,

Michelle

Another gift delivered at a time when I needed it most. I became like the blanket-carrying Peanuts character Linus with that prayer blanket; I kept it with me everywhere I went.

As to the nurses, I enjoyed them immensely. We had the best conversations. I remember one nurse in particular who worked the night shift on weekends because that schedule allowed her to spend more time with her preteen sons. She and I had many late night talks that afforded me the opportunity to share my experiences raising teenage boys and to let her know it doesn't have to be the horror story so many people make it out to be.

Other nurses got engaged while I was there, and I was able to tell them about my long and happy marriage and my parents' even longer one. With others, I talked about everything from dogs to faith. I know the nurses were a blessing to me, and I hope I blessed them. That may be the reason for my extended hospital stay, but I'll never be sure this side of heaven.

⚓ Wednesday, April 3, 2013, 10:01 a.m.

Just a very short note to let you know that I have to go back in for more surgery. Originally they said this afternoon, but now they say they're coming to get me soon. More details later.

Love,

Michelle

Knowing the pain that resulted from the last lung surgery, I was less than eager to undergo the same procedure yet again. I had made my peace with it, though, and wasn't afraid. Even when they showed up hours sooner than expected, I was just glad to get on with it.

Why did I stop to post on CaringBridge mere minutes before they whisked me off to surgery? It certainly wasn't because I had breaking news to share with the public. I shared it because I wanted people to be praying for me.

"Four things let us ever keep in mind: God hears prayer, God heeds prayer, God answers prayer and God delivers by prayer." – E. M. Bounds

⚓ Wednesday, April 3, 2013, 3:22 p.m.

I want to thank everyone for your prayers during this critical time on what was a major surgery. The name of the procedure is a thoracotomy with decortication. Translation, it was similar to the surgery that Michelle just had, only this time it was to fix her lung that had not totally expanded. When a lobe of the lung is removed the remaining portion of lung expands to fill the void left behind, and hers had not completely expanded. This should take care of the fluid and air leaking problem.

Michelle is currently in recovery and doing fine. Dr. Harville feels good about her surgery and says that based on her last CT scan there was no other option. Michelle will be in ICU for a day or two and then will be in a step down version of ICU. Her stay will be at least a week if everything goes according to plan. I have total faith that God is in control. This setback is for a reason. Our spirits are high as we are blessed with loving friends and family whose tremendous support and prayers help sustain us.

- David

I woke up from surgery with a breathing tube down my throat. The 30 minutes I had to wait before they could remove the tube were long and uncomfortable. The nurses seemed quite pleased when I was able to muster enough strength to help cough out the tube. I just wanted to get that thing out of there.

As David said, we were blessed with a tremendous amount of love and support. We also felt the many prayers going up on our behalf. Hard

⚓ **Saturday, April 6, 2013, 8:17 p.m.**

I hate to bother everyone so late but please pray for Michelle. She is currently in acute renal failure. I will know more tomorrow after I speak to her kidney doctor.

David

This was a scary time. I knew that acute renal failure was serious business.

As WebMD states, "Acute kidney injury (also called acute renal failure) means that your kidneys have suddenly stopped working. When your kidneys stop working, waste products, fluids and electrolytes build up in your body. This can cause problems that can be deadly."

I'm so glad that David rallied the troops for prayer. I've heard from many, many people who say they were diligently holding me up in prayer during this health crisis.

⚓ **Sunday, April 7, 2013, 10:39 a.m.**

I spoke to Michelle's kidney doctor today and he does not feel her kidney failure is medication related. Her blood pressure has been dangerously low at times with the systolic or top number down as low as 72. The doctor thinks this has shocked her kidneys.

They have taken steps to reverse her kidney failure and her fluid output has improved somewhat. The next 24 hours are critical and hopefully dialysis will not be needed. Michelle is feeling lousy and it is understandable after two major surgeries back to back within 30 days.

Several nurses have told me that thoracotomy procedures are the most painful surgery there is, and after seeing what Michelle has had to endure I believe it. As many of you know it is hard to see someone you love be in such pain, which is why we joyfully take great comfort in your prayers and kindness.

Hopeful and sincere,

David

In my PR job, I write a variety of materials for medical practices. In order to prepare the most effective piece, I typically perform a fair amount of medical research and often talk with doctors about the subject matter. I have written about a wide variety of topics and now possess a little bit of knowledge about many different medical conditions and treatments. I knew enough about dialysis to know it was something I wanted no part of.

To make matters worse, I felt horrible. This was not a fun time for me or my family.

⚓ Monday, April 8, 2013, 7:31 p.m.

I am glad to say that I'm finally bouncing back after my latest surgery. Honestly, though, it's tough to hear the doctor say over and over again, "This is a very rare occurrence, but..." before going on to explain yet another complication they discovered.

I won't go into a multitude of details because at this point the main thing that needs prayer is for my kidneys to begin eliminating toxins. Right now, my outputs are good, but I'm storing up a lot of fluid, most of it toxic. If the situation doesn't improve by tomorrow, I'll have to temporarily go on dialysis to correct the problem.

I know that miracles can and do happen. I thank you for all of your prayers and support. They help!!

Praying for a miracle but trusting God no matter what comes my way,

Michelle

At this point I was glad to be feeling a little bit better, but I also was wondering what might happen next. It felt like the only news I got was bad. This was definitely one of those times when I felt like I was reaching out to God from the depths of a massive pit.

"The cords of Sheol surrounded me; the snares of death confronted me. In my distress I called upon the Lord, and cried to my God for help; He heard my voice out of His temple, and my cry for help before Him came into His ears." Psalm 18:4-6

⚓ Tuesday, April 9, 2013, 8:33 a.m.

"Praise the Lord, oh my soul, and let all that's within me praise His holy name."

Those lyrics, from the song "Praise the Lord" by Kristene Mueller, have been going through my mind since last night. Then this morning, one of my nurses came in and said, "Praise the Lord!" Now that the nephrologist came in and confirmed her report, I am VERY grateful to report that I don't need dialysis! My kidney function has vastly improved. Thanks be to God!

I'm not out of the woods yet, as I still have a lot of leakage from my lung, but Dr. Harville's PA told me that it is to be expected. That to make it better, the surgery would first make it worse. I'm fine with that. I'd rather feel bad for a season and spend extra time in the hospital than leave a dangerous situation in place and be at home.

Please keep up the prayers – for both kidneys and lung. They clearly make a difference.

With much thanks and love,

Michelle

The lyrics to that song were rolling around in my head before I got the good news. As I faced the grim diagnosis of acute kidney failure and all that could accompany that dangerous condition, God gave me the gift of songs in the night and a heart full of praise. It was very reassuring when the nurse came in the next morning echoing those words of praise. The roller coaster ride continued. How wonderful it was to celebrate this trip back up.

"Thou didst draw near when I called on Thee; Thou didst say, 'Do not fear!'" Lamentations 3:57

⚓ **Friday, April 12, 2013, 3:28 p.m.**

It's been too long since I've given an update. For that, I apologize.

I continue to do better every day and feel my strength coming back. The nurses are all amazed at how I'm able to walk up and down the halls without assistance. The nurses, by the way, are great. They really spoil me! They wash my hair because they know I love it so, and they regularly take me out to the courtyard to enjoy the sunshine. Those little things mean a lot and make the stay here much more tolerable.

In fact, I find it amazing – and believe it's a blessing from God and your prayers – that I'm perfectly content to sit here and wait to get well. Ordinarily, I'd be climbing the walls. The pain is mostly under control, but when it's time for my pain meds I can really tell it. Right now, I'm rather uncomfortable.

I am so thankful to be pulling through so many challenges, and I know that I really took for granted that I would have the surgery, hurt a bit, get over it and move on. It hasn't been that easy, but I am beginning to move on, and for that I am so, so grateful.

I know there's a reason for the continued delays, and I trust God to work through them. Thanks for praying for us during this tough time. We could never thank you enough for all the support that has come our way.

With much love,

Michelle

I can't say enough about how wonderful the nurses and certified nurses' assistants were. The shampoos and outdoor excursions really helped boost my spirits, which I know helped the healing process. I laugh now to think about where I went while looking so wretched. One day when the courtyard was closed, we crossed a rather busy street so we could access another outside patio. Now, when I drive down that street, I wonder what I would think if my path were crossed by some wild-haired woman wearing a hospital gown and carrying a chest tube.

The kitchen staff also was very accommodating. Because I can't eat anything with lots of fat or sugar, I often had to order something outside the regular menu. They came up with many good options, including a fresh fruit platter with cottage cheese that was delicious.

⚓ Saturday, April 13, 2013, 6:19 p.m.

"Be still and know that I am God..." Psalm 46:10, NIV

I've had to practice being still a lot these last few years, even more so these past few weeks. For the past hour I've been trying to stay in the exact same position because when I move even the slightest, I can feel the chest tube moving around. It feels like someone has a wrench on my insides, turning it for all they're worth. Fortunately, this doesn't happen often, and right now the pain has passed. I feel pretty good most of the time, especially by staying absolutely on time with my pain medications.

The doctors are all very pleased with the progress with my kidneys. My kidney function and blood counts continue to get better every day, and we're definitely out of the danger zone with the kidneys. However, I do have Fred Flintstone feet and huge, puffy legs! I have never had swollen legs and feet, even when I was pregnant. It's funny to look down and see these puffy appendages sticking out from under the blanket.

While my kidneys improve, the leak in my lung is being stubborn and continues to be a problem. When Dr. Harville stopped by today, he mentioned consulting with Dr. LeMense, a pulmonologist, on Monday to discuss the possibility of doing a procedure to place a valve (or valves) on the tear in my lung to help speed up the healing process.

Of course, I'm all for speeding up the healing process, but I have to be honest and say that the thought of yet another procedure isn't the least bit appealing. I feel like my body has been through quite enough traumas these past few weeks.

So I'm asking that you pray that my lung will heal itself without the need for another procedure and that God be glorified through it all.

Wherever He leads, I'll go. Even if it means another procedure. But it sure would be nice to get where I need to be without one.

Thanks again for your faithful prayers and support!

Safely in His arms,

Michelle

For me, being still is not an easy task, but it is one I definitely had to master during my extended hospital stay. I really hoped I wouldn't need yet another procedure, but I was prepared to do whatever it took to get better.

⚓ Monday, April 15, 2013, 6:52 p.m.

I had another good day today and continue to regain my strength. My lung is doing a little better but is not yet healed. Dr. Harville stopped by a little while ago and said that for now we will continue to watch and wait to see if my lung will repair itself. This made me quite happy!

Thanks so much for your prayers and support, and please keep them up! I know that God can heal my lung in an instant if He chooses. As I mentioned already, I want His will and His timing. It just sure would be nice if they align with my desires.

With much love,

Michelle

I believe Dr. Harville was hoping that my lung would heal as much as I was.

⚓ Wednesday, April 17, 2013, 8:09 p.m.

Onward and forward. Here we go again!

As you know, I was really hoping to forego another procedure, but as it now stands we're going forward with inserting valves to help seal up the leak in my lung. The procedure is scheduled for tomorrow at noon.

When Dr. LeMense, the pulmonologist who is performing the procedure, walked in my room today he said, "Congratulations. You've got the loudest air leak I've ever heard. I heard you from the hall." Dubious honor, indeed. He showed me the valves they will use, which look like a tiny metal bug with very sharp edges. The procedure is conducted through a bronchoscope that goes down my throat – no incision needed! They use small balloons to detect where the lung is leaking and attach the valves to the lung to hold it together until it seals on its own. The entire procedure should only last 30 minutes to an hour.

This is a fairly new procedure; only seven have been done to date. I'm ready to move forward, though, and finally get over all this and get on with living. Please pray that the procedure goes well and that they are able to completely seal up the leak. There is a chance that they could have to go back in to add more valves in a few days if everything doesn't seal up properly after tomorrow. Obviously, we hope that can be avoided.

If all goes well, they will watch me for two or three days, remove the chest tube, and then I'll be ready to go home.

Maintaining the hope,

Michelle

Dr. Gregory LeMense was right about my air leak being loud. While I was exaggerating a bit by calling it Niagara Falls, the machine that removed fluid and air from my lung sounded a lot like an aquarium. After I met with Dr. LeMense, I felt much better about putting in the valves. David, however, was very concerned. I believe it was related to all that had happened with his mother nearly a year before. Her doctors kept assuring David that everything would be fine, but it never was. Dr. Harville seemed a bit depressed by it as well. He entered my room with his shoulders slumped and said, "Couldn't this be happening to any other patient besides *you*?"

At this point we were all beginning to wonder what might happen next.

⚓ Thursday, April 18, 2013, 2:19 p.m.

Just a quick note to let you know that surgery went well. They put in three valves and are very optimistic about success. Since I'm still a bit sedated and connected to lots of stuff, I'm not writing much.

Thanks for your prayers!

Love,

Michelle

The procedure went well, but they weren't able to seal off all the leaks. Dr. LeMense explained that sealing off the fourth leak would have taken up too much lung capacity, so it was better to leave it to heal on its own. Despite the small remaining air leak, I was glad to have another procedure out of the way.

⚓ Friday, April 19, 2013, 2:30 p.m.

I just met with Dr. LeMense, the doctor who put in the valves yesterday. He said my lung sounds really good. There is one small leak, but they think it will seal itself.

Right now, we remain in "watch and wait" mode. The good news is that the doctor said we are in a MUCH better place today than we were yesterday. The Pleur-Evac, the machine that draws fluid and air from my lung and sounded like Niagara Falls, barely makes a peep now. Earlier today I kept checking for a problem with the tubing because I couldn't believe it was so quiet.

Now we're keeping the machine turned off all the time. The next step will be to clamp off the chest tube to make sure my lung functions okay without it. After clearing that hurdle, I'll be headed home. In the words of Dorothy, "There's no place like home!"

Watching and waiting,

Michelle

After the successful air valve procedure, I felt like I was really making progress and was anxiously anticipating that final air leak going away so I could go home.

⚓ Monday, April 22, 2013, 11:38 a.m.

After enjoying a long walk this morning and settling back in my chair to read, I felt quite content. I was simply enjoying the thought that I would soon be nearing the end of this odyssey that began with surgery on March 5.

I started to think about things like finding shoes for Drew's wedding. And getting alterations to my dress, which was a bit too big when I bought it and is now undoubtedly way too big. Not to mention a much needed visit to the salon for a haircut and color. I'm beginning to resemble Cruella De Vil! My thoughts were interrupted when a physician's assistant came in with news. He did the poorest job of conveying information you could ever believe. Before I share his news, I want you to know that it's not nearly as dreadful as he made it sound.

He said, "There's been a development. Remember all the goo they took out of your lung when they did the surgery a few weeks ago?

The cultures just came back and they're showing signs of being positive for TB. You'll have to be in isolation for six to eight weeks."

My nurses came in and said not to worry, that the odds of it being TB were very, very remote and that it likely showed up that way because of the cancer. Wisely, the nurses immediately put in an order for the infectious disease specialist to come talk to me.

Once I talked to the specialist, I was fine. Basically, there is some kind of bacteria growing in the "goo" that came from my lung. They have to watch it for about six to eight weeks to be sure it's not TB, which it likely is not. This discovery in no way changes when I get out of the hospital. It only means that I've been moved to an isolation room and that anyone who comes around me has to wear a mask for precautionary measures. I'll have to go through some sort of treatment with antibiotics and wear a mask when out in public until they determine exactly what the bacteria is.

I won't lie. The original news shook me to the core. I thought I was going to be trapped in the hospital for weeks on end AND miss Drew's wedding. I was hoping to talk to the infectious disease specialist before I talked to any of my family, but my mother called soon after I received the bad news. She prayed the sweetest prayer, "God, we don't understand but we trust you."

I don't understand why every time I feel like I'm moving forward something else comes along, but I do trust God that He is in control.

I am still waiting for the doctors to see me today and do something with this chest tube. They had talked about clamping it off, saying that if I am able to do okay with it clamped off, they could remove it. I'm ready to get that show on the road.

I also know that I can't control any of this except that I must be diligent in following doctor's orders. I am eating (the mostly bad hospital food) so that I get the nourishment I need, taking long walks at every opportunity, and faithfully doing my physical therapy and breathing exercises. My oxygen levels are almost always 100 percent, and all my other vitals are "perfect."

I have gotten so many sweet, sweet cards, and they really lift my spirits. One from a coworker arrived today at the hospital. It quotes Proverbs 18:10: "The name of the Lord is a strong tower, the righteous runs into it and is safe." Amen.

In the safety of the strong tower,

Michelle

Up to this point, I had stayed strong through everything they threw at me. This, however, was the breaking point. I remember sitting there in despair thinking I was going to be stuck in the hospital forever and miss my son's wedding. I may not be one for tears, but this brought lots of them.

Soon after I received the devastating news, a conversation played in my mind. I could almost hear the devil saying to me, "Surely you don't trust God now. Renounce him."

"I won't," I cried.

This back-and-forth continued for a few minutes.

To some it may sound crazy, but I believe real spiritual warfare took place in my room that day. I stood firm, but it was a draining experience.

My next thought was I didn't want to tell my family until we were better able to sort out the details. My mother called only a few minutes later. I hated to dump any more bad news on her. She already had suffered with me through so much, and I think everything bothered her more because she had to mostly stay home to take care of my dad instead of being with me. She took the news like a trouper, though, and her prayer was perfect.

The nurses and CNAs all were so kind. They rallied around me, offered encouraging words and helped move the considerable stockpile of paraphernalia that had accumulated in my regular room to an isolation room up the hall. Once I was inside, the door slammed shut with conviction. Alarms would go off if the door was ajar because of the scare that my disease would infect others.

"For our struggle is not against flesh and blood, but against the rulers, against the powers, against the world forces of this darkness, against the spiritual forces of wickedness in the heavenly places." Ephesians 6:12

⚓ **Thursday, April 25, 2013, 7:14 p.m.**

As I recall, Dorothy had her share of troubles before she finally made it home. Witches, flying monkeys, all kinds of scary things. Yes, I can identify with Dorothy!

At any rate, I am very happy to report that the latest news from my doctor is good. The plan is for me to go home tomorrow or Saturday at the latest. Hooray!!

Unfortunately, my small air leak remains. Because it's being so stubborn about healing, I'm going to go home with the chest tube in place. This morning they were planning to swap out the Pleur-Evac – the giant plastic case that connects to the chest tube and that I carry with me everywhere I go – with a smaller, easier to transport version. However, the order was messed up and they didn't have the right piece of equipment. Ugh!

It was at this point that I had to again take a deep breath, remind myself that God is in control and that there could be a very good reason why the delay was necessary and actually beneficial to me instead of just another nuisance.

Dr. Harville said he hopes the smaller version will come in tomorrow and that they can swap them out and send me home. If the smaller version doesn't come, he thinks he'll just send me home with the giant box and swap it out in his office on Monday. He knows I'm ready to be out of here and is working hard to make that happen. The Saturday departure date was mentioned in case there are any "glitches" tomorrow. Guess Dr. Harville is ready for about anything with me by now!

As to the TB scare, I'm still treated like Typhoid Mary in an isolation room, and I'm taking twice as many antibiotics (about a dozen pills) because they're actually treating me for TB and something else until they know for sure what it is, which should be in about a week. The antibiotics make me feel a little bad, but so far I'm tolerating them okay.

The pulmonologist is of the opinion that the test was a false positive. He said that there were four cultures done and that only one came back positive and that it just doesn't fit in with the bigger picture. Hopefully that is the case and once they discover that, I can stop taking all the antibiotics and be done with it. That'd be wonderful!

Several of you have asked about Drew's wedding date. It is set for May 18. So, I've got to get my act together by then. Hopefully without a chest tube. But chest tube or no chest tube, I plan to be there!

I've gotten so many sweet cards, emails and phone calls. Others have sent food to David and the boys. And I know that there are many, many of you praying for me every day. I am so touched! To all of you, I cannot thank you enough!

This has indeed been a tough battle. It feels good to be getting (hopefully) nearer to the end.

Marching on,

Michelle

The tuberculosis scare was a royal pain. Before the diagnosis, I went on several walks a day that covered virtually the entire hospital. Those walks helped me mentally and physically. After the diagnosis, I had to wear a face mask whenever I ventured outside my room. The nurses and I knew if I really had TB, the horse already was out of the barn. I would have infected most of the hospital before I was ever diagnosed. Nonetheless, protocol mandated that on the rare occasions I was allowed to leave my room, I did so wearing a mask that made it nearly impossible to breathe.

In my old room I enjoyed fairly regular visits with friends and family. Like the walks, they boosted my spirits. Now, warning signs on my door discouraged visitors and required them to don a face mask before entering the room. I told my cousin Tracy, who had been a frequent and fun visitor, not to bother coming over.

All the little things that made my hospitalization bearable were being stripped away one by one. It added insult to injury when a box arrived with what was supposed to contain the chest tube that was my ticket home. The nurse excitedly opened the box only to discover the wrong item had been delivered. We were back to square one on the chest tube. I was weary.

⚓ **Friday, April 26, 2013, 11:32 a.m.**

The hospital staff has moved heaven and earth trying to find the device I need to go home with the chest tube. I just got word that they finally found it, and it is being shipped overnight. I go home tomorrow!

I know tomorrow isn't as good as today, but I'm happy nonetheless. One more day doesn't seem so bad after more than a month.

Thankfully,

Michelle

I was touched and impressed by how hard the hospital staff worked to locate the chest tube, and it felt good to finally see light at the end of the tunnel. I wasn't about to let one small delay bring me down.

⚓ **Saturday, April 27, 2013, 8:52 a.m.**

I hoped that the next post I sent would be telling you that I'm home, but that's not the case – yet. There's nothing major going on, just pesky little details that could potentially delay my departure. I need your prayers!

The new box has not yet arrived by FedEx, although it is supposed to be here today. Also, there is some confusion with the medications I have to take for the TB and how all that's going to work once I'm discharged.

I know that prayer changes things. Please pray that these obstacles will be removed and that I can go home.

Thanks!

Michelle

I was taking no chances this time. I wanted everyone to be praying for good results.

⚓ **Saturday, April 27, 2013, 10:40 a.m.**

The box just arrived! One hurdle out of the way! Praise God!

- Michelle

I can't describe how happy I was to hear the box had arrived. The nurse asked if I wanted to walk with her to pick it up, and I happily tagged along. It was a fairly long walk, made all the more difficult by the stupid mask, but I didn't care. That box meant I was finally going home.

⚓ **Saturday, April 27, 2013, 1:15 p.m.**

They are preparing my discharge papers now. Heading home soon!

Hallelujah! Thanks be to God! Thanks for all your prayers!

One happy girl,

Michelle

Although the discharge process began early in the afternoon, it was late evening before I finally got to leave. There were problems with prescriptions for the antibiotics, and I still needed to have someone switch out my Pleur-Evac. With it being a Saturday, I started to get a little concerned that no one was coming, and I might be stuck in the hospital another day. I was quite pleased when I saw Dr. Harville come through the door. I also was impressed he would take the time on a Saturday evening to handle a mundane task that could have been carried out by a physician's assistant. After all that had gone on with me, he probably was afraid to let anyone else near me.

After I got home, my brother Kevin and some of his boys delivered a delicious meal prepared by my mother. I enjoyed their company and the meal. My mother's cooking is wonderful anyway, but her food tasted especially delicious after eating only hospital food for more than a month.

⚓ **Monday, April 29, 2013, 9:15 a.m.**

It is good to be home! I ended up not getting home until about 7:00 Saturday evening because of delays at the hospital. But I can tell that I'm getting better even in the short time that I've been here.

It is so good to sleep in my own bed and to sleep through the night without having people come in the room to check my vital signs, take blood, give me breathing treatments, and all the other things they bugged me with at the hospital. And with yesterday being such a rainy day, it was the perfect opportunity to catch up on my rest. I slept until 9:00 and then took two naps. Nothing like sleep to restore the body and soul!

As I sit here looking out the window, it amazes me how much time has gone by since I went to the hospital. It was snowing the day I was readmitted to the hospital. Today, I look out and see beautiful shades of green and thriving trees that had been bare. Time indeed marches on.

As I said, I'm doing much better. The only real problem I have is the chest tube. With it still in place I have a hard time getting comfortable, and it's hard to move around because I have to carry the little plastic box with me everywhere I go.

Looking forward to the time that I bloom and blossom again like the trees and plants coming alive before us this beautiful spring.

"Don't you know that day dawns after night, showers displace drought, and spring and summer follow winter? Then have hope! Hope forever, for God will not fail you." – Charles Spurgeon

Please pray that this last remaining air leak will heal so that I can get rid of this chest tube. While you're at it, please also pray that the TB test was a false positive so that I can stop taking a dozen antibiotic pills every day.

Hoping for healing,

Michelle

Being away so long gave me an even greater appreciation for how good it felt to be home, and I could tell I was already doing better just from being there. Those antibiotics, however, really put a damper on

my recovery. In the hospital, they let me take the antibiotics at night because they upset my stomach and made me feel lousy. Taking the pills at bedtime meant I could sleep off the worst of the side effects. Once released, however, government regulations mandated that someone from the Health Department witness me taking them. That meant swallowing the pills at home during the day.

I will say again there's something majestic about spring. Seeing the earth shake off winter and come to life with all its color always reminds me that life comes after death and dawn comes after night. I definitely felt like I was coming back to life after the longest, coldest season I ever had endured.

⚓ Thursday, May 2, 2013, 3:28 p.m.

Can you join me in saying, "Argh!"?

Yesterday, thanks to our dear friends at the Health Department, I was as mad as I've been in years. Today did nothing to change my irritation level. I am dealing with a bureaucracy that seems to have no end, and it's driving me crazy.

As you know, I tested positive for TB at the hospital. Actually, one of four cultures tested positive; the others were negative. Since then, I've been treated like Typhoid Mary, under quarantine and taking loads of medicine; which, by the way, I have to take under the watchful eye of a Health Department employee. (Most TB patients are drug addicts, homeless or previously incarcerated. I understand why they would need to be watched, but really? I can't be trusted to take my medicine?)

Anyway, I was told in the hospital that I would have blood test results back by yesterday and culture results back today and that if they came back negative that would be the end of it.

Yesterday I learned that the blood test results came back negative. (Good news!) However, they also said that until I give them three sputum samples (coughed up stuff) that come back clear I won't be deemed TB-free even if the culture comes back negative. The problem is there isn't anything to cough up. They even gave me a breathing treatment at the hospital that made me cough until I was gagging, and I still couldn't get anything to come up besides the graham cracker I had eaten earlier that day.

As to the culture that was to be ready today, I just learned that they couldn't get a definitive result. So, they are trying again to culture the sample. Who knows when that will be done.

It seems I'm locked on some kind of crazy merry-go-round that won't stop. I keep hearing benchmarks to the end, and they keep changing the rules and moving the finish line. And the requirements seem increasingly impossible to meet. To say that I am frustrated would be an understatement. I have an appointment Thursday morning with the Health Department doctor who makes the final decision as to when I'm released. I hope that goes well.

Yes, I know this isn't one of my positive, upbeat posts, but it does feel good to vent!

Actually, I can't help myself. I will be a bit positive. I am feeling really good and still see improvement every day. So, overall, things are improving and for that I am very thankful. Now, if we can just get the Health Department to make some sense!

Frustrated but keeping the faith,

Michelle

I've heard it said that adversity doesn't build character it reveals it. I'm ashamed to say my shortcomings and sinful nature were all too transparent in several of my dealings with the Health Department. On the day I got so mad, problems started before the health care worker ever arrived.

The lady delivering my medicine was filling in for the man who usually came by, and she had trouble finding our house. Once she got on our street, she called to say that she wasn't sure which house was ours. Even though I told her we were at the very end of the cul-de-sac, I could clearly see her parked in front of a neighbor's house down the street. As I talked to her on the phone, I stood on the front porch and waved. It wasn't easy to be moving around, so I was out of breath, sore and irritated by the time I managed to flag her down.

Once she came inside, I noticed the lady's uniform was filthy; it looked like it came from the bottom of a garbage can. It was wrong and judgmental, but based on my initial impressions, I deemed her to be stupid and lazy. That impression no doubt impaired my ability to graciously handle the news about the sputum samples. I told her it was the most ridiculous thing I had ever heard and I was sick to death of dealing with all of it. I didn't scream, but I was clearly angry and she knew it. When I later told my mother that the lady looked scared even though I never raised my voice, Mom said, "Yes, but you were probably giving her your look; that look speaks volumes on its own."

It's not often that I get mad, and I never feel better after losing my temper. In this instance, I expended far too much energy being angry when I should have been focusing all my efforts on getting better. Worse yet, I was brutal and unloving in my critique of the health care worker. As a friend asked, "How would Jesus have reacted to this woman and her clothes?" I know the answer. Jesus would have loved her. As a Christian, I have been called to love her as well. I know I mess up often and sometimes royally. Thankfully, I also know that I am forgiven.

"If we confess our sins, He is faithful and righteous to forgive us our sins and to cleanse us from all unrighteousness." I John 1:8

⚓ Monday, May 6, 2013, 1:37 p.m.

Things are looking up!

I saw Dr. Harville today, and he thinks my air leak is getting a lot better. Still not gone, but I'll take better. And, while he thinks it could be a few weeks before the chest tube can come out, he has a way to use a different device the weekend of the wedding so that I don't have to go to the wedding with the Pleur-Evac. Hooray!

Next up is an appointment with the Health Department infectious disease doctor on Thursday morning. Here's hoping that goes as well – or even better – than today's appointment!

Thanks for your continued prayers and support!

Love,

Michelle

It was refreshing to get good news from Dr. Harville, and I was so relieved to learn there was a solution for dealing with the chest tube. My sister joked she could bedazzle my Pleur-Evac for the big day, but it wouldn't have been funny if I had to carry around a big plastic box connected to a long tube at the wedding.

⚓ Thursday, May 9, 2013, 9:45 a.m.

I had my appointment with the doctor at the Health Department this morning, and it's a good news/bad news kind of situation. Should I have expected less?

The good news is that every test they've done so far has indicated that I don't have TB. This has provided enough proof to get me out of isolation. Hooray!

The bad news is that the culture they are growing has not yet grown out enough for them to get a definitive answer on whether or not I have TB. So, I still have to take all the antibiotics. Boo!

As I said to David when we left the Health Department, all my progress is in baby steps. It's hard being patient, but that's what I'm going to have to do. I'm sure there are many lessons for me to learn here, and I'll be a better person for it in the end.

Thanks for your continued prayers and support!

Free at last,

Michelle

Things were looking up. This latest news about no longer being in isolation meant I could finally schedule an appointment to get my hair done, and I wouldn't have to wear a face mask to the wedding.

⚓ Friday, May 10, 2013, 2:20 p.m.

"Is anyone among you suffering? Let him pray. Is anyone cheerful? Let him sing praises. Is anyone among you sick? Let him call for the elders of the church, and let them pray over him, anointing him with oil in the name of the Lord." James 5:13

After the TB diagnosis in the hospital, my mother mentioned this verse and said maybe I should consider being prayed over and anointed with oil. I agreed that it seemed like a good idea and wondered why I hadn't thought of it sooner.

At any rate, yesterday David and I went out to Sevier Heights Baptist Church, the church we've been visiting for some time. Five pastors anointed me with oil and prayed over me. It was a beautiful and uplifting experience. To make it more special, one of the pastors mentioned that the oil he was using came from Israel and was given to him by a dear friend who died of cancer. As it turns out, his dear friend was Breck Ellison, a longtime family friend. Breck's widow, Gail, remains close to our family.

I asked specifically that the pastors pray for my air leak to heal and for the TB culture to grow to the point that we could get an accurate diagnosis. I left thinking that I was already at peace with things happening slowly, and that God would heal me in His time not mine. I certainly didn't want to think of the prayer time as trying to "twist God's arm" into moving at my pace. I was ready to wait.

Imagine my shock when I got a message just now saying that the culture came back and I don't have TB! Praise God! Even though I was fully prepared to wait weeks for the diagnosis, here it is. I am so very thankful!

And, my air leak seems to be improving. I can still tell I have a small leak when I cough, but it seems to be lessening. Who knows when it will completely seal, but I thank God for the progress that has happened to date.

"O taste and see that the Lord is good; How blessed is the man who takes refuge in Him!" - Psalm 34:8

Praising Him,

Michelle

The many weeks leading up to this point were dark to say the least. Just writing about the period beginning with the March 5 surgery was painful and depressing. After reading back through all the dismal news, I was tempted to sneak in some humor somewhere to lighten up those bleak pages. I realize now that the darkness of those days is the reality of that time, and it would diminish my story to try making it more palatable or an easier read.

I also realize I arrived at church that day pretty much a broken woman. I was physically and emotionally exhausted and on the verge of tears the entire time we were there. When one of the pastors asked how my faith was doing through all of this, I told him it was strong. He said that he could see it in my eyes, which was good to know. I knew I had faith, but I looked and felt so dreadful I wasn't sure what I was projecting to others at this point.

When David and I left to go home, I was relieved and hopeful. Knowing the anointing oil came from Breck Ellison made the entire experience even more memorable. I really didn't expect any kind of immediate results, but I knew I had been obedient when God called me to have this anointing, and that was enough.

⚓ Monday, May 13, 2013, 2:06 p.m.

My baby steps forward continue. I had a good visit at Dr. Harville's office today. The leak is getting better, but it is still there. Dr. Harville said that ordinarily he'd consider taking steps to move toward removing the chest tube this week. Since Drew's wedding is this weekend, however, we don't want to run the risk of anything going wrong and keeping me from being there. (Please pray that rain stays away on Saturday evening. Their reception is outside in some gardens!)

We agreed to leave the tube in place and go with the different valve as we discussed last week. At least I won't have a long tube and box at the wedding!

If all goes well, I should have the chest tube removed next week or the week after. Once the tube is out, I should feel a lot better.

Thankful to be moving forward,

Michelle

I don't typically visit websites that include forums where people share their experiences with cancer and surgery because I inevitably end up comparing myself to others or thinking about potential problems – neither of which is good. The other day, however, I landed on one of those websites when I was looking up something about the spasms I had following lung surgery.

I noted a few people mentioned having more pain where their chest tube had been than at the incision site. Until I read that, I wondered why I had so much pain running up my left side. I now realize the pain follows the same path where the chest tube resided all those weeks. Also, I had chest tubes inserted on three different occasions over those months. It stands to reason I'd be sore.

The new chest tube valve was a plastic device that was about the size and shape of a hot dog. They taped a surgeon's glove over the end of it to catch any fluid that came from my lung. It looked like a blue rooster hanging from my side, but at least it could be hidden underneath my clothes.

In another sign that God cares about the little things, months before the wedding I bought a dress online at Macy's. I'm more of a last-minute person, so it was very unusual for me to have planned ahead and made this purchase. When I went to have the dress altered, the lady making the alterations said I couldn't have chosen a better dress to hide the tubing. Not only did I have a dress, I had the perfect dress for my needs. Finding that dress while randomly surfing the Internet seemed like a fluke. I now think it was God's way of providing for a need before I knew the need existed.

"… for your Father knows what you need before you ask Him."
Matthew 6:8

⚓ **Monday, May 20, 2013, 7:23 p.m.**

Saturday's wedding was a very special day, and I am so very grateful to have been there. It was touching to see the love that Drew and Sam (short for Samantha) have for each other and for the Lord. Their future together is indeed bright.

Rain prevented a garden wedding reception, but we implemented Plan B and everything went wonderfully. The bride kept a good attitude and said if only she could get some wedding photos in the gardens she would be happy. The rain broke long enough for them to get photos in the gardens, which I know will be fabulous! I'll share a few when I have them.

I felt pretty good for the wedding, although I was a little sore from switching out my usual box and tube with the valve. It was worth the pain to avoid dragging around that contraption all night. By Sunday the tube readjusted, and the pain went away.

I saw Dr. Harville today, and we are definitely making progress. I currently have the tube clamped off, which is the same as if it were removed. I go tomorrow for a chest X-ray to make sure everything looks okay with the tube clamped. If so, we'll be able to take it out this week. Hooray!!

Words can't describe how good it feels to be nearing the end of this odyssey. I'm going to be patient, though, and continue to move slowly and behave. I sure don't want to go backwards at this point. I said the other day that this is the "new me." I now accept help when it's offered and admit when I can't do things. Another lesson learned, and a valuable one at that. I'll try to make the change permanent.

To God be the glory, great things He hath done!

Looking forward to being tube-free,

Michelle

The wedding was a wonderful time of celebration with friends and family. The pastor who conducted the ceremony did an excellent job of telling the story of Drew and Sam's love for each other and their commitment to God. The Laurel Theater was an ideal venue for the wedding and reception, and I was so glad Drew had the foresight to insist on a Plan B. I also was thankful they were able to get some photos in the gardens. Like the bride, those photos are stunning.

Drew and Sam celebrated their one-year anniversary on May 18, 2014. They are happy and doing well. Sam recently graduated with her master's degree, and they moved a few hours away so she could take a job with Young Life. Even though I hated to see them leave, I want them to be where God wants them. And I'd rather Drew be married to Sam and living three hours away than be with the wrong woman even if they stayed in Knoxville.

⚓ **Thursday, May 23, 2013, 3:27 p.m.**

My baby steps are finally paying off. Earlier today, they pulled out my chest tube. Hooray!

I feel so much better already, and I had a much easier time driving home. With the chest tube in, it hurt every time I turned my head to check for traffic or if I moved around much at all.

Not to worry, though. My newfound freedom doesn't mean I'm going to go crazy. I'm taking next week off, and after that the doctor has cleared me to work two to three hours a day. I'll start slowly and build up from there.

I went to an Executive Women's Association meeting yesterday. It was so good to see everybody and have an opportunity to thank the members for their amazing support. But I have to admit, it wore me out. I had to take a rather long nap yesterday afternoon. Believe me when I say I'm well aware of my limits.

Looking ahead, I know that I'm still not out of the woods. I have lots of doctor's appointments coming up and will need another procedure to remove the valves they inserted to seal up the air leaks. But for now I think I'll focus on the positive and say, "Free at last, free at last!"

Thanks so much for your continued prayers and support.

"Even when our situation appears to be impossible, our work is to hope in God. Our hope will not be in vain, and in the Lord's own timing help will come." – George Mueller

Glad to be tube-free,

Michelle

    I have to brag on the ladies of Executive Women's Association. The organization has more than 150 members, all of whom are top female executives. These busy professionals have been amazing in the love and support they've poured on me throughout my sickness. They have showered me with cards and emails, visited me in the hospital, brought food by my house and carried out my job duties while I was hospitalized. I can't say enough how much their support has meant to me.

    It was good to have that chest tube removed. I have to admit I was a little leery before they pulled it. I realized there was a possibility my lung could collapse once the tube was removed, and I'd be back to where I was before. Fortunately, that didn't happen.

⚓ Thursday, May 30, 2013, 10:51 a.m.

It's been a while since I last posted, so I'll give a brief update. On Tuesday I saw Dr. LeMense, the doctor who put in the valves to stop my air leaks. When he walked in the room he feigned shock and said with a laugh, "You look human!" As if I needed any reminders of how bad I looked when I was in the hospital.

At any rate, he and I both agreed that we should err on the side of caution, so I'm going to see him again in six weeks to discuss taking out the valves. Given the fact that the other air leak never fully healed, I'm in no hurry to remove the valves that we know are keeping my lung intact.

The doctor explained that an air leak is not a problem so long as it doesn't cause the lung to collapse. That's why we were able to remove the chest tube even though I still had a small air leak. When the chest tube was clamped off, my lung didn't collapse, letting the doctor know that the lung had scarred and healed enough to hold it in place. We're hoping the same is true for the spots where the valves are. In case you're wondering, the valves have to be removed because they make it harder for me to breathe and can sometimes cause infection or bleeding.

At my appointment, I asked the doctor several questions about how much pain I still have and how much activity I should be doing. He said, "Remember. You had two major surgeries very close together, you had the valves put in, and you spent a long time in the hospital. This is going to take some time to get over." He then added with a grin, "You don't do anything halfway, do you?" The good news is that I am getting better, albeit at a slower pace than I would like.

I have managed to walk to the end of my street the last two nights. I hope to increase it to two times up and down the street soon and move up from there. My instructions for activity are to use common sense. Stop if something hurts but do as much as I feel like doing.

One good thing about my recovery time is that in slowing me down it has allowed me time to catch up with some dear friends. I just had the best conversation with Mary Miller, a friend from way back. I haven't talked to her in years. I've also noticed that other phone conversations are longer than typical for me. I usually use the phone like a walkie talkie, say what needs to be said and hang up.

I said just yesterday that I'll try to strike a better balance between work, rest and play when I go back to work full-time. It's easy to say but so hard to do. We'll see how it works out.

That's about it for now. I have an appointment with my oncologist later in June, where I'll learn more about where my cancer stands. Dr. Harville said that they didn't find any cancer in my lymph nodes, which was very good news. Now we'll just have to see if the tiny spot on my right lung is causing any problems.

Thanks for your continued prayers and concern. The more I talk to people the more I realize that we all have so many obstacles to face in our lives and there are so many pressing prayer concerns. I am honored and humbled to remain on so many prayer lists.

Keeping the faith,

Michelle

When I started out on that short walk down our road, I thought about the marathon our city hosts each year. I remembered several individuals who said they went from being total couch potatoes to competing in that marathon. Those runners shared a common thread – they all had to start somewhere, and their journey began with the first step. Thus inspired, I took my first steps down our road. Each time I would get to the end of our street, I would look longingly up the giant hill that I had previously climbed with such ease. "I'll get you one of these days," I promised the hill.

When I eventually graduated from our road, I took the easier and flatter route that led to the entrance of our subdivision. While I longed to make that uphill climb, the new route proved quite enjoyable because it allowed me to meet some neighbors whose paths I had not previously crossed.

I don't know if it was the result of my obvious vulnerability or because I so openly shared my trials on CaringBridge, but during this time many people approached me with some very pressing prayer concerns. There were times when I felt almost guilty that people were praying for me when there was so much hurt in the world. When I thought about it realistically, though, I knew God is bigger than that. We should never limit our prayers based on some misguided notion that we might ask God for too much or that an answer to our prayer might prevent someone else's prayer from being answered.

⚓ **Sunday, June 9, 2013, 1:55 p.m.**

For those of you who have followed my blog for a long time, you may remember Fergie, the evil dog we got for my parents. She bit everybody she came around and we had to give her back.

Well, we had another "swing and a miss" in the dog world this weekend. While I was in the hospital, David and I started talking about getting another dog. My cousin Tracy knew some people who were thinking about giving away their Sheepdog because they didn't have enough time to spend with her.

We saw an adorable picture and soon made plans to try her out. I was really excited. This dog didn't bite anybody and was as sweet as advertised, but something about her made my allergies flare up uncontrollably. With my lung compromised as it is, a major allergy attack is not a good thing. We realized within hours of bringing her home that we had to get the dog out of the house, so back she went.

I spent all day yesterday in bed coughing my head off. I felt pretty lousy. I'm clearing up today and seem to be getting over it.

This was yet another wakeup call that I'm far from "back to normal" and that I'll have to be extremely cautious about everything I do.

I did start working about two hours a day last week. It felt good to be back in the office. I plan to up the hours a bit this week and next and perhaps be back to regular hours by the last week of June. Not to worry, though. If I have to go slower than that I am fully prepared to do so. This is one survivor who'd prefer no more setbacks!

Thanks again for your continued prayers and support!

Thankful to be breathing better,

Michelle

During dark times, it often helps to have something positive to look forward to. I believe that was the impetus behind our discussions about getting a dog while I was in the hospital. It really made little sense to consider getting something to take care of when I was in no shape to even take care of myself, but it was fun to look at dogs and dream of a new furry companion. When Tracy mentioned the Sheepdog, it seemed like a great idea.

My allergies began to kick in soon after I met this sweet, pony-sized dog, but I didn't pay attention. Not long after getting her home, however, there was no denying she was causing problems. I couldn't stop coughing and had difficulty breathing. That episode was probably a good thing because it did an excellent job of reminding me I was still recovering and needed to take it easy. Even now, I still can tell I'm not back to normal. I tire much easier than I used to, and I have to be careful not to do too much.

⚓ **Wednesday, June 19, 2013, 8:49 p.m.**

"Our Christian hope is that we're going to live with Christ in a new earth, where there is not only no more death, but where life is what it was always meant to be." – Timothy Keller

This quote was in today's devotional from *Jesus Today*, and I just loved it. That's the hope I was thinking of when I chose HOPE as the title of my blog. Not necessarily the hope that I'd be cured and all would be well here on Earth, but that ultimately I will be healed and all will be well for eternity.

I continue to improve every day. I've seen lots of doctors since my last post, and they are encouraged at how well I'm progressing.

I saw the infectious disease doctor last week. She said I have Mycobacterium avium complex (MAC) lung disease, which is why I had the original misdiagnosis of TB. Treatment involves lots of antibiotics, but not as many as I was taking for my supposed case of TB. As fate would have it, the very afternoon I saw the doctor I also had lunch with Lisa Shouse, a good friend who has had the same disease. She gave me lots of good information and advice. Rather than immediately start taking the medicine, I decided to first talk to Drs. Harville and Antonucci. I just didn't completely trust the infectious disease folks after all that happened before.

I saw Dr. Harville, my surgeon, on Monday. He said my chest X-ray looked by far the best it's looked since the first surgery. While there, I asked about some odd lumps in the area between my ribs. He said the lumps are caused by air that's accumulating there. His nurse said some patients have air leak up to their faces, causing them to swell and crack. Ugh! I'll take air in my midsection over air in my face any day!

Dr. Harville also talked about the possibility of more surgery on my other lung but said he'd defer to Dr. Antonucci, my oncologist, on how to proceed. Finally, he referred me to physical therapy to try to address the significant pain I have in my shoulder.

I saw Dr. Antonucci yesterday. As always, he was very thorough and full of good advice. He said I probably got MAC lung disease while my immune system was compromised from chemotherapy. He's had other patients with the same problem. He also said the disease is likely what caused a lot of the post-surgical issues. He advised I take the medicine and treat the disease. Since I totally trust his opinion, I'm going to start taking the dreaded antibiotics and hope they don't make me feel too bad.

On the positive side, Dr. Antonucci said that, considering all that went wrong with the prior lung surgery, he just wants to wait and watch for now. He added the CEA counts (cancer markers in my blood) will be a really good tool for watching because they reacted very strongly last time when there wasn't a lot of cancer activity.

I agree with Dr. Antonucci that waiting on surgery is the best course of action. I'll have more surgery if and when it's needed, but I'm in absolutely no hurry to have anybody messing with my lungs.

This update turned out to be much longer than I anticipated. I'll close by saying I've been cleared to work up to six hours a day and am very thankful to feel up to getting back in the groove of things.

As always, thanks for caring!

Bouncing back,

Michelle

How easy it is to get discouraged in today's world. From problematic people to economic hardship, disease, disaster or even death, there are so many things that make us long for better days. When my friend and colleague Bob Wilson recently died, I commented that I was sad, not sad for Bob because I knew he was in a far better place, but sad for those he left behind, particularly his wife and daughter who lost someone so dear.

When I think about my own death, which I realize may come sooner than my friends and family would like, I am encouraged by the fact that I will have no more pain. At the same time, I am bothered by the thought of leaving them to suffer pain at my passing. It is one of those areas where I have to let go and trust God. For all I know, He plans for me to live to be 100. If not, I hope it is a comfort for others to know that a glorious, eternal and pain-free future awaits everyone who accepts God's free gift of salvation.

"And He shall wipe away every tear from their eyes; and there shall no longer be any death; there shall no longer be any mourning, or crying, or pain…" Revelation 21:4

⚓ Wednesday, June 26, 2013, 9:08 p.m.

I got a phone call with good news today, and I just have to share it! My oncologist's office called with the results of the test that detects cancer markers in my blood. My CEA count was 0.3 – down from the 20s before I had surgery. Normal is anything 5 or below.

When I saw the doctor last week, he said he wouldn't be alarmed even if the counts were still high because my body has been through so many traumas, which makes the news even better! It means the surgery was successful, and the other tumor in my right lung isn't causing any problems at the moment. Now, I am able to sit back and relax a bit. I would say I can sit back and breathe, but breathing is still a bit of an issue for me. David now calls me Wheezy, after the asthmatic penguin in "Toy Story."

Despite my labored breathing, all continues to go well. I started working full-time this week. So far, so good. I also went to physical therapy Monday. I have frozen shoulder and a couple of other maladies that are common in people who have had lung surgery. I start actual therapy Monday. They said it will probably take six to eight weeks to see any real improvement, but it's not a problem. By now, I'm used to waiting.

I continue to be uplifted and amazed at all the love and support that comes my way. I feel your care and prayers every day!

Wheezy but well,

Michelle

Since the surgery, I am like a walking air quality sensor, able to detect even the slightest problem with the air I'm breathing. Earlier today, I was at my mom's house while a workman was cutting through some marble. Even though he was several rooms away and there was no visible dust in the air, I wound up coughing and struggling to breathe. I get the same way if I'm around any kind of smoke or if the air is particularly humid or dry. When you get down to it, I have trouble breathing most of the time, likely because of the past surgeries and the fact I still have tumors in my right lung. Looking on the bright side, at least I'm still breathing.

⚓ Monday, July 8, 2013, 8:03 p.m.

I remember a sermon I once heard on pain. The pastor said there are times when pain can be good. As an illustration, he talked about how people who are paralyzed can seriously injure themselves without realizing it because they don't feel pain.

I guess I thought about that sermon in light of what I'm currently going through. Today marked week two of physical therapy. It's excruciating. I have places on my left side that hurt to barely touch. To treat those tender areas, they're doing something called Astym therapy. It involves taking an instrument that looks kind of like a shoe horn and running it up and down my whole side and around my shoulder blade. Fun stuff.

Also, I'm in week two or three of the dreaded antibiotics for MAC lung disease. They're fun, too. My stomach, which isn't in great shape anyway, isn't pleased with the introduction of antibiotics. And on Saturday I ended up in bed all day with a migraine. I'm now taking a daily probiotic in hopes of calming my stomach. As to the migraine, the pharmacist recommended I drink lots of water and be sure to eat something when I take the antibiotics. And there's always the hope that the migraine was random and had nothing to do with the medicine.

My mother said my body is probably saying, "What are you doing to me now?!!" She's right. It seems like every time I start to get back on my feet something else takes a swing at me.

But I know these temporary discomforts will bring about a better long-term solution just like the temporary discomforts of chemo, radiation and the surgeries. Already I'm noticing a bit of improvement on the physical therapy front. It didn't hurt quite as much today as it did last week, and the therapist said she already sees some improvement in my mobility.

I told the therapist about a dream I had the other night. In it, I dived in an ocean and swam and swam. When I came up for air I excitedly said, "My physical therapy worked! That didn't hurt a bit!" She said she liked that positive attitude. I like the fact that while I may not be able to dive in and swim right now, I can still enjoy it in my dreams and look forward to the day when I am well enough to be as active as I like.

As I've mentioned before, I talk to so many people who have so much pain in their lives. Not always physical, but painful nonetheless. With that in mind, I'll close by sharing a verse that really speaks to me:

> Therefore we do not lose heart, but though our outer man is decaying, yet our inner man is being renewed day by day.
>
> For momentary, light affliction is producing for us an eternal weight of glory far beyond all comparison, while we look not at the things which are seen, but at the things which are not seen; for the things which are seen are temporal, but the things which are not seen are eternal.
>
> 2 Corinthians 4:16-18

Praising Him through the pain,

Michelle

This was again one of those times when I felt like I was going three steps forward, two steps back. Every time I seemed to move ahead, something would knock me back again.

When I think about all the pain I endured and how so much of it was necessary to get better, I am reminded there are many times when we need to face something painful in order to achieve healing. My frozen shoulder was the result of my reluctance to move my left arm after surgery. It hurt to move my arm, so I just stopped moving it. It was a natural response to avoid pain, but it only ended up making the pain that much worse.

In a broader sense, I believe far too many relationships are fractured because people tiptoe around a problem rather than enduring the temporary pain that comes from bringing it out in the open. I'm not suggesting we go around throwing hand grenades at every situation, but there are times when an honest, productive discussion is in order. I'm a peacemaker, and I much prefer that things be calm and that people be happy. There have been times, however, when out of love and respect for the relationship, I've had some tough conversations with David, my sons or others.

⚓ Tuesday, July 16, 2013, 7:35 p.m.

In my last post I said that pain can be good. Turns out I'm putting that theory to the ultimate test.

The Astym treatments, which were bad enough on their own, were only the beginning. Now that I've built up some tolerance to those, they've added a fun little technique called "dry needling."

Dry needling involves inserting very long needles into the muscles that are knotted up. Apparently, when the muscles go into spasm and twitch that is good because they will eventually begin to loosen. At one point my muscle twitched so hard it bent the needle. I nearly came off the table. If I had any military secrets, I would have gladly shared them at that point.

When they finally finished, I was covered with sweat and feeling a bit sick. I was so sore I could barely drive home. The good news is I recovered enough to go on a walk later yesterday evening, and I'm not nearly as sore today as I feared I would be.

Another fear – that the antibiotics would make me very sick – does not seem to be coming to pass. I can't say I feel spectacular taking so many antibiotics, but I haven't had any more migraines, and my stomach isn't as messed up as it was in the beginning.

All in all, I'm doing very well. I continue to gain strength every day, and I still hear from more than one person a day that they're praying for me. In a sermon Sunday the pastor said something along the lines of, "You can pay me no greater kindness than to keep me in your prayers." Amen to that! I continue to be humbled and honored that so many people care enough to keep me in their continued prayers. As I often say, those prayers carry me through every day.

Feeling the power of your prayers,

Michelle

Pain was definitely a big part of my life following lung surgery. There's not much good I can say about it, although I can say I now feel like I can face about anything. Each time you endure more pain than seems humanly possible, you are strengthened for whatever battles lie ahead. Tremendous pain and setbacks also help keep things in perspective. If you've climbed Mount Everest, you're less inclined to make a mountain out of a molehill.

⚓ Wednesday, July 24, 2013, 6:50 p.m.

In last week's post I regaled you with tales about my physical therapy exploits. I'm happy to report that they added no new torture techniques to my treatment this week. In fact, while today's therapy session hurt, it wasn't nearly as painful as others have been. And my range of motion is improving. While they still make frequent comments like, "Wow. Look at this! No wonder she hurts," all in all things on the physical therapy front are beginning to look up.

I saw Dr. LeMense, the lung doctor, yesterday. He's ready to remove the valves. Yes, the valves they had to put in to stop my lung from leaking. I was a little apprehensive at first, but he changed my mind by telling me three things:

1. The longer the valves are in place, the riskier it is to remove them.
2. When the valves come out, my breathing should greatly improve.
3. He's going to biopsy my lung and do another culture to see if I really have MAC lung disease. He doesn't think I do. If the culture comes back negative, I'll be able to stop taking all those nasty antibiotics.

As soon as he told me that, I said, "Sold! Sign me up for the procedure." I'm going in Monday morning to have the valves removed. It's a simple outpatient procedure with no cutting involved. Everything is done through a bronchoscope that goes down my throat. The only concern is that if the leaks aren't healed I could end up with another collapsed lung. We don't think that will happen. Please pray that it doesn't.

Monday night I'm doing a radio interview for a Christian radio station in California. (Thank you, Lynn Bennett, for suggesting me for the show!) I look forward to the opportunity to share the good news about all that's happened through my journey and hopefully give some of the listeners a renewed sense of hope. I know I haven't come this far for nothing, and I really want to use my story to help others.

On Tuesday, David and I celebrate our 30th anniversary. I can't imagine life without him and can't say enough about the support he's given me as I've struggled with this illness. I am blessed. Blessed to have a great husband, family and friends, and blessed to still be here to enjoy them.

Healing a little more each day,

Michelle

People thought I was crazy to agree to a radio interview the night of my procedure, but it went well. I enjoyed the opportunity to share my story and give God the glory for what He has done in my life. I hope this book brings even more of those opportunities.

⚓ Monday, July 29, 2013, 3:15 p.m.

Good news! The procedure went fine, and all is well. Thanks for all the prayers – I could really feel them! When time was nearing for the procedure, the nurses said they were going to give me some "I don't care juice." One of them said, "She looks like she's already had it." Then, they all remarked how calm I was. It's true. I had no worries going in for the procedure. So, thank you!

Disclaimer: This post may contain grammatical errors or typos. I'm still a little groggy from the sedation, and because I'm too lazy to get my glasses, I'm not seeing all that well either.

Groggy but good,

Michelle

By the time of this procedure, I was practically a celebrity at Fort Sanders Regional Medical Center. In addition to having spent an inordinately long time there, I also had to go back weekly for chest X-rays and then again for this procedure to remove the valves.

The first few times I went for X-rays, I could barely function. By the time I traversed the distance to the check-in desk, I was out of breath and in desperate need of a wheelchair. The patient services representatives soon got to know me, and they often commented on how good it was to see me getting a little healthier each week. We had friendly chats about our faith, families and all kinds of things.

The staff members who took my chest X-rays also were very friendly. While I was hospitalized, they came in each morning to snap an image. The same lady would enter my room each day with a pleasant and booming, "Good morning, Mrs. Henry!" When I was finally out of the hospital and came back for another X-ray, she said she had been thinking about me and was glad I was doing better.

When I went in to have the valves removed some of the nurses and technicians remembered me from the prior bronchoscopies. In addition to commenting on my calm demeanor, they said it sure was good to see me looking so much healthier than I did when they last saw me. I knew I was in bad shape and looked dreadful following the lung surgeries, but I was reminded just how bad I looked every time people were so amazed to see me looking so much better.

As to my calm demeanor prior to the procedure, I am convinced the many prayers that went up on my behalf helped allay any fears and carried me gently through that day.

⚓ Thursday, August 8, 2013, 8:05 p.m.

Have you ever heard of someone being kicked out of physical therapy? Now you have. Actually, to say that I've failed physical therapy is a little premature, but I'm dangerously close.

When I saw the therapist Monday, he was concerned my shoulder may be so frozen that no amount of therapy will do any good at this point. He said if that's the case it's not fair to put me through so much pain when it isn't going to help. He based that concern on measurements they take of my range of motion, which seem to be stuck. I suggested the problem stemmed from having the procedure to remove the valves from my lung. I could tell that my muscles were a lot tighter right after that procedure.

At any rate, since I had a little bit more motion when they measured yesterday, we're going to give it another week before I get the boot. If I do get kicked out, I'll be sent home with exercises to maintain the range of motion I've achieved and wait for my body to heal more before trying more physical therapy. That could take at least nine months.

I can't say that I would miss the torture sessions, but I am ready to just get on with it and get better. Another option is to have surgery to correct the problem, but there's no way I'm having surgery for my shoulder. I've spent enough time on the operating table.

On a positive note, I can tell I'm breathing better since the valves were removed. I even expect to soon be walking up the big hill in my subdivision instead of taking the easier, flatter route I've been taking of late. Don't worry. I won't overdo.

I see my oncologist next week. I don't expect any breaking news from that visit, but I'll be sure to share an update if there's anything to report.

Thanks for continuing to care.

The physical therapy failure,

Michelle

I appreciated the physical therapist's honesty. Knowing that my insurance was covering all of my expenses, he could have kept me coming even though it wasn't going to do any good.

⚓ **Thursday, August 15, 2013, 8:59 p.m.**

Look away – I'm hideous. Okay, maybe that's a bit of an exaggeration, but there is something going on with my face. Over the weekend I noticed some small blisters on the side of my nose. They later merged into a dime sized sore. When I saw Dr. Antonucci on Tuesday, he thought it might be due to the massive amounts of antibiotics I'm taking.

Now, the left side of my face is swollen, I have three more spots over my lip that look as if they'll turn into blisters, and the side of my face is red. I'm beginning to think it may be due to a spider bite. I'll know more tomorrow when I see the nurse practitioner in my internist's office. If it is a spider bite, they'll likely prescribe more antibiotics. I need more antibiotics like I need another visit to the doctor's office.

I also have to see my eye doctor next week. Apparently one of the antibiotics I'm taking can cause severe damage to the eyes. See why I'm anxious to stop taking these things? I'm hoping the results of my lung culture come back soon, and they are negative so I can stop taking so much medicine.

Overall, Dr. Antonucci was pleased with my progress. I won't have results from my most recent blood work until next week, but the results from the blood drawn about six weeks ago showed all is going well. The doctor said he's going to hold off doing any scans for now and just keep an eye on me, knowing that the cancer markers in my blood are highly sensitive and a good early detection tool.

Oh, I almost forgot. I was kicked out of physical therapy, but only temporarily. I'll do home exercises for about six weeks and then go back to see if my body is ready for more treatment. If not, we'll wait six more weeks and try again.

Other than this episode with my face and the problems with my shoulder, I really am getting better. I can feel my strength and breathing improving all the time. The body's ability to heal itself is amazing.

A bit disfigured but not disheartened,

Michelle

You know how it feels to have something wrong with your face? Any bump feels 10 times its normal size, and it seems like everyone is staring at it. On the morning of this post, I was embarrassed by the blister on the side of my nose. It was not terrible, but bad enough that I thought it warranted an explanation. Shortly after arriving at work I complained about the blister, but my colleagues assured me it wasn't as bad as I thought it was. By that afternoon, however, they were urging me to see a doctor. My face had swollen considerably and was bright red on one side. It also was a little sore.

After being dismissed from physical therapy I was sent home with exercises, which I faithfully executed on a daily basis. I am pleased to report I now have almost full range of motion in my left shoulder.

⚓ **Friday, August 16, 2013, 4:11 p.m.**

I remember how excited I was to get chicken pox when I was a kid. "Look, I got 'em!" I exclaimed, knowing that it meant I'd get to stay home from school for a while and enjoy some pampering.

I can't say I shared the same sense of fervor when I was diagnosed with shingles today. That's right. Shingles. On my face. Ugh! (Everyone who's had chickenpox carries the virus in nerve tissue near the spinal cord and brain. Years later, it may reactivate as shingles, a painful rash.)

I've started a prescription that should help clear things up in about a week or two. In the meantime, I have been told to take it easy and rest.

Please pray for protection of my left eye. The shingles are dangerously close to getting in my eye, and that could cause some long-term problems. A secondary concern is scarring on my face. Obviously, I don't want that either.

Thanks so much for your continued prayers and support.

Keeping the faith,

Michelle

Cancer, frozen shoulder, kidney failure, MAC lung disease, shingles. My hairdresser, Nancy Mitchell, joked it looked like I was going through the medical dictionary and trying out everything in there. By this point, it sure felt like it.

I always had heard how painful shingles can be, but I was far more concerned with how I looked than how I felt. I think my pain was lessened because I already was taking medicine to alleviate nerve pain. Either that or all the pain I went through up to that point set a fairly high bar of tolerance.

⚓ **Tuesday, August 20, 2013, 9:01 p.m.**

Don't worry. I don't have any new diseases or afflictions. Actually, I am pleased to report the medicine is working wonders, and I'm doing much better. The blisters are healing well and barely hurt at all anymore. The swelling in my face has gone down, too. I no longer look like a battered wife.

We're still waiting for the culture to grow out so we can get a report on the MAC lung disease. Hoping to have good news to share on that end soon!

"Our light and momentary troubles are achieving for us an eternal glory that far outweighs them all." 2 Corinthians 4:17, NIV

Buoyed by your prayers and support,

Michelle

The shingles turned out to be not so bad after all. The medicine worked wonders, and I was grateful.

⚓ **Monday, August 26, 2013, 7:19 p.m.**

I was waiting to post hoping I'd have even more good news to share. Since I haven't heard anything more on the culture I'll give a quick update.

I saw the eye doctor Thursday morning, and he said my eyes look great. The shingles stayed out of my left eye, and there's no evidence the antibiotics have caused any damage at all. Hooray!

I also got the test results from by blood work. My CEA count (cancer markers in my blood) remains excellent – 0.4. Normal can be as high as 5.0.

I'm almost completely over the shingles. My energy is coming back and almost all the sores have completely gone away.

Though it's tough getting knocked down over and over, it's always good to bounce back. And I cannot overstate how encouraging it is to have so many people supporting me.

I'll give an update on the culture when I have one. If I get news that there is no MAC lung disease, you may hear the shouts of joy from here.

Nearly shingles-free,

Michelle

When things are going well, it's easy to take them for granted. In ordinary circumstances, a good report from the eye doctor would hardly register. Add possible damage from shingles and harsh antibiotics into the equation, however, and that good report becomes cause for celebration. I was very pleased and thankful that my eyes had suffered no harm.

Years ago, I had Lasik surgery. Before the procedure, my vision was so poor that I saw at 20 feet what most people see at 800 feet. After the procedure, my vision was perfect. I am now slightly nearsighted, but nothing like before. I appreciate my good vision and don't want anything to hamper it.

⚓ Wednesday, September 11, 2013, 3:47 p.m.

Cue the Rocky music! Remember the scene in the movie when Rocky made it to the top of the stairs? I feel a bit like that right now for a couple of reasons.

First, my routine colonoscopy today came back completely clear! I'd be less than honest if I didn't admit to a little apprehension going into the test. I knew that even one polyp would indicate potential problems, and I couldn't bear to think about another cancerous tumor. I wasn't petrified with fear, but I was flooded with relief when Dr. Edmunds gave me a big thumbs-up as soon as I recovered from anesthesia. (That propofol is good stuff, by the way.)

Second, for many months now I've been working to build up my stamina and lung capacity. I started by walking to the end of my street and added from there. I've always had the goal of making it to the top of my subdivision. For those of you familiar with Kesterbrooke Boulevard, you know it is a formidable hill to climb. I've been headed up the hill for more than a month now, going a little farther each time. Last week I finally made it to the top! Every time I get there, I stop and enjoy the beautiful view and thank God that He continues to heal and restore me.

I still await final results of the culture, but that news is also looking good. Dr. LeMense called last week to say the cultures are still negative but need to grow out one more week for a definitive answer. I hope to have a final answer Monday.

The roller coaster continues. I have to say it sure feels good to be going back up!

"The Sovereign Lord is my strength; He makes my feet like the feet of a deer, He enables me to go on the heights." Habakkuk 3:19, NIV

Enjoying the view from the mountaintop,

Michelle

After so many long, hard months and so much bad news, it was wonderful to bask in all the good news coming my way. The importance of a clean colonoscopy was not lost on me. I knew it was a strong indicator that all the steps we took to rid my body of colorectal cancer were effective.

Setting and reaching the goal of walking to the top of my subdivision was exhilarating. As I walked the last stretch at the top, one of my neighbors asked if I was really feeling okay. "I'm up here, aren't I?" I said with a smile. I couldn't think of a better sign that I was doing better than okay.

"Heal me, O Lord, and I will be healed; save me and I will be saved, for Thou art my praise." Jeremiah 17:14

⚓ Monday, September 23, 2013, 8:20 p.m.

Yippee! Hooray! Hallelujah!

Today I finally got the good news I've been waiting for – the cultures came back negative, which means I can stop taking all those nasty antibiotics. It's a pretty big deal. Without this good news, I would have been forced to take a bunch of strong antibiotics for about a year or more. They could have caused serious side effects, such as damage to my vision or liver.

Also, I saw my surgeon, Dr. Harville, last week. Before releasing me from his care, he said he's very happy with the end result but mine was the most bizarre case he's ever handled. Like the other lung doctor said, I don't do anything halfway.

For now, we're just going to keep a very close eye on the tumor that remains in my right lung. As long as it behaves, we'll leave it alone. If my cancer markers show signs of activity, they'll go in and take it out. Because of the tumor's location any additional lung surgery should be much less complicated than what I had before, but I'd rather not test that theory.

I have to say, sharing good news is much easier than sharing so much bad. There for a while, I had people afraid to open their emails.

For now, expect fewer posts as I shouldn't have much to report. I think I better hurry and write my book before I get any more chapters to add.

Shingles-free, MAC-free and breathing better,

Michelle

"Taste and see that the Lord is good; blessed is the one who takes refuge in him." Psalm 34:8

My body bears a lot of scars, some from the tomboy days of my youth and many from the various surgeries and procedures I have endured. In addition, the antibiotics caused a fungus to form on my skin that killed the pigment in many places. My arms and legs now are adorned with lots of ugly white spots, yet another kind of scarring.

While I would much prefer to have a scar-free body, I recognize every scar is a reminder of what I've been through and the miraculous way God has carried me through. My scars are a signpost of His faithfulness.

⚓ **Saturday, October 26, 2013, 11:30 a.m.**

Today's journal entry isn't about my health. My mother asked that I share the latest news about my dad. He moved to hospice Wednesday, and we don't expect him to last much longer.

As we enjoy this crisp fall day and the beautiful colors of the changing leaves, I am reminded that my dad's passing brings us to another season of life. A season without the patriarch who for so many years and with such great devotion has led the Ironside clan.

Dad has been leaving us for some time now, with Alzheimer's and other ailments sapping his strength and his ability to enjoy daily living. Knowing he has suffered so much for so long makes it easier to let go. The knowledge he'll be in a far better place helps tremendously.

When we went to visit Dad yesterday, he kept staring at the ceiling and pointing up. He could barely talk, but he kept looking at me and saying the word, "Wonderful." I believe he was seeing the wonderful place where he will soon be headed. A place where he knows no more pain, no more sorrow, no more tears. We'll join him there one day, and it will be a beautiful reunion. For now, we are bracing ourselves for the farewell that is coming soon.

As to my health, I'm still doing well and feeling better every day. It's funny, though, once you've had cancer twice it always lurks in the back of your mind. A couple of weeks ago I had been telling someone about how coffee stopped tasting good to me a couple of months before my first cancer diagnosis. The next day when I sat down to drink a cup of coffee, it tasted terrible. "Oh, no," I thought. "The cancer's coming back." I was quite relieved when I discovered the pack of sweetener that should have gone in my coffee still sitting on the counter.

Please keep my mom and my family in your thoughts and prayers. Even though we know this is for the best and have the assurance my dad is going to a far better place, there still will be tough days ahead.

Trusting God,

Michelle

At first I didn't understand the meaning behind my father looking up and repeating the word "wonderful." Upon further reflection, though, it seemed obvious he was catching a glimpse of heaven. I was thankful to have been present for that moment. Another good moment came when Dad saw Evan. Following a temporary flash of recognition, Dad gave Evan his last big smile. Evan and my father enjoyed a special relationship. That smile was a tremendous farewell gift for my son.

Our family, already close, pulled even closer as we faced the loss of my father. The morning of this post, we gathered at the football field to watch the athletic exploits of my nephews Kai and Mugisha. It was comforting to enjoy the simple pleasures of a beautiful fall day and a football game well played by some youngsters. It was a good reminder that, although we would feel the pain of loss, life would go on.

Another pleasant reminder that life goes on came at Christmas when my mother invited all of her older grandsons to go through Dad's closet to see if there were any clothes they wanted. They all found something they liked and came downstairs in sport coats and dress slacks looking very dapper and standing proud. My father was very particular about his clothes and had quite the haberdashery. Mom says it does her heart good to see her grandsons decked out in the clothes that Dad always loved.

⚓ Tuesday, October 29, 2013, 1:08 a.m.

Late yesterday evening I came across a really cool print that pictured a ship in the midst of a storm with the words "It Is Well with My Soul." That song has been rolling around in my head ever since.

My father's earthly struggle ended only a few hours ago. It was tough saying goodbye to him and especially hard to see my mother bid farewell to her partner of 54 years.

Nonetheless, "It is well with my soul" and with my mother's soul as well. Thanks for your prayers and words of encouragement. As always, they help us weather the storm.

Praising Him for the gift of peace,

Michelle

As we planned my father's funeral, my brothers said they wanted to speak at the service. I knew I had things to say but also knew it would be nearly impossible for me to stand and speak at such an emotional moment. I therefore volunteered to write something for the program. As I sat down to write, my mind was flooded with all the things I wanted to communicate. How do you sum up what your father's life meant to you in a few short paragraphs?

After struggling with what seemed to be an impossible task, I did what I always do when my flesh is weak; I prayed that the Holy Spirit would work through my weakness so that all the glory would go to God. My prayer was answered, and these words flowed quickly and effortlessly:

> "I have been crucified with Christ; and it is no longer I who live, but Christ lives in me." Galatians 2:20
>
> Galatians 2:20 was Dad's favorite verse, and he lived it every day from the time he was saved at age 35. He lived it when he loved his children and devoted himself to his family, never once complaining he was orphaned at a very young age, never knew his parents and was raised by an uncle not much older than himself.
>
> He lived it when he gave so much to charity that the IRS came knocking on the door, convinced they would detect some kind of fraud, only to find that *they* owed *him* money.
>
> He lived it when he stood for what was right, even when it wasn't popular. There was nothing lukewarm

about Dad, and people rarely felt neutral about him. They either loved him fiercely or hated him with a passion, but even the "haters" usually came around and loved him in the end.

He lived it when he bowed his head in prayer and thanked God before every meal, even when his body and mind were failing him and the thought of food disgusted him.

He lived it through a faithful and undying love for his wife of 54 years, a lady he loved so much that he repeatedly asked her to marry him when his mind no long remembered that they were wed.

He lived it in his last days when he held up his hand, looked toward the heavens and said, "Wonderful."

We loved our Dad and will miss him greatly, but we rejoice knowing that he is in a place where there will be no more pain, no more sorrow, no more tears, and we will see him again one day.

"O death, where is your victory? O death, where is your sting?" 1 Corinthians 15:55

At least 900 people came by the church to give their condolences, and many shared stories of how my father had impacted their lives. We knew Dad lived a life for God, but we never knew half the things he did to serve others. Dad didn't draw attention to himself as he did good deeds; he didn't have buildings erected in his name or submit his picture to the paper when he donated money or volunteered for worthy causes. My father didn't care about being noticed by men; he knew his reward was with his Father in heaven.

"Beware of practicing your righteousness before men to be noticed by them; otherwise you have no reward with your Father who is in heaven." Matthew 6:1

⚓ **Wednesday, December 11, 2013, 7:43 p.m.**

It's been almost four years to the day that I first learned I had cancer, making today's phone call from Dr. Antonucci's office telling me that my blood work was perfect all the more encouraging. As I've said before, it's not like I'm walking around terrified that cancer will rear its ugly head, but it is always good to get reassurance that for now it's at bay.

The plan is for me to have another PET scan at the end of the year to make sure the tumor on my right lung is behaving. I say that's the plan because my insurance company thinks otherwise. Dr. Antonucci says he will stay after them until they agree to the procedure. Knowing him, I'd say he will convince them it's necessary.

Many people have asked about my mom. She is doing amazingly well, as is the rest of the family. We often pray for peace, but when it truly comes I think it surprises some people. It's not that I don't care that I have cancer or that my family and I don't care that my father died, it's that we've been blessed with the gift of peace that passes all understanding. For that, I am truly grateful.

I pray that you and yours will experience the gift of peace throughout this Christmas season and in 2014.

"Peace I leave with you, My peace I give to you; not as the world gives do I give to you. Let not your heart be troubled, neither let it be afraid." John 14:27

Celebrating,

Michelle

As Christians, we are called to be different. We are to be light in the darkness and the salt of the earth. Yet, when we are different, many people, Christians included, act like we're a bit crazy or that we're not being honest about how we feel.

A lot of people seem surprised at how well my mother is doing. Some have made comments that make her feel almost guilty that she's not wallowing in despair. One difference is Mom was mourning the loss of my father for years before he died; he had been leaving us for such a long time and was suffering so much that it was a relief to know his suffering had ended. The other difference is she is receiving the gift of peace that God promises every believer. That same gift is there for all of us, but it is up to us to receive it.

God's peace has accompanied me throughout my battle with cancer and resides with me now, even though I live with the knowledge that cancerous tumors reside in my right lung. I'm not living in peaceful oblivion; I know all too well the dangers associated with my disease. I am resting in the knowledge that God is in control and trusting Him with the details.

⚓ **Thursday, January 17, 2014, 7:13 p.m.**

The other morning I thought of a sermon illustration I heard many years ago.

> One day when Amy and her grandmother were going through an old jewelry box, Amy found a pearl necklace. The young girl draped the necklace around her neck and admired her reflection in the mirror. "Look, Grandma, it's so beautiful!"
>
> "Those aren't real pearls, but the necklace looks pretty on you. I'll let you have it if you promise to take good care of it," said her grandmother with a gentle smile.
>
> "Oh, thank you! I promise I will!"

Amy kept her promise. She was careful to take off her pearls before swimming or taking a bath, and she kept them in a special box on the rare occasions when they weren't around her neck.

Amy's father noticed how much she loved the pearls and admired how she took such good care of them. As he tucked her in one night, Amy's father asked, "Do you love me?"

"Yes, Daddy. I love you bunches and bunches!"

"Then give me your pearls."

"Not my pearls, but you can have Beatrice. She's my favorite doll, and she's real pretty."

"That's okay, sweetie," he said before giving her a soft kiss and turning out the light.

A few nights later, her father asked again. "Amy, do you love me?"

"You know I love you, Daddy."

"Then give me your pearls."

"What if I give you my new drawing set? The markers are like new, and it's a lot more fun than a necklace."

"That's all right," he said tenderly. "Daddy loves you. Sleep tight, little one."

Several nights later when he came upstairs to read her a bedtime story, Amy's father noticed her lip was quivering and a few silent tears spilled down her cheeks. Before he could ask what was wrong, she handed over her pearls. "Here, Daddy. These are for you."

As he took the pearls in one hand, he reached in his pocket with the other. It contained the real pearl necklace that he had been waiting to give his daughter all along.

I share this and believe it came to mind because I recently felt called to give something up. For the past five years, I've been working three part-time jobs. People told me I was crazy, but I insisted I liked it. And I did.

But then something happened. My father died. It made me value life all the more and really think about how close I came to dying in 2013. Then, I had a three-week break around the Christmas holiday and stopped moving long enough to reflect on how short life is and how important it is that I live mine with purpose.

What had been a gentle tug became a burning desire to write the book I've been talking about writing – a book that tells the story of my journey these past four years and all that God has done in my life. I knew I had to make a change. But could I hand over my "necklace"?

It turns out I could. I turned in my resignation at the Urban League, the four-day-a-week job, and am ready to spend that time writing my book. It is definitely a new chapter in my life, literally and figuratively. I am bursting with words that have been rolling around in my head and anxious to start "putting pen to paper."

I haven't been handed the "real pearls" yet, but I did have the blessing of having two godly women share the same Scripture and words of wisdom with me, and it felt like the heavens had opened up so that God could tell me I did the right thing.

I'll close with the same admonition the sermon illustration did, "What are you holding onto?"

"If you, then, being evil, know how to give good gifts to your children, how much more shall your Father who is in heaven give what is good to those who ask Him!" Matthew 7:11

Trusting Him,

Michelle

For now you kind of know how the story ends: I survive. I say "kind of know" because I'm not even sure how or when my story will end. The cancer that started in my colon, spread to my liver and then moved to my lungs still lurks in the right lung.

My most recent PET scan, a highly sensitive scan used to reveal the presence and severity of cancer and other disease, indicates I have two tumors in my right lung that have gotten a little larger and are showing more activity. At some point I expect I'll be facing more surgery. Lung surgery is what nearly killed me last time; so I truly don't know how this story ends.

When you get down to it, though, no one really knows how or when their story will end, so, in that regard, you're not that much different from me.

This morning our pastor preached the first in a series of sermons about Christ's death and resurrection. As I heard him preach, I recognized he had just given me the ending to my book. My story of hope in the midst of a storm would not be possible without Christ's death and resurrection. What Christ accomplished on the cross is at the crux of everything I am and everything I believe.

You may have been reading my book with the attitude, "That faith stuff may be okay for her, but it's not for me." I applaud your efforts to stay with me this far. Now, please consider the possibility that all that "faith stuff" is real. Jesus Christ died on a cross as payment for my sin and yours. He offers the free gift of salvation to anyone who genuinely calls on Him for salvation.

In Luke 23, beginning at verse 39, we read that two thieves were hanged alongside Jesus. One hurled insults at Him, but the other said, "Jesus, remember me when You come in Your kingdom!" To that thief, Jesus replied, "Truly I say to you, today you shall be with Me in Paradise."

The gift of salvation is free; there is nothing we can do to earn it. But we must accept it.

"But as many as received Him, to them He gave the right to become children of God, even to those who believe in His name." John 1:12